T0373809

The Philosophy of Theoretical Linguistics

What is the remit of theoretical linguistics? How are human languages different from animal calls or artificial languages? What philosophical insights about language can be gleaned from phonology, pragmatics, probabilistic linguistics, and deep learning? This book addresses the current philosophical issues at the heart of theoretical linguistics, which are widely debated by not only linguists but also philosophers, psychologists, and computer scientists. It delves into hitherto uncharted territory, putting philosophy in direct conversation with phonology, sign language studies, supersemantics, computational linguistics, and language evolution. A range of theoretical positions are covered, from optimality theory and autosegmental phonology to generative syntax, dynamic semantics, and natural language processing with deep learning techniques. By both unwinding the complexities of natural language and delving into the nature of the science that studies it, this book ultimately improves our tools of discovery aimed at one of the most essential features of our humanity, our language.

RYAN M. NEFDT is an associate professor of philosophy at the University of Cape Town. He works in the broad area of cognitive science with a specialisation in the philosophy of linguistics. Notable publications include *Language, Science, and Structure* (Oxford University Press, 2023).

The Philosophy of Theoretical Linguistics

A Contemporary Outlook

Ryan M. Nefdt
University of Cape Town

CAMBRIDGE
UNIVERSITY PRESS

Shaftesbury Road, Cambridge CB2 8EA, United Kingdom

One Liberty Plaza, 20th Floor, New York, NY 10006, USA

477 Williamstown Road, Port Melbourne, VIC 3207, Australia

314–321, 3rd Floor, Plot 3, Splendor Forum, Jasola District Centre,
New Delhi – 110025, India

103 Penang Road, #05–06/07, Visioncrest Commercial, Singapore 238467

Cambridge University Press is part of Cambridge University Press & Assessment,
a department of the University of Cambridge.

We share the University's mission to contribute to society through the pursuit of
education, learning and research at the highest international levels of excellence.

www.cambridge.org
Information on this title: www.cambridge.org/9781316514252

DOI: 10.1017/9781009082853

First published 2024

A catalogue record for this publication is available from the British Library.

*A Cataloging-in-Publication data record for this book is available from the Library of
Congress*

ISBN 978-1-316-51425-2 Hardback

Contents

Figures

Tables

Preface

Philosophy and linguistics have had a long and storied history together. Analysing language has been central to philosophical analysis since ancient times and well after the so-called Linguistic Turn of twentieth-century analytic philosophy. With the incorporation of more logical techniques and models before and after the advent of the generative tradition in linguistics (*circa* 1957), the data and tools of each discipline become almost indistinguishable at times. This is apparent especially in the case of model-theoretic or truth-conditional semantics where both philosophers and linguists have contributed equally to its foundations. But the connections between these subjects don't only follow the purely mathematical path designated by proof theory and model theory, respectively. There are deep philosophical issues embedded in sociolinguistics, cognitive linguistics, and evolutionary and computational approaches to language. These topics often go underexplored.

In the present work, the aim is to mine the significant philosophical resources and puzzles at the heart of the linguistic enterprise, across frameworks. Perhaps the most philosophical work has been done with generative grammar in mind (both in terms of internal accounts and external critiques). Naturally, generative theories and the philosophical questions they pose will be covered in this text. However, our focus won't be on the mainstream linguistic theory exclusively. Questions over formal approaches to pragmatics, the role of constructions in grammar, sign language phonology, deep learning, complexity-theoretic views on language evolution, and many others will be addressed.

The goal is to provide not only a songbird's-eye view of the interconnections between different subdisciplines and frameworks of linguistic theory but to showcase common problems and present novel analyses of the study of language that only a contemporary philosophical overview can offer. Each chapter can be considered a sustained, self-contained argument based on the subfield at hand. The reader shouldn't expect the standard arguments for and against specific views to be rehashed without qualification here. Such claims will only receive emphasis when they contribute to the agenda of unearthing the connections and theoretically interesting divergences between accounts or revealing the commitments of theorists. References to those classical debates will be included in the *Further Reading* section at the end of each chapter.

The length of each chapter will in part be determined by the amount of philosophical work already present on the relevant topic, however inchoate that literature may be. This, of course, produces an imbalance in which syntax, semantics, and pragmatics seem to receive more investigation than topics such as phonology, sociolinguistics, and computational approaches do. Despite the inherited imbalance, I aim to do justice to these latter subfields by highlighting the unique philosophical issues that often go unnoticed in the philosophical work on linguistics as well as possible connections with the subfields that generally command more of the reflective real estate.

Thus, the primary target of this book is advanced students of either philosophy or linguistics and experienced practitioners at the intersection between these fields. Despite, or rather because of, this integrated focus, there will be enough explanatory resources for those unfamiliar with various topics to follow the narrative and argument. In spite of any author's best efforts at comprehensiveness, some topics will fall beyond the present scope. Where this is an unavoidable choice, it'll be flagged, and where it's deemed an omission, I beg the reader's compassion at the sheer task ahead.

The study of language is both a behemoth and a chimera. There's a plenitude of diverging theories of everything from syntax to lexical semantics to phonological structure. There are also around eighty years of analysis, frameworks, data, and reflection (and that's ignoring American Structuralism, historical linguistics, and much of the Stoic and Arabic work on early grammar). In order to keep the task manageable, I'll therefore devote myself to only contemporary accounts of various theories. For instance, when discussing generative grammar, my attention will be focused primarily on Minimalism as it's the dominant instantiation of the general programme. 'Cognitive linguistics' will refer mostly to extant versions of the theory such as construction grammar. 'Formal semantics' will cover model-theoretic as well as dynamic approaches and so on. Active research will supersede historical reflection, except in cases where leaving out the latter will create an inescapable lacuna (such as in Chapter 5 on pragmatics).

At the end of the book, the reader should have a clear grasp of the theoretical landscape in linguistics across prominent frameworks and formalisms. More importantly, the reader should have a renewed appreciation for the philosophical fecundity of the broader field of theoretical linguistics, both its contemporary outlook and its future prospects.

Acknowledgements

There are many people to thank at various institutions across the world. Before I attempt to acknowledge those intellectual debts, I should mention the funding bodies that made this project possible: the Oppenheimer Memorial Trust's sabbatical research fund, the National Research Foundation of South Africa's Presidential Rating Fellowship, and the Vice-Chancellor's Future Leaders Fellowship at the University of Cape Town. Thanks to the generous support of these fellowships, I was able to take the time and find the resources for the completion of this book.

I'd also like to thank audiences at various universities including the Massachusetts Institute of Technology (MIT), Durham University, the University of Miami, Universitat Pompeu Fabra, the Max Planck Institute for Evolutionary Anthropology, and the Norwegian University of Science and Technology.

I'd especially like to thank Louise McNally, Marco Baroni, Giosuè Baggio, Martin Haspelmath, and Zoltán Szabó for comments and corrections specifically on the present manuscript or issues directly therein. My extended list of expert interlocutors on the various topics of the monograph include Geoff Pullum, Jeff Pelletier, Emmanuel Chemla, Michael Kac, Kate Stanton, Dieuwke Hupkes, Henk Zeevat, Reinhard Blutner, Manuel Carpintero, Wolfram Hinzen, and Gemma Boleda. Of course, over the years, I've been lucky enough to meet many amazing linguists, cognitive scientists, and philosophers who have all contributed to my thinking on the subject.

I owe a huge debt of gratitude to Helen Barton at Cambridge University Press for her guidance and support during the process of making this book a reality. My research assistant, Matt White, also deserves special mention for his careful reading of the entire manuscript and more careful comments on its content.

Lastly, I'd like to thank my family for their support. My wife, Anastasia, always knew what to say when I inevitably claimed a chapter was impossible to complete or the book would never be finished. My dog, Barcelona, also always seemed to know when a walk was needed to clear my thoughts.

1 Introduction

1.1 What Is Theoretical Linguistics?

Defining theoretical linguistics, the remit of the present philosophical investigation, is a surprisingly fraught task. I say 'surprisingly' because one might expect that the domain is specifiable in terms similar to other fields prefixed with the same modifier. *Theoretical* physics is contrasted with experimental physics in terms of the kinds of methods and tools used in its exploration. For instance, theoretical physicists often make use of mathematical frameworks such as group theory to identify properties of symmetry or invariance in natural structures. They can incorporate sweeping idealisations in pursuit of laws of nature (Cartwright 1983). On the other hand, experimental physicists, such as those in big data cosmology, focus their efforts on applying statistical techniques to questions related to the origins of the universe. Experimental physicists more generally conduct real-world experiments (including simulations) to test and confirm theoretical posits or hypotheses. In a different vein, *theoretical* philosophy differs from *practical* philosophy in a shift in emphasis from abstract reality to practical, quotidian matters. In some cases, the distinction is captured by the difference between descriptive and normative contexts. Practical philosophy involves what we *ought* to do while theoretical philosophy aims to uncover what we *in fact* do (or *might* do in other possible worlds). Of course, this characterisation is overly simplistic.[1] There are fields that live in both worlds such as metaethics or mathematical physics. There are also fields where the distinction doesn't seem to hold such as biology and chemistry.

The nomenclature of philosophy and physics is equally unhelpful in the case of linguistics. Theoretical linguistics is indeed a descriptive enterprise, but so is experimental linguistics. In some cases, such as generative grammar, discrete mathematics characterises the methodological core of the practice. However, in others, such as probabilistic linguistics, continuous mathematics is favoured (Bod *et al.* 2003). Similarly, the status of experimentation is unclear in

---

[1] For one thing, the new conceptual engineering movement in philosophy aims at replacing or ameliorating 'defective' concepts. See Isaac *et al.* (2022) for an introduction to the new field.

linguistics. Corpus studies are becoming more prominent in theoretical contexts with some theorists like Marantz (2007) even suggesting that the intuitions of linguists stand proxy for corpus data.

Methodology alone won't settle the target and scope of theoretical linguistics. Where normativity plays a role, it's unlikely to be one that distinguishes between theoretical and other fields of linguistics. Various theoretical approaches, from generative grammar to dynamic syntax, embrace different tools and methods, some formal and others empirical.

Haspelmath (2021) discusses a similar issue when he distinguishes between 'theoretical', 'general', and 'particular' linguistics. 'Theoretical', for him, cannot be contrasted with experimental since experimental work in linguistics often serves to push theory. He finds the distinction between 'theoretical' and 'applied' preferable since work in language pedagogy, automatic speech processing, and speech therapy set out to contribute to the resolution of practical problems and 'not necessarily in furthering theoretical understanding' (Haspelmath 2021, p. 4). But this is tricky: language pathology has a long history of informing theoretical pursuits. Asphasia studies or the general study of the linguistic effects of brain damage, for instance, have cemented theoretical distinctions and concepts like function versus content words, syntactic versus paratactic constructions, and the modularity of mental grammars.[2]

The distinction Haspelmath seems to be making is that the domain of theoretical linguistics (for both the general study of language itself and that of particular languages) is theory-driven in some fundamental way. But 'of or related to theory' assumes a neat dichotomy between theory and observation, which has been justly problematised in the philosophy of science. The more advanced the tools of observation, the more blurry the lines between observation and theory become. Think about the assignment of grammaticality to minimal pairs of sentences for a moment, either through introspection or corpus studies. Screening off syntactic well-formedness from semantic and pragmatic features is already a theory-laden activity. It presupposes autonomous syntax, which is a posit of a particular kind of theory (usually a generative one). Is an electron microscope a theoretical tool, enhanced observation, or both? Measurement is inherently theoretical. There's no clear distinction to be had between theory and observation, between science and facts.[3]

Despite the difficulty of the task, it's important to identify the field we're aiming to investigate. In some ways, the task has been made easier by the theoretical dominance of generative grammar in linguistics. Many excellent philosophical treatises have thus almost exclusively focused on it in their

---

[2] For a historical overview of the role aphasia studies have played in theoretical linguistics, see Elffers (2020).
[3] See Kukla (1996) for an argument that neither realists nor antirealists in the philosophy of science need to avail themselves of it.

reflections: Newmeyer (1996), Ludlow (2011), and Rey (2020), to name a few. However, I don't plan to take generative grammar as metonymous for, or exhaustive of, theoretical linguistics. It's not the only game in town, nor was it ever. It's just one of many theoretical approaches to a distinct set of questions. Therein lies the clue as to my intended interpretation of the term 'theoretical linguistics'.

Theoretical linguistics is ultimately an explanatory project. The trouble is that the project has often been confused for its explanans, such as generative grammars or hierarchical tree structures. However, there are many and varied tools at the disposal of the theoretical linguist, well beyond these latter options. A better way to identify the project, in my view, is by appreciating its explananda, or the targets of its explanations. Thus, the way forward, as I see it, is to identify theoretical linguistics with a set of core theoretical questions.[4] These questions can be and are studied by means of numerous methods and approaches. They're unified not in approach but rather in their targets. The guiding set of questions is:

1a. *What is Language?*
 b. *What is a language?*
2. *How do we acquire languages?*
3. *How is linguistic communication possible?*
4. *How did language evolve?*

To be a theoretical linguist, of whichever variety, you have to attempt to answer some, if not all, of these questions in a coherent manner. An applied linguist can get away without clear or scrutinised answers to the above sorts of questions. Of course, this interpretation doesn't constitute a necessary and sufficient set of conditions. I believe such a task would be largely fruitless. Nor does it cover every specific question a theoretical linguist might be interested in. We'll see more specific sub-questions in the following sections. It's my contention that they do all ultimately aim to produce answers to the general questions listed above. In Chapter 7, we'll come closest to views that diverge from this prescribed agenda. Computational approaches often have engineering goals in mind with human-level competence acting as little more than a benchmark, the so-called gold standard. Nevertheless, in keeping with the aims of this book, we'll still ask whether or not new approaches in artificial intelligence and computational linguistics can offer insights into the aforementioned theoretical questions. I'll argue that they do.

What's more important is that there's a distinct logical hierarchy in the list. The success conditions for any linguistic theory will depend on how one

---

[4] These are similar to Chomsky's (1965) nested adequacy conditions, with the addition of his later evolutionary bent and a focus on explaining communication, which is the focus of pragmatics and sociolinguistics.

answers (1), and the answer to (1) will determine the range of possibilities available for answers to (2) to (4). For instance, generative grammar (or biolinguistics) assumes that language consists of a modular mental system responsible for narrow syntax. Languages are specific settings of this system activated by varying external stimuli (from different language communities). Acquisition is largely explained by an innate module in the brain specific to our species. Communication is an exaptation. Language evolved for thought, and since it's mostly syntactic in nature, an operation like the set-theoretic one of 'Merge' can do the job of explaining its sudden emergence some 100 thousand years ago (Berwick & Chomsky 2016).[5] Of course, this particular sequence is negotiable at every turn. The package changes if we start with the idea that language is a mathematical representation of conventions in particular speech communities. David Lewis (1975) attempts to provide such a synthesis. Acquisition can essentially include sociolinguistic principles and discoveries with in its remit. Successful explanation along these lines would involve finding the correct model of the community's linguistic conventions.

However, methodologically, there can be convergence. Platonists, like Katz (1981), differ in their answer to (1) but insist that the methodology (of generative grammar) remains constant. In fact, they argue the methodology better fits their ontological paradigm (Postal 2003). In the next subsection, we move on to a discussion of one of the chief tools for answering these questions in the theoretical linguist's arsenal, namely, that of a *grammar*.

1.2   Grammar and Grammaticality

Most introductory linguistics textbooks start with a caution and a disclaimer: 'Prescriptivists keep out! Science ahead'. The idea is that the notion of a grammar is historically associated with various injunctions on writing and speaking 'properly' – 'Don't split your infinitives', 'Don't end sentences with prepositions', 'Avoid passives', and so on.[6] Students of a language need to disabuse themselves of these restrictive claims. The task of a grammarian is then not to prescribe arbitrary stylistic rules of 'proper usage' but to uncover the rules that govern *actual* usage. It's unclear whether or not linguists are solely interested in describing actual usage. Indeed, some corpus linguistics is directed at identifying patterns or regularities within various corpora, but for the most part, theoretical linguists see their tasks as inductive and ampliative. In so doing, they're invariably confronted with possibilia, or unactualised types of sentences, and constructions that are predicted and sometimes prohibited by the rules they

---

[5] We'll see more of this view in Chapter 2.
[6] See Pullum (2014) for a history of the 'fear and loathing' of the English passive, for instance.

describe. What makes this process interesting is that this might be the point at which normativity creeps into the field (Kac 1994; Itkonen 2019; Pullum 2019).

In demarcating the space of acceptable or unacceptable strings of any language, one isn't only describing a state of affairs but prescribing certain legal and illegal operations. For example, if the only rule of English was that a Verb Phrase = Noun + Finite Verb, as in *Geoff sings*, then although hundreds of thousands of sentences would immediately be licensed, many other forms such as those involving determiners, adjectives, prepositions, and so on, would be banned or relegated to the inimical category of the 'ungrammatical'. Whether a grammar is a normative or descriptive device is a tricky philosophical question, one that often receives very little attention by linguists or even philosophers. Inferentialism in the philosophy of language and logic takes normativity to be central to the generation of meaning.[7] It enters linguistics via proof-theoretic semantics (Brandom 1994; Francez & Dyckhoff 2010; Peregrin 2015). Before we can approach this issue more broadly and what relation modern grammatical theory might even have to old-school grammar instruction (still alive and nitpicking in various popular writing books), we need to define what a grammar is and what role it plays in theoretical linguistics.

The 'orthodox' or mainstream generative view has it that 'grammar' plays multiple roles in the theory of language. Nevertheless, one overarching role, upon which Chomsky (1965, 1981, 2000) has repeatedly insisted, is that a grammar is a theory of a language, in the sense of a 'scientific' theory. For him, the target of theorising is our knowledge of language understood as a stable mental state of the language faculty. The overall job of linguistic theory is then to illuminate the structure of this knowledge or mental state. Specifically, there are two senses of 'grammar' common in the generative literature. The first kind of grammar attempts to map the contours of the mature state of the language faculty attained by an individual cogniser (her 'I-language'), while the second demarcates the settings of a deeper underlying universal patterning or the innate initial state of all language users. As Chomsky states, '[a]dapting traditional terms to a special usage, we call the theory of the state attained its *grammar* and the theory of the initial state *Univeral Grammar* (UG)' (1995b: p. 12). We'll see much more of these ideas in Chapter 2.

If linguistic theory is indeed scientific in any strong sense, then we might expect laws or regularities to emerge from our investigations. This expectation has led to at least two further trends in the field (that track the two senses above). The first and earliest has been the focus on syntax as a core aspect of the language faculty. One reason is that syntax is rather well behaved, math-

---

[7] There's a distinctive Wittgensteinian flavour to this framework, not only in the use-based theory but also in the later Wittgenstein views on mathematics as a 'network of norms' (Wittgenstein 1953, VII §67).

ematically speaking. Early twentieth-century formal logic provided numerous insights into proof theory with the work of Post, Turing, Gödel, and Carnap, to name just a few prominent examples. Many of these results translate very well to the study of syntactic structures. In fact, formal language theory was invented as a subfield of linguistics that was directly informed by both logical structure and natural language constraints. Some early results, such as Chomsky (1956), aimed to show that natural language syntax outstripped the bounds of finite-state grammars and required context-free rules with transformations. Later work used data from languages such as Dutch and Swiss-German to show that context-free grammars were equally insufficient given the possibility of cross-serial dependencies (Shieber 1985). I'll return to some of these details in the next subsection, but for now, the basic idea is that syntactic complexity can be precisely characterised in terms of formal languages (generated by formal grammars). The trick is then to show that some natural construction, formally specified, exceeds the limits of a particular formal language by showing that it cannot be generated by the associated grammar. Here, particular patterns in particular languages inform the grammar qua scientific theory.

The second trend to emerge from the 'scientific expectation' was the search for linguistic universals, the ultimate regularities to be found in linguistic nature. Successfully identifying regular law-like patterns in cross-linguistic reality would go a long way to supporting the claim that grammars are theories of language that ultimately illuminate some sort of UG. If all languages, the world over, prescribe to a set of formally identifiable constraints, then studying these constraints might indeed reveal the underlying structure of language itself (Language with an uppercase 'L'). Despite decades of valiant attempts, languages (with a lowercase 'l') proved recalcitrant to such universal characterisation (see Evans & Levinson 2009 and Chapter 2).[8] The result was that more and more abstract properties were considered as candidates for universality. One popular such proposal is that *all natural languages are recursive* (Hauser *et al.* 2002). However, recursion is a formal property of grammar or representation. Iterative structures in natural language need not be represented as recursive (Lobina 2017). Furthermore, there's some question over where exactly recursive structure lies. As an aspect of the computational component of the UG, the claim becomes almost unfalsifiable since no particular language would offer counterevidence, whether or not it possessed the hallmarks of surface recursion like centre-embedding or propositional contexts like *Joan said that Irene believed that Angelika thought that …*

---

[8] Some have followed Greenberg's 1963 infamous attempts at finding linguistic universals. Fascinating as this list is, it mostly comprises conditional patterns, many of which are not syntactic. Not to mention the initial sample was composed of around thirty of the world's eight thousand extant languages.

This picture of the science of language can change with the role and definition of grammar. Some theorists such as Tiede & Stout (2010) and Nefdt (2016, 2019) have argued that grammars are more akin to formal models than scientific theories. The change of perspective has some profound consequences. For one thing, models are indirect representations of a target phenomenon. What this means is that grammars themselves (or some of their aspects) could be nonveridical. So instead of 'reading' the structures of the model as reflective of linguistic reality directly, one can appreciate a looser relationship between grammars and reality. For instance, the debate over the universal nature of recursion becomes a discussion over whether recursive structures are artefactual aspects of the model used or actual explananda of the system under investigation. This possibility has a knock-on effect on debates concerning the infinitude of natural language since it opens up the further possibility that talk of linguistic infinity is a mere simplification device similar to treating a complex system as *essentially infinite* in computer science even if it's in fact finite (see Savitch 1993; Nefdt 2019).

Another effect of this shift in interpretation involves the success conditions of grammars again. For instance, if formal semantics is in the business of assigning models to sets of sentences, then counterexamples would refute the models and require expansion (assuming nonmonotonicity). Theories can be more recalcitrant to contravening data, according to some linguists (see Chapter 7 for more).

To add to the complication, whatever our philosophical interpretation of grammar, the notion of 'grammaticality' can be somewhat detached from it. Interestingly, it seems less possible to detach grammaticality from the normativity debate, though. Assuming that grammaticality is a property of individual expressions or subexpressions of a language, what makes a sentence grammatical? The answers can converge and diverge whether you view grammars as scientific theories or models. However, determining the grammatical sentences does seem to involve deciding whether grammars are mental devices, reflections of community standards, or some hybrid of these and other options. For instance, if grammaticality is grounded in conventional practices of a linguistic community, then its application seems to be normative. Saying *I is hungry* is incorrect by the standards of the community since grammatical agreement between subject and copula is the norm.[9] Saying *Ek is honger* in Afrikaans is fine since that language has long since abandoned verb–subject agreement (and inflection from its parent language Dutch). If grammaticality is a property of formal expressions derived from a mental module or generative grammar, then certain violations might belong to the realm of performance

---

[9] Ungrammatical or unacceptable constructions are usually marked with an asterisk in the top-left corner of the sentence.

and not grammatical competence (see Chapter 7). You might say *I is hungry* because you're drunk, or trying to be funny, or both. We'll get to the competence–performance distinction later. But as Manning (2003) points out, this doesn't help when nonstandard usage is at play. Standard grammar rules tend to divide grammatical and ungrammatical strings absolutely (even if the grammar is undecidable).[10] The problem is that there are constructions and phrases that pop up all over human language (and corpora) that would be deemed simply ungrammatical in this strict generative sense (i.e. not generated by any discrete rule). Manning identifies one such construction, namely, *as least as*. This construction sounds strange at first but robustly appears across various texts. He claims that generative grammar (which he calls a 'categorical linguistic theory') is prescriptive in the sense that it places hard boundaries on grammaticality when these boundaries are much fuzzier in reality. Many theorists realise that grammaticality itself might be fuzzy. This possibility doesn't, however, rule out successfully using apparatus to tame it in discrete or binary terms. Historically, others have embraced the fuzziness and either advocated fluid grammatical catogories, or 'squishiness' (Ross 1973), or a fuzzy logic to capture it (Lakoff 1973). Others yet either reject grammaticality itself (Sampson & Babarczy 2013) or hope for theoretical illumination on the distinction between grammaticality and acceptability (Sprouse 2018), the latter more amenable to fuzzy characterisations than the former.

Of course, Chomskyans themselves can admit the possible gradable nature of grammaticality or acceptability at the performance level while arguing that discreteness is a useful idealisation nonetheless at the level of competence. Whether grammaticality is modelled discretely or continuously, deviations from the rules (or statistical generalisations) appear to elicit some normative force. The point generalises to deep issues about linguistic methodology going back generations. What do you do when your intuition-derived examples, and eventual laws, conflict with data from corpora? Deny the latter on pain of giving the descriptive game away?[11] Some American structuralists, like Charles Hockett, believed linguistics had to do both jobs at once: characterise corpora of utterances and explain unuttered possibilia. In a move inspired by Goodman and the normative theoretical device of reflective equilibrium (a bedrock in moral and political philosophy), Pullum claims the following of the epistemology of syntax:

The goal is an optimal fit between a general linguistic theory (which is never complete), the proposed rules or constraints (which are not quite as conformant with the general

---

[10] Given a string w and a formal language $L(G)$, there's a finite procedure for deciding whether $w \in L(G)$, that is, a Turing machine that outputs 'yes' or 'no' in finite time. In other words, a language $L(G)$ is decidable if G is a decidable grammar. This is called the 'membership problem'. See Jäger & Rogers (2012).

[11] As we'll see, mainstream linguistics might co-opt the competence–performance distinction to avoid this issue altogether (see Chapter 2) or a 'Galilean' strategy in science (see Chapter 7).

theory as we would like), the best grammaticality judgments obtainable (which are not guaranteed to be veridical), and facts from corpora (which may always contain errors). (2007, p. 37)

Theory development can then follow the Quine–Duhem thesis and the scientific holism it advocates. Confirmation depends on a tapestry of interconnected components, not individual linguists' judgements or speech corpora, wholly. Pullum offers this kind of picture as a response to Sampson's (2007) project aimed at both ridding linguistics of introspective data and divorcing grammatical theory from grammaticality entirely (along with the grammatical–ungrammatical distinction). In so doing, he unequivocally states: 'I take linguistics to have an inherently normative subject matter. The task of the syntactician is exact codification of a set of norms implicit in linguistic practice' (Pullum 2007, p. 39).

Grammar, grammaticality, normativity, and linguistic theory all seem to be interconnected. Before we return to those issues briefly below, we need to address one further (and related) tool that has proven powerful in the linguist's arsenal, that of formalisation.

1.3   Formal Approaches

Contemporary linguistics, as a discipline, is unique in many ways. One of the most interesting aspects of the field, one that sets it apart from many of the social sciences and humanities, is how highly formalised it is. This is apparent in syntax, which drew from work in proof theory, but phonology, semantics, and even pragmatics have all been modelled by formal apparatus of various kinds (e.g. optimality theory is one framework that has been used to formalise all of these subfields). Chomsky famously stated that:

Precisely constructed models for linguistic structure can play an important role, both negative and positive, in the process of discovery itself. By pushing a precise but inadequate formulation to an unacceptable conclusion, we can often expose the exact source of this inadequacy and, consequently, gain a deep understanding of the linguistic data. More positively, a formalized theory may automatically provide solutions for many problems other than those for which it was explicitly designed. (1957, p. 5)

Since then, precision has been the cornerstone of the enterprise.[12] But is there a reason beyond the rhetoric? Is formalisation more than just a tool in the language sciences? Let's evaluate both the 'negative and positive' sides of Chomsky's above claim.

---

[12] Precision and formalisation were, of course, present in the linguistics done before Chomsky as well. Hilbert's programme in metamathematics greatly influenced early linguists like Bloomfield, Hockett, and Harris (see Tomalin 2006). But the formalism played a slightly different role later on, as we'll see.

There are, of course, many positive reasons for formalisation in the sciences more generally. Besides precision, formal theories tend to be explicit about the claims that are made. This feature in turn allows others to build on or critique those theories with more confidence. Mathematics has been 'unreasonably effective' at wrestling the hidden structure of the natural world into submission. This is especially true in physics where group theory, graph theory, and linear algebra have all proved successful in unearthing countless discoveries over the centuries (Wigner 1960). Philosophers, on the other hand, honed formal logic for the construction of their arguments and even used it to extract ontological consequences from their domains of inquiry (recall Quine's influential dictum: 'to be is to be the value of a bound variable' (1948)).

In linguistics, generative grammar was one of the disciplines at the helm of the classical cognitive revolution (Miller 2003). One of the core insights of this paradigm shift in the study of mind was the computational theory of mind, or CTM. The classical version of CTM proposed that the mind can be understood as a computational system or Turing machine of some sort. Chomskyan linguistics embraced not only the letter of CTM but also its punctuation. Formal grammars are formalised as recursive devices that enumerate potentially infinite sets via a finite set of rules. In fact, the $[\Sigma, F]$ or rewrite grammars of *Syntactic Structures* were modelled on post-production systems, Turing-complete recursive enumerators (see Pullum 2011). 'Each such grammar is defined by a finite set Σ of initial strings and a finite set F of "instruction formulas" of the form $X \rightarrow Y$ interpreted: "rewrite X as Y"' (Chomsky 1957, p. 22). A philosopher might recognise a similar procedure here to natural deduction in which you derive a certain formula or conjecture from an initial alphabet and the repeated application of the rules of inference. The field of formal language theory (FLT) became the dominant instantiation of Chomsky's statement at the start of this section. And although FLT has moved from mainstream linguistics to computational approaches (see Chapter 7), early results of the structure and complexity of natural language drew from it significantly.

Take, for instance, the proof of the context-freeness of natural language alluded to above. Without the formalisation of linguistic structure via formal grammars, actual proofs about the structure of language would have been impossible. A tempting thought might be that syntax can be well captured by means of a Markov chain or a simple statistical process involving initial states and transitions between them in sequence. This much is suggested by Saussurean structuralism.[13] Consider the finite state automaton (FSA) in Figure 1.1.

FSAs recognise regular languages (the least complex class of formal languages in the original Chomsky Hierarchy). In the diagram, $q0$ represents

---

[13] 'One of the principles defended by Saussure in the *Course in General Linguistics* is the principle of the "linear nature of the signifier" (1959, p. 70; 1916, p. 103), by which Saussure intends to say that words, like sentences, are concatenations of signs along a linear temporal axis (the time it takes to pronounce a word or sentence)' (Egré 2018, p. 670).

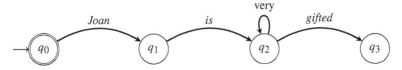

Figure 1.1 Finite state automaton

the input state while $q3$ represents the output (sometimes indicated by a full stop). This kind of formalism has produced significant results in information theory, and as a model of language, it would represent a behaviourist's dream: stimulus and response at its finest. Adding probabilities to the transitions serves as the basis of word-to-word sequencing and earlier predictive processing. A few interesting facts about FLT can already show us why human language cannot be represented by this kind of machine. Every automaton is an accepting machine. It can be paired with a particular formal grammar and language. Furthermore, what it accepts are sequences of strings of a certain complexity. It was argued in Chomsky (1956, 1957) that there are very common patterns in English that already outstrip the power of finite-state automata, namely, patterns of the $a^n b^n$ variety. Less abstractly, certain kinds of syntactic patterns show particular dependencies between units. *The man the woman saw left* fits the mould of the aforementioned pattern. The key to understanding why these sorts of dependencies, and the phenomenon of 'embedding' itself, cause so much difficulty is the appreciation that natural language syntax is a bit like a 'Matryoshka', or Russian nesting doll. Units aren't like Leibniz's *monads* (which were unique, indestructible substances making up the universe) but decomposable phrases that allow for further decomposition. The structural picture that goes with this idea is more like a tree than a line (see Figure 1.2).

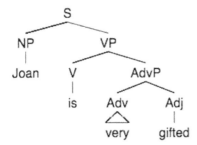

Figure 1.2 Tree for *Joan is very gifted*

The kind of grammar that produces these kinds of structures is phrase structure grammar.[14] The rule systems associated with them are 'context-free', which is a ring above the regular languages in terms of complexity. This means they can represent patterns that finite-state or regular grammars cannot,

---

[14] This class of automata is the pushdown automata with this neat feature called a 'stack' that acts like a little internal memory for the machine.

especially the ones that have embedded constituents.[15] This makes them more expressive since they capture the patterns of the regular languages and more. So why don't we go for the most expressive grammars? In this case, these formalisms would give us the recursively enumerable languages accepted by Turing machines, basically, the machines that can compute any algorithmic computable function whatsoever. Well, it comes down to what the purpose of grammars were supposed to be, that is, they were supposed to generate *all and only all* the sentences of a language. Finite-state grammars don't get us the first 'all' and more complex grammars take us beyond the 'only all'. Now, of course, there's evidence to suggest that context-free or phrase structure grammars don't get us the first 'all' either (Shieber 1985). This argument, based on the syntax of Swiss-German, is a little out of the neighbourhood for us right now, and, in fact, Chomsky (1956) already anticipated that phrase structure grammars wouldn't do by themselves. They needed to be supplemented with transformation rules that could convert one kind of structure into another, for example, an active sentence into a passive.[16] Specifically, in transformational grammar, which characterised the 'Standard Theory' in generative grammar (Chomsky 1965), to get the syntactic structure of a sentence, you start with a 'kernel sentence' derivable by a context-free grammar or rewrite grammar (such as VP → V, AdvP above), then you apply syntactic transformations that insert, move, delete, or alter elements in the structures to which they apply.

This is all to say that formal grammars and formalisation have taught us, and can teach us, a lot about language at a very abstract level. But philosophically, it's even deeper than this. Remember, linguistics was a big player in the classical cognitive revolution (Miller 2003; Bever 2021). One of the core principles of this programme was that the mind is basically like a computer (at the software level). Thus, FLT, automata theory, and formal syntax all contributed to an understanding of what kinds of structures this mental computer was running on, specifically, when it processed language. This is part of the reason that linguistics started to look a lot like computer science. The other part of the reason is an insight attributed to the linguist Wilhelm von Humboldt (1836) that language 'makes infinite use of finite resources'. Chomsky, and others, have claimed that recursion theory (or computability theory) is the only way to make sense of this uniquely linguistic property. Hence, generative grammars with recursive rules.

Lastly, the computational analogy goes both ways. As Müller (2018, p. 6) notes:

---

[15] Constituents are, again, those units of language that seem to act together. For example, they can usually be moved or fronted in English as in *that book, Irene coveted*. There are a number of other 'tests' for constituency common across syntax textbooks.

[16] I've used phrase structure and context-free synonymously here. But there's reason to separate the notions; see Manaster-Ramer & Kac (1990).

[a] further advantage of precisely formulated theories is that they can be written down in such a way that computer programs can process them. When a theoretical analysis is implemented as a computationally processable grammar fragment, any inconsistency will become immediately evident.

This last point tracks well with results in FLT that very often follow the pattern of showing why a particular grammar, formalism, theory, or structure isn't the right one, or at the right level, for particular purposes. Formalisation is a vastly important tool for theory building, but it can be even more useful as a debugger.

It's not only syntax that has undergone massive formalisation: semantics also benefited from the introduction of highly formalised models. If syntax drew inspiration from proof theory, then semantics looked to another side of logic, namely, model theory. Model theory is the mathematical study of interpreting structures or models of formal theories. Led by figures in philosophy like Richard Montague and David Lewis, formal semantics incorporated tools and insights from modal logic, type theory, and lambda calculus to model meaning as the functional complement to syntactic theory. Barbara Partee, the mother of formal semantics, is credited with saying 'lambdas really changed my life' (Partee 1996, p. 24).[17] This kind of mathematical life-changing experience is unsurprising in a field founded by a mathematician who infamously wrote:

There is in my opinion no important theoretical difference between natural languages and the artificial languages of logicians; indeed I consider it possible to comprehend the syntax and semantics of both kinds of languages with a single natural and mathematically precise theory. (Montague 1970, p. 373)[18]

The road from formalisation to mathematisation to Platonism is paved with good scientific intentions. But despite the claims of a few philosophers and linguists,[19] most researchers in the language sciences embrace a different side of the field, one that aligns it less with logic and mathematics and more with fields such as physics, biology, and anthropology. It's to this face of linguistics that we now briefly turn.

1.4   Linguistics as an Empirical Science

One way in which to approach the question of the balance between formal versus empirical components in linguistics is by asking yourself this question: if all the mathematical facts about formal languages were settled, what would be

---

[17] Besides helping with naming complex set-theoretic objects associated with syntactic objects, lambdas aid in transforming syntactic objects like VPs into truth-conditional functions. We'll return to the tool of functional application in Chapter 6.

[18] Thomason (1974, p. 2) further claims that Montague held the view that 'syntax of English, for example, is just as much a part of mathematics as number theory or geometry'.

[19] Notably, Jerrold Katz (1981, 1996) and Paul Postal (2003, 2009).

left of linguistics? To hard-line platonists, the answer might be nothing. To most others, though, it's a panoply of possibility. Linguists study communication, phonetics, sign languages, and conventional regularities inherited from linguistic communities over time. Although some of the foundational tools have been borrowed from discrete mathematics, statistical and social scientific approaches have also played a role in some of the most important discoveries of the field.

Consider the famous case of class-based linguistic variation across societies. Intra- and inter-class regularities have been documented in speech patterns, register, and lexicon. For instance, '[Labov] soon established that when the collective pronunciation of a certain vowel changes without being noticed by the speech community, it is likely that upper-working class or lower-middle class women are leading the change' (Woschitz 2020, p. 163). His work on African American Vernacular English (AAVE) was groundbreaking. Chomskyans generally reject dialect studies as peripheral to linguistic theory and a nonstarter to scientific research on language. So-called external or E-languages are considered political more than scientific objects. But Labov showed that studying neglected (and oppressed) dialects of English, such as those spoken by working-class African American communities in the USA, provides a theoretical window into phenomena as diverse as structural variation, language contact, and language change. For example, Labov (1969) uncovered an interesting regularity that when copula contraction is permitted in Standard English, AAVE allows deletion (and the other way around). Furthermore, when contraction isn't possible, then neither is deletion. Consider the following:

1. Barbara said *she's* going/*Smart, that's what she's.
2. Barbara said *she* going/*Smart, that's what she.

His methodology wasn't mathematical. In fact, he used methodological innovations such as peer-group recordings to identify phonological as well as grammatical features across dialects and class structures. On a more systemic level, in a slightly more recent article, Labov (2010) argues that contrary to the contemporary trajectory of many oppressed languages toward extinction, residential segregation has reversed this fate for AAVE. Variability is key to understanding sociolinguistics. It doesn't deal in laws or mathematical certainty but contextually triggered phenomena, like when a linguistic environment triggers code-switching behaviour. Shifting from a job interview to a party with friends is likely to affect your register in systematic and measurable ways.

Contemporary biolinguists consider language to be a 'biological object' and claim to embrace the biological sciences as an alternative to formal logic and mathematics (we'll evaluate these claims more carefully in Chapter 8). Similarly to Labovian methodology, biology, for researchers like Berwick & Chomsky (2016), is more of a case study than the law-foraging expeditions of physics or mathematics. The regularities one discovers are often unstable and subject to change. Language is essentially a brain state, and our knowledge of neural circuitry is relatively nascent. Friederici *et al.* (2017) identify the Broca area (BA 44) as the brain centre of syntactic processing (as well as the dorsal pathway). '[W]ith respect to Broca's area, the activation of BA 44 as a function of syntax has been confirmed in many studies across different languages' (Friederici *et al.* 2017, p. 714). More specifically, they link these areas to the 'Merge' postulate of later generative grammar. Merge is an operation that takes syntactic objects and composes a labelled (unordered) set containing these objects, iteratively. Merge is meant to capture the allegedly universal property of the hierarchical structure of syntax, that is, sentences are composed of embedded phrases that can themselves be embedded, represented by a tree-like structure. The tools of biolinguistics are supposed to include fMRI studies, computed tomology, and other techniques used in event-related potential (ERP) research, in which direct brain responses are measured with specific stimuli. However, neuroscientists emphasise the property of neural plasticity, which militates against strong causal and structural claims about the brain (Silberstein 2022). In addition, in biolinguistics, unlike Labovian sociolinguistics, most contextual and environmental factors are abstracted away. Biolinguists often aim to verify the generative architecture of the language faculty, replete with autonomous syntax and externalised interfaces characteristic of the Minimalist Program (Chomsky 1995b). They hope to do this by means of empirical investigation, using the techniques of neuroscience inter alia.

Corpus linguistics, invigorated by computational tools Saussure could only have dreamed of, homes in on speech corpora and interconnections or collocations between data points. A prominent example of this approach are vector-space distributional models in semantics. Instead of a meaning or semantic value being defined by the association of a word or expression with a discrete set-theoretic object as it is with formal semantics, semantic values are represented as vectors, or, more abstractly, meanings of linguistic items are modelled 'as points or regions in some "meaning space"' (Erk 2020, p. 71). Here, statistical collocational data provides the background for representing semantic structure. A simple case is 'count-based spaces' in which a vector is a sequence of numerical values used to measure the meaning of a word in terms of the words that co-occur with it across multiple contexts. The underlying assumption is that words with the same or similar meanings occur within similar contexts. By representing a word as a matrix of similarity scores within these contexts, we can thus get to its approximate meaning. This perspective breathes new life into Firth's (1957) famous adage that 'you shall know a word by the company it keeps'.

Finally, even in some cases where formalism seems to be doing a lot of the work, such as Optimality Theory (OT), there's a distinctive instrumental flavour to the analysis (Prince & Smolensky 1993). In OT, the basic architecture

Table 1.1. *Basic OT structure*

	Input	Constraint 1	Constraint 2	Constraint 3
	candidate 1	*!		
	candidate 2		*	
☞	candidate 3			*

contains a generator (GEN) that generates an infinite number of outputs or candidates for representation for each input of the grammar. The evaluator component (EVAL) then chooses the optimal output from the set of outputs through a set of ranked, violable constraints, or CON. CON is considered to be universal while the rankings are given by particular languages. In phonology, the inputs are representations from the lexicon and morphology and the outputs are phonetic transcriptions. The basic structure is given in Table 1.1.[20]

In a sense, OT relies on pure combinatorics. It's similar to a mathematical decision procedure. Nevertheless, in spite of the formalism, phonology is very grounded in actual human phonetic possibilities. The candidate list is finite given that phonemes are finite and their combinations limited in real-world languages. The ranked list of constraints is an empirical matter divined from linguistic fieldwork and experimentation.

Even the theoretical linguistic work based entirely on the intuitions of linguists can in part be seen as an empirical exercise, if we follow Devitt's (2006) convincing line of argument that linguists' intuitions aren't Cartesian introspection but rather scientifically honed skills for spotting linguistically relevant structure. The analogy asks us to compare the impressions of a lay person looking over a dig site to that of a paleontologist with years of experience. Naturally, the latter will immediately ('intuitively') see scientifically relevant fragments in ways inaccessible to the novice.

The notion of 'conservativeness' in the nominalist tradition in the philosophy of mathematics is helpful here (Field 1980). The idea is that mathematics aids the sciences in all the ways I mentioned in the previous section on formalisation. More precise models, clearer results, and easier debugging. But the science is *conservative* with relation to mathematics when every claim can be stated without it, in principle. In practice, of course, this makes scientific life very difficult but still possible. More precisely, it suggests that at some high level, the mathematics is dispensable. In other words, all the consequences of the scientific theory (nominalistically stated) derived from the mathematical theory are already consequences of the former without the latter. OT phonology can

---

[20] A star indicates a constraint violation, an exclamation mark after the star means a fatal violation, and a pointing hand an optimal candidate. Sometimes, there's more than one optimal candidate.

most certainly be stated without the tableaux. It's harder to see how this could be for the results of computational corpus linguistics (and part of the reason the original programme was put on hold for a few decades). But again, the statistics are merely meant to reflect the underlying regularities. What's more tricky is the question over the results of FLT and whether the proofs of relative complexity of natural language grammars and constructions are stateable without the formalisms. They're certainly stateable by means of *alternative* formalisms.[21] But the problem is that if mathematical models provide *structural* explanations in empirical sciences and FLT is purely structural, then there might be no remainder for the theory without the maths.[22] We won't settle this question here. In fact, some theoretical linguistics, such as the aforementioned biolinguistics, aims to retain a deep mathematical core of language (Merge or 'narrow syntax') while advocating a naturalist scientific persuasion to the field at large.

Many of the issues discussed in this opening salvo will return within specific contexts in later chapters.

1.5   Cognitive or Social Science?

If linguistics is an empirical science, the next natural question concerns what kind of empirical science it is. The mainstream literature assumes, with Chomsky (1965), that the study of language is the study of (a part of) the mind. Thus, linguistics, on this view, is a cognitive science. Even more, linguistics is often taken to be the study of a particular module of the mind/brain called 'the language faculty'. Of course, this move isn't mandatory. Cognitive linguistics assumes a more domain-general approach to linguistic structure that eschews some of the uniqueness claims of generative theory (Lakoff 1991).[23] Either way, language is considered something internal to the language user. Chomsky infamously stated in *Aspects*:

Linguistic theory is concerned primarily with an ideal speaker-listener, in a completely homogeneous speech-community, who knows its (the speech community's) language perfectly and is unaffected by such grammatically irrelevant conditions as memory lim-

---

[21] For a comparison between generative-enumerative theories of syntax and model-theoretic alternatives, see Pullum (2013).
[22] See Leng (2021) for a recent argument to the effect that mathematical explanations are structural explanations in the sciences generally, and Nefdt (2021, 2022) for a structural realist account of linguistics specifically.
[23] Itkonen (2006) criticises cognitive linguistics as inheriting a fallacy of equivocation from generative linguistics in its definition of 'conventional mental conventions' (Lakoff 1987; Langacker 1991). He argues that cognitive linguistics needs a social normative grounding in order to be successful.

itations, distractions, shifts of attention and interest, and errors (random or characteristic) in applying his knowledge of this language in actual performance. (1965, p. 4)

The idea behind this idealisation was an empirical assumption that many of the mechanisms involved in memory limitations and linguistic dysfluencies of other sorts are independent of those involved in the generation of syntactic structures. What's interesting is that this idealisation not only idealises the internal state of the cogniser but also the state of her community. Essentially, this interpretation of the scientific target of linguistics later developed into an object known as *I-language* in which 'the state attained is a computational (generative) system' (Chomsky 2000, p. 78). The 'I' stands for *internal*, *intensional*, and *individualistic*. The first term simply reiterates the internalism of the field. The second emphasises the need to study grammars qua functions that generate the infinite sets of expressions of language. Lastly, we have the individualistic nature of the scientific object of study. As linguists, we're to be solely interested in the goings-on within the heads of individual speakers and not their environments or relations to others. Part of the motivation for this circumscription is that the alternative, an E(xternal)-language, is allegedly scientifically untenable. Some oft-cited criticisms of this latter possibility involve the politically determined boundaries between languages, poverty of stimulus, and the idea that it might entail an infeasible 'theory of everything' (Chomsky 2000).

Nevertheless, the dual suggestion of a social normative dimension of an empirically based science of linguistics (Sections 1.2 and 1.4) allows for the further possibility of viewing the field as a subfield of social science. There are at least three ways to take this suggestion: (1) incorporating sociolinguistics within theoretical linguistics more firmly, (2) establishing a science of E-language, or (3) exploring the constitutive social normative aspects of language. These options need not be mutually exclusive, of course, even if they're usually packaged that way. Let's explore each briefly.

Sociolinguistics, or option (1), Labovian or otherwise, entails a social ontology but not a normative scientific perspective. Language might be a social object but its properties are identifiable at the social level by statistical, corpus, and/or general social scientific methods. It's a descriptive science. Option (2) takes languages to be external public objects. They're constituted by social conventions. For instance, Dummett holds that 'a speaker has "mastery of a procedure, of a conventional practice"' (1993, p. 69) of a community of speakers when she knows a language. This, to him, is necessary for communication. However, the way to study this social convention need not differ from the tools of standard linguistics or the logical methodology of analytic philosophy of language. Again, without further argument, normativity doesn't enter the picture directly. By contrast, option (3) embraces the normativity.

Itkonen (1978, 1997) motivates the idea that language is a normative social entity and that 'autonomous linguistics' studies it. 'The grammarian does not describe what is said or how it is understood, but what ought to be said or how it ought to be understood. And because the norms (or rules) of language that determine these "ought"-aspects cannot be individual … they must be social' (Itkonen 1997, p. 54). Here, he relies on Wittgenstein's famous argument that the very idea of a private language is incoherent.[24]

In a more contemporary setting, inferentialism adopts a similar normative picture of language and meaning. They too are heavily influenced by Wittgenstein's philosophy. Peregrin (2015), following Brandom (1994), holds that language is constituted by normative inferential rules determined by the 'game of giving and asking for reasons'. Very quickly, as speakers in a community, we're constantly engaging in linguistic (and other) activities that establish 'commitments' and corresponding 'entitlements'. For example, when I make a statement like *Jarda stopped smoking*, I'm automatically committed to a host of other sentences like *Jarda was a smoker*. In terms of methodology, contemporary inferentialism shares features with early proof theory in that it embodies the attempted development of the proof-theoretic approach that characterised the logical constants (in Gentzen-style proof theory, for instance) to also include the nonlogical vocabulary of natural language. This is often referred to as 'strong inferentialism' in that it doesn't restrict the inferential analysis to moves from language to language but also the possibility of inferential rules that govern language–world relationships (following Sellars 1954).[25]

There are issues with both the cognitive scientific and the social scientific interpretations of linguistics. Methodologically, standard linguistics differs from other cognitive sciences and, besides sociolinguistics, from the tools of the social sciences to boot. Ontologically, language has cognitive characteristics as well as a social conventional side. Even Chomsky admits that 'the state of knowledge attained may itself include some kind of reference to the social nature of language' (Chomsky 1986, p. 18). The task is to find a way to pursue both goals without neglecting either. In Chapter 2, I set out one means of achieving a union between these desiderata.

1.6   Outline of the Book

Each forthcoming chapter has at its core a philosophical argument concerning a particular linguistic domain or, in the case of later chapters, the relationship between linguistic domains and other fields. These arguments aren't offered as consensus views or adumbrations of the theoretical questions of the particular topic.

---

[24] See Chapter 6 for more on Wittgenstein's view of language.
[25] See Nefdt (2018b) for a discussion of the links between proof theory and inferentialism.

In Chapter 2, I'll argue that the central pursuit of theoretical linguistics is the determination of what makes a language a possibly human one. This will take us into the work on recursion, statistical universals, impossible languages, and ultimately bring us to a novel modal metaphysics for linguistic possibility.

Chapter 3 delves into syntactic metatheory. Specifically, I attempt to find a common thread between vastly different contemporary syntactic frameworks from generative grammar and Jackendoff's Parallel Architecture to radical construction grammar and dependency grammar. I'll argue that there's a basic explanatory project in syntax, broader than most accounts but precise enough to offer a genuine point of contact between rival approaches.

The burgeoning field of metasemantics is the focus of Chapter 4. The main pursuit is directed at identifying a viable metasemantic grounding for the field. In this process, I introduce a contextual continuum that connects dynamic and distributional approaches to mainstream formal semantic ones. I also discuss lexical decomposition, underspecification, and supersemantics.

If the syntax–semantics interface looms large in the previous chapter, the semantics–pragmatics distinction occupies Chapter 5. Pragmatics has often been considered 'the waste-basket of semantics'. However, in this chapter, we consider new and old ideas on the semantics–pragmatics interface as well as how these ideas map on to contemporary linguistic pragmatics in the form of relevance theory, OT, game theory, and Bayesian approaches.

The main theme of Chapter 6 is phonology and sign language. The philosophy of phonology is an often-neglected subfield, yet, many of the formal foundations of generative grammar have roots in the methodology of phonology. I'll argue that phonology (broadly construed to include sign, gesture, and haptic modalities) opens up the possibility of thinking of language in terms of a philosophical action theory.

In Chapter 7, we move to a controversial companion to theoretical linguistics. In fact, the central issue of the chapter is whether new approaches in computational linguistics and natural language processing, such as deep learning, have something significant to offer the theoretical study of language. My answer will involve a detour into the philosophy of science, the neglected scientific goal of prediction and its relation to the explanatory project of theoretical linguistics.

The penultimate Chapter 8 will delve into the philosophy of language evolution. Instead of surveying the myriad theoretical options of this topic, we'll challenge the minimalisation trend of the mainstream linguistic approach and argue for a complexity-theoretic interpretation of the scientific target of the field in its stead.

Chapter 9 will conclude with a brief discussion of some topics not covered in depth and an overview of the interconnections between chapters.

Further Reading

Book-length treatments of the philosophy of linguistics are rare. But the following brief list offers readers, new and old, strong introductions to some of the topics covered in this chapter so far.

- A volume by Ruth Kempson, Tim Fernando, and Nicholas Asher (2012), *Philosophy of Linguistics* (Elsevier Ltd), is an excellent place to start with general overviews of philosophical issues lurking within various subfields of linguistics. It contains a number of high-level introductions to issues in the philosophy of phonology, language evolution, computational approaches, syntax, and semantics, written by experts in their respective fields. The coverage is broad, but the depth is strong enough to be accessible to the general reader as well as the seasoned practitioner.
- In terms of formal or mathematical approaches to linguistics, a classic text is still Barbara Partee, Alice Meulen, and Robert Wall's (1993) *Mathematical Methods in Linguistics* (Kluwer Academic Publishers). It covers a large number of tools from within set theory and logic that have been specifically incorporated into linguistic theory in both syntax and semantics. The final set of chapters is especially useful for a deeper understanding of formal language theory, automata theory, and the Chomsky Hierarchy of formal languages.
- For a slightly more recent compendium of mathematical modelling in linguistics, Edward Keenan and Lawrence Moss' (2016) *Mathematical Structures in Language* (CSLI Publications) offers a comprehensive account that includes phonology and a model of Modern Korean. It also covers a lot of the same material as the Partee *et al.* book, such as lattices, set theory, and FLT.
- A more philosophical treatment of the relationship between the formal sciences and linguistics can be found in Marcus Tomalin (2006) *Linguistics and the Formal Sciences* (Cambridge University Press). This book not only serves as a thorough historical overview of the philosophical and mathematical origins of generative grammar but also of its connections to Bloomfieldian formal methods, Hilbert's metamathematical programme, and Goodman's constructional system theory. The evolution of recursion within various epochs of generative grammar is also covered in a careful and precise manner.
- A different take on the relationship between linguistics and philosophy is provided by the recent edited volume by Daniel Altshuler (2022), *Linguistics Meets Philosophy* (Cambridge University Press). This book targets specific phenomena from both philosophical and linguistic angles. The introductory chapter by Barbara Partee is especially illuminating on the history of the interactions between the fields.

- Lastly, Noam Chomsky's (2000) *New Horizons for the Study of Mind and Language* (Cambridge University Press) is perhaps one of the most lucid interactions between philosophy of language and theoretical linguistics in circulation today. In it, Chomsky lays out the philosophical underpinnings of contemporary generative linguistics. He discusses the flaws of traditional philosophical work on language within the analytic tradition and details his alternative naturalistic view of language and linguistics, in which language is considered to be a 'biological object'.

2   What Is a Possible Human Language?

We know a lot about natural languages. We know facts about their structure and typology. We've isolated specific brain regions responsible for processing specific parts of speech. We might even be able to tell why people say *uh* instead of *um* in some situations.[1] Despite this undeniable progress, there's still a big-picture question that's generally gone underexplored: what is a possible human or natural language?

This question is central to the enterprise of theoretical linguistics. An adequate answer would give us traction on issues in language evolution, acquisition, and the philosophy of language. There have been some notable attempts at addressing this general region of theoretical space. Hockett's (1960) famous design features are one source of insight. Comparative work on human and nonhuman animal communication also offers further resources (and, in some cases, doubt about Hockett's original neat dichotomy). However, uniqueness and possibility aren't identical. To know which features *actual* human languages exhibit isn't to answer the question of what possible features our languages *could* express. Nevertheless, uniqueness isn't orthogonal to the kinds of questions we're asking here. On the formal side, there's been some interest in questions of how many possible languages there are. Pullum (1983) refers to the idea that a given linguistic theory limits the number of possible grammars to a finite upper-bound as the 'finiteness result'. If this sort of result were true, it would also place a finite limit on the number of possible human languages. He shows that no such result holds water, formally speaking. He also argues that even if it did, it wouldn't be very interesting or important. I'm not sure I completely agree.[2] For one thing, it would count, *contra* Montague, as a theoretical difference between formal and natural languages since formal languages are certainly infinite in number. We'll get into some issues with formal languages and natural languages below. But again, the cardinality of natural languages won't directly concern us here and, as Pullum rightly remarks,

---

[1] Clark & Fox Tree (2002) analyse large corpora to hypothesise that *uh* indicates a minor delay and *um* a major one.
[2] To be fair, Pullum gets to this conclusion with relation to acquisition studies and the like.

'even if the class of possible grammars were finite, children could not make use of this fact. The cardinality of the relevant class, even of core grammars, would be unimaginably vast' (1983, p. 462). In other words, finitude shouldn't be confused with paucity, tractability, or learnability.

In this chapter, I plan to deconstruct the notion of possible human or natural language. My plan, in Section 2.4, is to use an analogy with modal metaphysics to argue for a view of possible languages in terms of accessibility relations given to us by linguistic theory. Before I can do this, I need to address some related concepts in theoretical linguistics. In Section 2.3, I want to link the concept of 'naturalness' in philosophy and investigate whether it can be of use in demarcating the space of possibility as a kind of filtration in terms of learnability. In Section 2.2, I'll discuss the recent literature on impossible languages as an indirect way of answering our quandary. I'll expose some of the controversial assumptions in this research and ultimately claim that it'll be of little help to our present quest (despite its other merits). But before any of these tasks can be adequately pursued, we need to be more clear on what we take a language to be. This will be the topic of the next section.

2.1   Universal Language and Particular Languages

There's a vital distinction at the heart of linguistic theory, across formalisms and frameworks. This issue has already been hinted at above with relation to Haspelmath's (2021) separation between 'general' and 'particular' linguistics. To oversimplify, general linguistics pertains to language as such or *Language* (with a capital 'L') while particular linguistics pertains to *languages* (lower-case 'l'). The distinction isn't just a matter of orthography. It tracks an important difference in scientific target. Chomskyans tend to view the separation as that between Universal Grammar (UG) and individual grammars or *I*-languages (internalised representations of the individual states of the language faculty of idealised cognisers). But that's not the only way to carve out the difference. A Language could be defined platonically, based on abstract rule systems and then the ways in which people use such systems, similar to how they use natural number systems, to define the possible instantiations. A public language theorist could identify the total set of social conventions, which can be considered linguistic, and then distinguish between individual realisations in particular communities of speakers.

Haspelmath (2021) goes as far as to suggest that there's a paradox in theoretical linguistics. The idea is that the only way to access Language is via languages. 'We want to explore and understand the nature of Human Language, but what we can observe directly is particular languages' (Haspelmath 2021,

p. 10).[3] To me, the 'paradox' seems like a common methodology situation in the empirical sciences. Understanding biological organisms requires us to investigate particular specimens and generalise to a type such as *Drosophilia* or *Mus musculus*.[4] On the other hand, if biolinguists are on to something, then we could possibly access UG directly through neuroscientific experimentation, at least in principle. But, as Marr (1982) influentially argued in the case of vision, information processing happens at various levels. Thus, even if we could pin down the hardware or implementational level, we'd still need to understand the algorithmic and computational levels. In other words, we need to specify the general nature of the problems we want to solve computationally and then identify the algorithms that could possibly do the trick given the physical systems or mechanisms with which we're dealing. Biolinguists assume that this system is the human brain, but cognitive linguists often opt to extend the remit of cognition (including linguistic) to the entire body and beyond, which complicates the implementational level. Either way, the question of what a possible human language is involves all the levels, not just the hardware or biological level.[5]

Interestingly, the movement in generative linguistics has been away from complexity towards simplicity to the extent that UG has been reduced to the Merge (and Move) operation under Minimalism (Chomsky 1995b). On the contrary, if we assume that Language is just Merge, and Merge is a set-theoretic operation that produces unordered sets of syntactic objects recursively, then Language is mathematically limitless. Of course, the idea in its original context is that Merge (or something like it) is more likely to have evolved within a short period of time than the highly complex multi-modular linguistic architectures of erstwhile frameworks such as Government and Binding (for example Berwick & Chomsky 2016). We'll return to this issue in Chapter 8. But for our purposes, reducing Language to an unordered algorithm on elements that can operate iteratively to infinity doesn't, by itself, set a clear boundary on what's possible.

The relationship between Language and languages is indeed a complex one. One avenue we might explore to assess this relationship is the research on linguistic universals. This would offer us a direct route from individual languages to universal patterns shared by all languages, that is, Language itself.

---

[3] There's a parallel here with the ancient platonic worries about how we might have access to the perfect *Forms* of things if we're mired by the imperfect nature of our everyday objects and instantiations.

[4] This is also part of the reason model organisms were cultivated within controlled environments; see Ankeny & Leonelli (2011) for an overview.

[5] For example, Frank *et al.* (2012) show that the neurolinguistic models that have been used as evidence for hierarchical structures in syntactic processing can be explained just as well by means of flat dependency-like structures. Same hardware and computational problem, different algorithm.

In practice, we don't need to assume anything about a cognitive universal substrate or biological instantiation in this kind of typological exercise. All we need is a large enough sample of grammars from distinct representatives of distinct language families, some metric of similarity, and perhaps a few computational tools to run the feature analysis. I say 'all we need', but this might not be enough. Even if it is, getting a large enough sample size for our universal instantiation would be a very tall order. In essence, this procedure suggests that there's a possibility of an underlying mathematical induction at play. Assume all languages have property P, then show P holds for the base case (probably English, given the linguistic bias in journal publication), then prove the inductive step or the claim that if the property holds for some nth language, then it holds for (n+1)th language.

It's not clear what properties would be within our candidate induction. According to linguists like William Croft (2001), natural languages are more like distinct species than homogeneous natural numbers. There are no universal categories, and translating one construction type from one language to another isn't a theory-neutral exercise.

Across languages as well, constructions appear to define different categories (Dryer 1997): Absolutive–Ergative does not match Subject–Object; the Verb category can be either more inclusive (including 'Adjectives' as well) or less inclusive (where a small set of 'Verbs' combines with other elements to produce the translation equivalents of English 'Verbs'). (Croft 2013, p. 4)

This is an extreme position, aptly named 'radical construction grammar'.[6] But even setting this position aside, inductive or statistical universals can only get us so far. The *actual* is a useful guide to the *possible*, but not an exhaustive one. Statistically, most languages are SVO (subject–verb–object) or SOV (subject–object–verb); verb-initial configurations such as VSO or VOS are more rare, with object-initial languages almost unattested. Specifically, some linguists have thought that OVS languages don't exist as they seem to reverse the linear order of externalisation. Are OVS languages impossible? Well, there seem to be some languages that exhibit this word order, with the most recent addition being South African Sign Language (SASL) (Vermeerbergen *et al.* 2007). However, it's not clear if these languages just allow for more topicalisation. Even if there were no known cases of OVS languages, what would that tell us exactly?[7] That all possible human languages are found in

---

[6] See Chapter 3 for a radical argument to the effect that radical construction grammar might not be that radical after all.

[7] Pullum (2018) tells an interesting story about how he met a student (and former missionary) in a class at University College London. Together, they discovered that a little-known Brazilian language called Hixkaryana might indeed be OVS. The more formal results are presented in Derbyshire & Pullum (1981).

the other configurations? Or perhaps that those languages have gone extinct for some reason? If the latter, then OVS was possible and thus is possible still, assuming human beings haven't changed their brain chemistry or environmental niches too radically in the past few thousand years. Furthermore, many of the world's languages have gone extinct before they could be studied sufficiently, casting serious doubt on the direct typological approach to universals.

Moreover, Evans & Levinson (2009) argue that diversity is more of a datum than universality could ever be. According to them, in the search for universality, typologists have instead found massive variation at every level of linguistic organisation. The idea that human languages are completely and comprehensively variable at every level is offered as a replacement research programme to the hunt for universals. I don't think accepting this possibility requires abandoning the pursuit for a more unified target in language evolution. Linguistic variability surely emerged after human language (or proto-language) did in some form. Thus, searching for patterns in the variation still seems like a viable project.[8] Evans & Levinson's suggestion would effectively eliminate the relevance of the present question into the nature of possible human language. In other words, there's no Language just languages, as Croft's theory would have it.

What we do get from the Croftian and Evans & Levinsonian positions is that the strategy of determining a *can* from an *is*, even if the *is* is feasible (which in this case is far from certain), isn't going to give us the insight we're seeking. This is because surveying extant constructions or properties of contemporary languages cannot fully determine the space of possible constructions and language. In fact, the research (including the Greenbergian variety) only really produces a picture in which 'there is no question that there are some very strong universal tendencies' (Dabrowska 2015, p. 7). We need additional assumptions to get from tendencies to possibilities (a framework I'll provide in the last section).[9]

Before we give up completely on the link between universality and possibility, or Language itself, let's consider the possibility that the true essence of Language lies deeper than the (cross-linguistic) surface. If the inference from particular languages involves statistical universals, then isolating formal properties of Language itself should focus on abstract design features

---

[8] Of course, to some Chomskyans, the appearance of variability is a scientific diversion. '[T]he appearance of complexity and diversity in a scientific field quite often simply reflects a lack of deeper understanding, a very familiar phenomenon' (Berwick & Chomsky 2016, p. 93).

[9] We might also worry, with Szabó (2022), that tendencies don't rule out exceptions, even contrived and inserted ones. His example is of ablaut reduplication in phonology in which an initial high vowel is replaced by a low one but never the other way around, for example, chit-chat, wishy-washy, flip-flop. Despite being a candidate for robust statistical tendencies or universal law across languages, it can easily be circumvented by merely inventing words and, with enough community support, inserting them into the language.

(even more abstract than Hockett's). If you recall from Chapter 1, we discussed the move from finite-state or regular grammars to context-free grammars. One of the reasons for the shift was that finite-state grammars couldn't handle embedding phenomena such as centre-embedding, ubiquitous across natural languages. In order to account for such phenomena, recursive rules need to be incorporated into the grammars. The production rules for context-free grammars are as follows:

1. $S \rightarrow aSb$.
2. $S \rightarrow ab$.

Note, the issue isn't about infinity as it's sometimes claimed. The simple finite-state automaton in Figure 1.1 of the last chapter contained a loop (for 'very') that would technically produce an infinite number of sentences. A boring infinity but an infinity nonetheless. The really interesting feature is captured by (1), in which S can be rewritten as a formula containing S. Generative linguists have homed in on this feature, suggesting that it and only it is the one true universal of language. All languages from SASL to Hixkaryana are recursive at base. In other words, every language has the built-in capacity for embedding, iterating, and compounding brought to you by the property of recursion. As Hauser *et al.* (2002) hypothesise:

All approaches agree that a core property of FLN [faculty of language in the narrow sense] is recursion, attributed to narrow syntax in the conception ... This capacity of FLN yields discrete infinity (a property that also characterizes the natural numbers). (p. 1571)

They distinguish between the 'faculty of language in the broad sense' (FLB), which is domain-general and dovetails with semantic, pragmatic, and other cognitive domains, and the 'faculty of language in the narrow sense' (FLN), which is a species-specific, domain-specific component of our genetic linguistic endowment, basically just containing the computational core of human language. This position (and the later version with Merge) marks the culmination of the concept of recursion from a technical modelling feature of formal grammars to a biocognitive component of the alleged *sine qua non* of the language faculty: narrow syntax. Tomalin (2007) describes the transition in the following way:

[I]n the earliest work, although recursive components were considered useful formal procedures that simplified the basic analytical framework, no strong claims were made concerning their biological status. Gradually, though, as the theory of GG developed ... the role of recursion within the GG framework began to acquire cognitive connotations, with the eventual result that ... it has been hypothesised that recursion is a genetically-embedded computational procedure. (p. 1785)

In terms of our present purpose, this view suggests that recursion is perhaps the only universal of language. We've already worried above whether recursion really gives us much traction on the possibly linguistic directly, but our next question is best negatively stated: can there be human languages without recursion? If there are possible human languages without recursion, then recursion isn't a necessary (or universal) property of human language. According to a controversial proposal by Daniel Everett (2005, 2017a), concerning the syntax of a little-known language (at the time) called Pirahã spoken by a small community in the Upper Amazon Basin, the answer is unequivocally yes. The controversy won't concern us here. Nor will I take a stand on the empirical issues that are largely orthogonal to our purposes (see Everett 2007, Nevins *et al.* 2009). What I want to focus on is one brand of response to Everett that I think highlights the level at which the universal recursion postulate is meant to be pitched. The line of counterargument goes something like this: it doesn't really matter if Pirahã or XYZ doesn't express features like centre-embedding or clausal subordination in their syntax; the property of recursion lies deeper than surface externalisations that can be prey to exogenous constraints. This means that in so far as the Pirahã people are human beings capable of human language, that is, they have UG, they have the 'capacity' for recursion.[10]

There are (at least) two interesting features of this kind of response worth considering here. One suggests that there's no amount of empirical or statistical investigation that can refute the recursion postulate. The worry is then that the claim is unfalsifiable. This is one of Evans & Levinson's main concerns, that '[t]he claims of Universal Grammar, we argue here, are either empirically false, unfalsifiable, or misleading in that they refer to tendencies rather than strict universals' (2009, p. 429). Claims of un/falsifiability are tricky. Firstly, a point that's sometimes elided outside of the philosophy of science, falsifiability isn't the hallmark of 'the scientific' that it once was. Secondly, and this brings out the tension between linguistics as a formal science versus an empirical science issue nicely (discussed in Chapter 1), empirical unfalsifiability might not rule out mathematical falsifiability. Smolensky & Dupoux's (2009) response to Evans & Levinson highlights this point further:

Counterexamples to des-universals are not counterexamples to cog-universals ... a hypothesised cog-universal can only be falsified by engaging the full apparatus of the formal theory. (p. 468)

---

[10] The history of the term 'recursion' in linguistics is complicated. The idea is that recursive functions introduce a property of self-reference. This involves two steps: one that specifies the condition of termination of the recursion or the base case, and a recursive step that reduces all other cases to the base. For some early attempts at formal definition, see Chomsky (1959b) and Miller & Chomsky (1963) for an elaboration of the terms 'language' and 'recursion' in linguistics. For a development of these ideas within recursive characterisations of particular linguistic constructions, see Langendoen (2008).

This brings us to the other interesting feature, namely, that the postulate moves us from the empirical to the formal domain of universals (also called 'deep universals'). Recursion is a formal property of Language itself, on this view. Thus, to be a possible human language is to be a recursive structure of a certain sort. But this structure need not be exhibited at the surface level. Dabrowska suggests that these deep 'invisible' universals make it unclear 'what would count as counterevidence for a proposal universal' (2015, p. 7). Well, obvious counterevidence would be of the cognitive-formal variety. For instance, if a linguist proposed that all natural languages fall within the context-sensitive ring of the Chomsky Hierarchy, that claim can be falsified by providing evidence that parsing with context-sensitive grammars is an NP-hard problem, thought to require $O(2^n)$ time to parse a sentence (n is the length of the input in words). It's a bit like certain geometric features preventing a particular engineering model from being feasible. The features might be formal, to do with angles or gradients or abstract volume calculations, but the effects are physical. Mathematical properties can and do constrain the range of possibilities in various domains – Language is no exception. Of course, the real issue is whether there are specific linguistic properties (even if these turn out to be formal) that constrain Language.

In Nefdt (2019), building on Tiede & Stout (2010), I argue that formal models and properties such as recursion need not reflect linguistic reality. If a grammar of a particular language, like English, requires recursive, context-free rules, this doesn't mean that English itself inherits this property. The natural sciences tout court utilise models with so-called nonveridical features all the time. In fact, discrete infinity itself, as I argue in that paper, has been used as a 'smoothing' device in order to make the mathematics of a system more tractable, a technique borrowed from computer science (Savitch 1993).[11]

To sum up, statistical or empirical universals provide us with generalised tendencies at best, while formal universals don't clearly delimit the space of possible languages nor unequivocally distinguish between linguistic models and linguistic reality. So where does this leave us with relation to the Language versus languages issue? In my view, Language is clearly a scientific abstraction from particular languages, just like mountains, plants, species, triangles, electrons, economies, complex systems, and other scientific objects are. In order to identify what a possible human language is, we need to accept the abstraction without reducing our subject matter to an a priori abstract object.[12] We need

[11] To make a stronger, more ontologically committing claim would require evidence that recursion is an actual property of natural language (the lack of stable empirical univerals notwithstanding). Sometimes, linguists make the recursion–infinity link, as we'll see in the next section, and others link creativity with infinity (Chomsky 1966).

[12] It's interesting to note that these ontological debates are largely absent in other scientific domains. No one in the cognitive neuroscience of memory asks how individual tokens or memories are related to some platonistic concept of Memory, divorced from its instantiations. I thank Wolfram Hinzen for this particular observation.

to stay general without losing our sense of reality or empirical science. Devitt (2013a) provides us with a usefully neutral characterisation:

What is a language? It is a system of representations or symbols that is constituted by a set of governing rules, and that a group of organisms use to communicate with each other. (p. 95)

As it stands, this conception lacks any overt ontological commitments.[13] Furthermore, the view I'll push in the later parts of this chapter will offer a means of capturing both the rule-bound nature of Language and the communicative dimension of languages.

Before we move on to the positive account, let's consider one last attempt at identifying the universal, this time indirectly via the idea of impossible languages. If we can develop a clear grasp on the linguistically impossible, surely possibility will follow by simple logic?

2.2   Moro on Impossible Languages

What is an impossible human language? This is the central question of the research of Andrea Moro, a prominent generativist and neuroscientist. Similar to my own interests, Moro sees the concept of impossible languages as a conduit to defining possible human Language. In the following section, I'll outline his fascinating perspective and experimental evidence. My eventual critique will be based on his underlying assumptions and some problems with the modal metaphysics of impossibility inherent in his work. However, this isn't to say that we cannot learn something important about possibility from Moro. In fact, I'll argue in the next section that his experiments provide us with one of the most significant insights from which to access our general modal inquiry.

There's a very simple idea at the core of Moro's concept of impossible language. Impossible languages are languages formally characterisable by linear ordering rules. To see why this is the negative hypothesis, we need to briefly delve into his base assumptions. Firstly, like many generativists, he considers recursion (and Merge) to be the defining property of natural language.

This specific way of combining discrete elements ad infinitum via recursion is one of the core aspects of human language and the one never found in any other animal communication code. (Moro 2016, p. 27)

Specifically, he considers the property on which this process is based to be that of discrete infinity. He goes on to suggest that this property is shared with mathematics and music. From this, all linguistic possibilities spring. In fact, Moro's claim can best be deconstructed as a cluster of essentially

---

[13] Devitt (2006) himself does go further to interpret this position nominalistically in terms of language as the physical output of mental linguistic competence.

linguistic properties: (1) hierarchical constituency, (2) structure dependence, (3) recursion, and (4) discrete infinity. Let's consider them separately for a moment.

Hierarchical constituency is a common concept in linguistics. The basic idea is that languages are syntactically composed of structural units that go together in specific ways. Constituents are groupings of linguistic items that can be moved, deleted, and replaced (with pronouns) without loss of grammaticality. They can also form answers to questions. A simple example of a constituent in English is a *noun phrase*, or NP, such as *the linguist* (contrast with *understands the*). You can easily replace it with a pronoun like *she* or *her* in most contexts, as in (4). It can also be moved to other positions such as the fronting example in (5).

3. The student understands the linguist.
4. The student understands *her*.
5. *The linguist*, the student understands.

However, it seems as though constituents are organised in a particular fashion. Given our favourite fact that phrases can be embedded within one another, it seems as though the organisation is tree-like in which the NP in (5) has been topicalised or moved to the top of the tree. With the advent of X-bar theory in the extended standard theory (Jackendoff 1977), the further idea is that there must be multiple levels of nonterminal elements (phrases) that need to be organised hierarchically in order to explain certain grammaticality judgements (see Figure 2.1).[14]

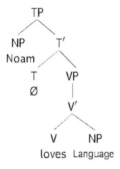

Figure 2.1 X-bar tree for *Noam loves Language*

As Poole notes,

[W]e discovered that your language faculty appears to structure phrases into three levels: the maximal projections or XP level, the intermediate X′ level, and the head or X°. (Poole 2002, p. 50)

[14] In Chapter 3, we'll challenge this notion, but for now, let's just assume it's correct.

The ideas of movement and hierarchical dependencies between words or constituencies, as in the verb phrase (VP) in Figure 2.1 that links *loves* and *Language*, bring us to the second concept: structure dependence. Hockett already had a general version of this feature ('Design Feature 9'), but generative linguists usually mean something a bit more by it. The generative concept is best understood in contrast to linear ordering. If we go back to Marr for a moment, we can see the line of argument quite clearly. Solutions to syntactic formation in natural language *could* have been based on linear order, as in the following sentence. Let's imagine the linear rule is something like 'move the verb to the left of the noun phrase'.

6. The man is happy.
7. Is the man happy?

Most English-speaking children learn how to construct interrogatives early on in their development. But if the linear rule is what they learn, then they should make mistakes of the following kind in turning (8) into a question:

8. The man who is tall, is happy.
9. * Is the man who tall, is happy?

Generativists claim that children just don't make these kinds of errors.[15] The conclusion is that even young children are already (innately) aware of the structure dependence of language.

   Both hierarchy and structure dependence feature prominently in phonology and morphology. 'Interestingly, not all structural phenomena involving hierarchy in human languages are recursive. Syllable structure is a prototypical example' (Moro 2016, p. 30). What's lacking in these domains is recursion (3) and infinity (4). Once we add these features, we not only have a clear picture of the quiddity of natural language but a testable concept of impossible languages.

An impossible language is one in which dependencies can be rigidly determined by the position of a word in a linear sequence. (Moro 2016, p. 30)

   Before we discuss the empirical ramifications of Moro's assumptions, let's zoom in on this alleged link between recursion and infinity. The claim is that recursive rules in a grammar result in a discrete infinitude of expressions (or structured descriptions/trees). I've already gestured above that recursion might be a property of a formal grammar, one which isn't necessarily true of the target domain itself. But there's a more direct reason to question the coupling based on an argument in Pullum & Scholz (2010). Their article

---

[15] This kind of data is also used to argue for the 'innateness hypothesis'; see Cowie (1999). We'll return to some of these issues in Chapter 7. However, it's not clear that linear-based bigrams cannot account for these kinds of examples simply in virtue of frequency facts (Reali & Christiansen 2005). The key question is whether or not young children have access to these data when they're learning language.

attempts to address the linguistic infinity postulate from various angles. They argue, among other things, that model-theoretic grammars don't produce any cardinality consequences for natural language (which lends further credence to my modelling view).[16] But I want to focus on a more specific technicality of generative grammars that they show with a toy example, namely, that recursive rules don't always entail infinite output.

Their toy (context-sensitive) grammar involves a set of terminals (words) {*They, came, running*}, a set of nonterminals {*S, NP, VP*}, a start symbol *S*, and the following rules:

- $S \rightarrow NP\ VP$
- $VP \rightarrow VP\ VP$
- $NP \rightarrow They$
- $VP \rightarrow came/They \ldots$
- $VP \rightarrow running/They\ came \ldots$

The surprising fact is that this generative grammar doesn't generate an infinite stringset. In fact, only two strings are generated: *They came* and *They came running*.[17] Every rule is used, no nonterminals (phrasal categories) are unproductive, and $VP \rightarrow VP\ VP$ isn't trivially recursive (in case you were wondering). Going further still, we have hierarchical constituency (I could turn those two strings into trees easily), structure dependence, and recursion but no infinity, of the discrete or discreet variety!

If you're concerned that this is a formal fluke of some sort, the issue actually goes deeper. As Pullum & Scholz note:

[I]nterestingly, for a wide range of generative grammars, including context-sensitive grammars and most varieties of transformational grammar, questions of the type 'Does grammar G generate an infinite set of strings?' are undecidable, in the sense that no general algorithm can determine whether the goal of 'a recursive procedure that generates an infinity of expressions' has been achieved. (2010, p. 120)

Thus, the link between recursion and discrete infinity is a more complicated matter than most generativists, including Moro, would like to admit. However, to appreciate Moro's empirical work on impossible languages, the only thing that's really needed is the property of structure dependence since his definition is based on its negation. Therefore, all there is to show is that rules and grammars based on linear ordering are impossible in some sense. Let's evaluate the experimental side of his argument, notwithstanding the formal assumptions.

Moro is interested in two kinds of related results, one from behavioural tests and the other from neuroscientific mappings using neuroimaging techniques

---

[16] See Chapter 3 for more on model-theoretic syntax.

[17] Technically, only two strings or derivations that terminate are generated.

such as fMRI. It's well established that a primary brain region that shows activation during syntactic tasks is the Broca area, especially the *pars triangularis* of the inferior frontal gyrus of the frontal lobe. Thus, his experiments aimed to test whether this region was activated in the same way when subjects were taught structure-dependent rules versus 'rules with rigid dependencies based on the position of words in the linear sequence' or 'impossible rules' (Moro 2016, p. 55). The design itself involved German native speakers learning two sets of rules in Italian and Japanese, respectively (the latter to eliminate any Indo-European contamination). One set, unbeknown to the subjects, was real and based on structure-dependent rules, and the other was impossible and based on linear dependencies. For instance, an example of an impossible rule was one in which the negative particle was placed in the fourth position of the sentence such as the equivalent of 'Andrea does the *no* experiment' in Italian. Another rule forced the first article of a string to agree with the last noun.[18]

The result was that:

[T]he amount of blood in Broca's area *augmented* when the subjects increased their ability to apply rules based on recursive architecture, whereas it *diminished* when the subjects increased their ability to apply rules based on linear order, regardless of which micro-language was involved. (Moro 2016, p. 56)

One immediate worry from the formal assumptions above is that given that Moro doesn't distinguish between a cluster of interrelated but theoretically independent properties (hierarchy, structure dependence, recursion, and infinity), his results don't clearly indicate which properties are prompting the increased brain activity. But let's set that aside for the sake of argument. There's another issue with the experimental conclusions. Moro's metrics for isolating possible versus impossible grammars (and rules) are learnability and neuronal architecture. But he openly admits two crucial things. The first is that syntax can be processed in other regions of the brain.[19] And the second is that subjects successfully learned the impossible rules, just not while exciting the neurons in the Broca area. This might be enough to establish one of Moro's chief aims: to show that the line between possible and impossible isn't socio-conventional in nature. Although if we accept the FLN–FLB distinction, then this conclusion isn't guaranteed either since the other brain regions could be responding to linguistic conventions. But combined, these admissions question the scope of the experimental results. It seems that the brain can process both

[18] They were also taught real rules of Italian such as the pro-drop possibilities the language allows as opposed to German (and English).

[19] This much is guaranteed by the property of neuroplasticity. See White *et al.* (2013) for an application to language learning.

structure-dependent and linear rules.[20,21] Moro's concept of impossible language is rendered rather *local* as a result. Local impossibility isn't by itself an issue. Sometimes, when we move discussions, we do so incrementally. Nevertheless, I think a more global notion of impossibility can be constructed based on the recent literature on impossible worlds (Berto & Jago 2019), as I hope to show in the final section. Furthermore, what we're really after is a clear distinction between languages that are human or natural and languages that aren't. This isn't provided by Moro's research.

What is apparent from Moro's experimental work is that the idea of learnability is central to our present question. It's on to this concept that we now move.

2.3   Naturalness, Learnability, and Usability

In the chapter so far, I've been using *natural* and *human* language synonymously. In order to proceed, I think we need to tread more carefully. In this section, I want to put forward an interpretation of 'natural' in natural language that grounds it in the concepts of acquisition and contextual usability. Before doing this, I think it prudent to disambiguate the term 'natural' from other possible contrasts and connections.

The first distinction often associated with natural language is that between natural and *formal* languages. Formal languages are artificially created devices for either the precisification of a target domain and/or a tool for providing structural explanations. Like natural languages, formal languages have characters, symbols, syntax, and semantics. They have a grammar in that their formation and interpretation rules are clearly specified (more so than in natural languages). Moreover, they can even contain recursive rules and hierarchical structure. They generally borrow their phonology from their natural counterparts. As mentioned in the previous chapter, some theorists, most famously Richard Montague, are attributed with the view that there's nothing theoretically divergent between natural and formal languages. Thus, tools devised for characterising the structure and semantics of formal languages are equally applicable to natural languages. In fact, this methodological principle lies at the heart of much work in early formal semantics of natural languages. The initial period saw the mathematical modelling of various natural language semantic constructions

---

[20] Moro refers to the former as recursive rules but there's nothing recursive about the particular training examples he used. This term only applies if we play fast and loose with the aforementioned cluster of concepts.

[21] Lexical functional grammar is a theory or formal-cognitive approach that takes syntax to be separated into c(onstituent)-structure and f(unctional)-structure. The former maps on to the properties of hierarchical constituency and structure dependence while the latter embraces linear order and functional roles. See Bresnan *et al.* (2016).

including quantifiers, indicative conditionals, belief statements, conjunctions, disjunctions, and embedded clauses. If this list sounds familiar, it's because many of these constructions are related to structures in formal languages such as quantifiers and connectives. Formal semantics formalised a fragment of English (and a select few other languages) using model theory and other tools from logic to some early acclaim. Nevertheless, 'extending this fragment' has proven difficult, especially to elements of natural language that seem to have no correlate in formal languages such as questions or imperatives.[22] Stokhof (2012) has a nice explanation for why the project of extending the fragment has hit a roadblock. To him, the issue is that Montague's theoretical equivalency between formal and natural languages only stretches so far as the subset of natural language in which the structures of formal languages reside, perhaps the truth-conditional parts. In other words, natural languages contain the elements of formal languages as proper subsets. Therefore, modelling those elements gives the impression of a successful enterprise, unsurprisingly. When semanticists attempted to move beyond this 'formal fragment', they encountered theoretical resistance.[23]

This is all to say that the neat distinction between formal and natural language isn't as apparent upon further scrutiny, at least when it comes to naturalness. The situation isn't improved by qualifying the natural with something like 'naturally occurring'. One might be tempted to draw the distinction in terms of which languages seem to pop up across linguistic communities or populations. You're certainly likely to find languages like English, Kiswahili, and Norwegian if you travel to different regions of the world. Put a few human beings together and they'll naturally develop a means of communicating with each other. The idea is that you won't be as likely to find propositional or predicate logic on your travels. But if Stokhof is correct, formal languages are naturally occurring since they're present in natural languages. Even if he isn't, then you still might bump into the odd formal language in your peregrinations. Arithmetic developed in different ways across cultures. If Peano was correct in his axiomatisation of the natural numbers, then you've probably encountered the language of Peano arithmetic specifically. Programming languages are also formal languages and they're ubiquitous in our interactions with devices like smart phones, ATMs, and computers.

Some linguists, especially of the generative persuasion, like to say that natural language is species-specific or unique to human beings. Again, even if

---

[22] See Karttunen (1977) for a classic account of question semantics in which a question denotes a set of statements that count as true answers to that question, and Groenendijk & Stokhof (1982) for development in terms of embedded questions. See Starr (2020) for a recent dynamic semantic account of imperatives.

[23] See Stanton (2020) for additional reasons why extending the fragment is unlikely to survive the computational bent of contemporary semantics.

this is true, it doesn't clearly distinguish between natural and formal languages. There aren't too many populations of monkeys, songbirds, or octopuses that use first- or second-order logic. The creation and manipulation of formal languages seem to be as unique to our species as natural languages are, perhaps more. This also militates against a simple equivalency between the terms *natural* and *human*.

So where to from here? It seems that formal and natural languages share significant structure and both naturally occur. Wherein lies the 'natural' in natural language if not in contrast with the 'formal' in formal languages? One clue, already given to us by Moro, is that natural languages are *learnable* for our species. But when linguists use this term, they mean something specific. For instance, some aspects of sign language are learnable to nonhuman primates. In other words, they can be taught how to use signs to construct simple expressions, usually bigrams like *eat-banana*. In the other direction, formal languages are clearly learnable too. Learning how to program involves learning how to use formal languages to encode certain kinds of instructions. Similarly, many philosophy and linguistics students learn formal logic in terms of the language of propositional and/or predicate logic. Therefore, learnability is usually associated with acquisition as a first language. Specifically, it's acquisition by a human child during a critical period that generally ends before puberty. It certainly seems as though formal languages cannot be acquired by children in the same ways that natural languages are. There are no communities of intuitionistic logic or C++ speakers.[24]

In a recent article, Szabó (2022) asks a similar question to ours concerning the difference between American Sign Language (ASL) and the Language of Peano Arithmetic (LPA). The latter, he argues, has dialects, recursive rules (in both syntax and semantics), and a lexicon containing an infinite set of variables and constants. Both ASL and LPA would fail on Hockett's first universal design feature, namely, that all human languages must possess a 'vocal-auditory channel'. It doesn't seem as though there are 'speakers' (in the strict sense) of either ASL or LPA. But we now know, and sadly this wasn't always the case, that sign languages are neither reducible to systems of gesture nor devoid of the hallmarks of natural language such as developed syntax, semantics, and pragmatics. So wherein lies the difference between ASL and LPA? According to Szabó, there are three immediate and interrelated distinguishing factors that make the former a possible human language and the latter not.

Firstly, ASL, like other human or natural languages, is linked to an interface with the sensorimotor system of the mind, sometimes referred to as externalisation. By contrast, 'LPA has no means of live articulation, which makes

---

[24] There's another contrast between formal, natural, and artificial languages. Esperanto is an artificial natural language given that it can be acquired as a first language by human speakers.

it unsuitable for face-to-face interaction' (Szabó 2022, p. 5). He goes on to suggest a link between this aspect of natural language and the so-called Strong Minimalist Thesis (SMT) in generative linguistics in which an I-language is viewed as the optimal solution to the interfaces with the sensorimotor (and conceptional-intentional) systems. Of course, Chomskyans see externalisation as peripheral and internal syntactic machinations as core to human language.[25]

Secondly, LPA is missing the capability of expressing 'perspectival thought'. The variables of LPA aren't designed or able to encode contextual parameters for interpretation as ASL and other natural languages are. Perhaps generalising a bit, formal languages like LPA don't have a pragmatic dimension. This suggests that how languages are used in linguistic communities is important to what they are and what makes them human. We'll return to this point subsequently.

Lastly, Szabó thinks that grammatical mood is essential for human language and another feature absent in LPA. The semantic difference that exists between imperatives, interrogatives, subjunctives, and indicatives is hard to conceive of outside of natural language. Simply adding syntax or lexical items to LPA won't be enough for such a feature to emerge in formal systems. There's something in all of Szabó's features that indicates the importance of communicative use as a marker of the humanly possible or natural.

Putting the two natural properties together, we get the claim that natural languages are both acquirable as first languages and usable as primary modes of communication within linguistic communities. Although these properties are often set up contrastively – core vs peripheral, FLN vs FLB, I-language vs E-language – they actually go together such that an internal language of thought without a conduit to the sensorimotor interface is as useless as a formal code without the ability to be used as a primary mode of communication. For Szabó, it's a matter of 'linguistic competence':

Syntactic competence may well be a matter of the language faculty being in a state where the parameters of Universal Grammar are set, while *semantic competence* is most likely the result of being party to a social convention underwritten by shared interest in communication. Linguistic competence requires both – a possible human language is one that could be both learned as a first language and used as a primary means of communication. (2022, p.9)

This conclusion suggests that Moro, and other Chomskyans, only have it half right. Impossible languages aren't just those that violate the assumed rules of syntactic competence but also the conventional rules of communities of

---

[25] '[C]ommunication is merely a possible function of the language faculty, and cannot be equated with it' (Friederici *et al.* 2017, p. 713), and '[a]t the neural level, core computations may be differentiable from a sensory-motor interface and a conceptual system' (Berwick *et al.* 2013, p. 93).

speakers. If a particular structure doesn't excite the Broca area but is usable by communities of speakers for successful communication, that language or rule cannot be impossible in any serious sense.

Since Lewis (1983), philosophers have been interested in the concept of *naturalness*. What makes a property more natural than another, perhaps more 'gruesome' or disjunctive, version? According to Lewis, properties are classes of possible entities. Some of these classes, a decided minority, are more *natural* than others. They 'cut nature at its joints'. Lewis thought that these perfectly natural properties are so useful, serviceable, and indispensable that they warrant primitive metaphysical status (and feature prominently in a number of his projects). Despite this, Lewis thinks that it's the job of the sciences to find the laws and natural properties endemic to the actual world.[26] In our case, linguistic theory has given us scientific traction on naturalness when it comes to languages in terms of acquirability and usability. Of course, outside of fundamental physics, we're not generally in the law-defining business, but special sciences can still identify the natural properties in their given domains. Furthermore, for Lewis, the class of natural properties also acts as a supervenient base for all other properties in that world. Again, what this means for us is that other linguistic properties will be supervenient on natural properties defined in the terms we've provided.

Thus, in this section, I've attempted to provide more details on the notion of natural in natural language. Now that we've dealt with 'language', 'natural' (and 'human'), we can safely move on to our final target concept of 'possible' and putting them all together.

2.4   A Modal Approach to Linguistic Possibility

Possibility is a concept that finds itself at the centre of a number of domains, philosophical views, scientific theories, quotidian speculation, and literary expression. Take Hockett's design feature of stimulus independence – often attributed to human language users exclusively. It says that all other animals utilise symbols in a manner that reflects their immediate environments (when they do). When a vervet monkey expectorates the call for 'snake', it does so when *and only when* it perceives a serpentine presence in its community. Similarly, when a meerkat sentry signals to its kin that a predator is nearby, the call isn't suppositional on pain of death or energy wastage. Even when a drongo bird tricks the meerkat community by mimicking their calls, usually to evoke a fleeing response leaving valuable prey unguarded, its deception is still stimulus-

---

[26] In fact, he thinks we need the natural properties to save his 'best system account' of the laws of nature, in which they're defined as regularities that figure in the ideal systems aspired to in science.

dependent (the stimulus in this case is the situation of unattended prey).[27] By contrast, our language use can express features of circumstances and scenarios that aren't only absent from the immediate vicinity but nonexistent (and even highly unlikely to be). In scientific discourse, counterfactual scenarios are ubiquitous, from Einstein's twin paradox in theoretical physics to Fischer's three-sex organism model in biology. 'The possible' seems to be an inescapable aspect of our cognition. In philosophy, modal logic formalises some aspects of our concept of modality or possibility while modal metaphysics attempts to describe and systematise the ontological consequences of the employment of the notion. In this chapter, I want to dip my feet into both domains for a specific purpose. I'll not only attempt to provide a formal framework for the discussion of what *possible* human languages are but also revisit the issue of what impossible languages might be, based on this framework. Let's begin with some basic terminology from the possible worlds literature and modal logic.

A possible world is usually viewed as a state in which or 'way things could have been' (see Stalnaker 1976 for an alternative). We have some traction, both diachronically and synchronically, on the way things have been or currently are, that is, the actual world. But it's uncontroversial to say that many events and features of our world *might* have been different. Hilary Clinton might have won the 2016 US presidential elections; the African National Congress (ANC) might have lost the South African presidential elections in 2020. These were both distinct possibilities. However, saying that the ANC might have won the US elections and Hilary Clinton might have been elected president of the Republic of South Africa seem to be much less possible. The changes to the actual world involved in the former possibilities seem to be minor (although the effects might not have been) while the changes in the latter are more significant. Adding physics- or biology-defying claims like the president of South Africa can levitate or regenerate a limb upon inauguration moves us towards the impossible. There seems to be a logic at play here. Some worlds are very possible, some are less, and some are downright impossible (unless we change the laws of logic, physics, or biology).

In modal logic, possibility is cashed out in terms of quantification over possible worlds. A necessary claim (indicated with '□') is one that quantifies over all possible worlds. In other words, it's true in all possible worlds. The usual candidates for necessary statements are mathematical ones like '10+12=22' or metaphysical claims such as 'Enoch is human'. Possible claims (indicated by '◇') are only true in some possible worlds and false (or have no truth value, depending on your view of vacuous truth) in others. Here, we find

---

[27] Again, cases such as the drongo might call Hockett's other uniquely human linguistic design features such as prevarication into question.

our presidential claims about the the USA and RSA, respectively. From this, we can already state the semantics of two useful modal expressions:

1. '$\Box P$' is true if and only if P is true at all worlds $w_1 \in W$.
2. '$\Diamond P$' is true if and only if P is true at some world $w_1 \in W$.

In (1) and (2), W is the set of all possible worlds and w_i indicates a possible world. Despite the formalism, we still don't really know much about W itself or the w_i's inside of it. For this, we need the concept of accessibility relations between worlds. These are usually modelled as labelled binary relations on possible worlds, as in: $w_1 \rightarrow w_2$. Basically, this just means that inhabitants of w_1 'can see' those of w_2. It's like a conceptual bridge from one state of affairs to another. So, for instance, if w_1 is the actual world and the statement D that denotes 'Donald Trump won the 2016 US elections' is true at that world and H denotes 'Hilary Clinton won the 2016 US elections' (true at w_2), then $\Diamond H$ is true at w_1 since it can see w_2. The world, w_3, in which Cyril Ramaphosa (the current president of South Africa) won the 2016 US elections might also be possible ($\Diamond$) from w_1, but it's further away, given the requirements on location of birth in the US, that is, how many changes to w_1 would be required to make it true. From this point already, we can see that modal notions are relative to the relations between worlds: they're restricted. Take 'nomological necessity' for a moment. This concept ensures that the worlds that can be reached or seen by the actual world are those worlds that maintain our laws of nature. Thus, Superman isn't absolutely impossible but his physics-defying abilities are impossible from our world, a claim that extends from the DC universe to the Marvel universe.

Systems of modal logic are created by adding axioms to propositional logic. If you add the following two axioms, you get system K (for 'Kripke'):

- Necessitation Rule: If A is a theorem of K, then so is $\Box A$.
- Distribution Axiom: $\Box(A \rightarrow B) \rightarrow (\Box A \rightarrow \Box B)$.[28]

Now, we're in the basic modal logic system. But to get some important properties of necessity and possibility, we need other axioms such as M ($\Box A \rightarrow A$). In fact, commonly used systems are S4 and S5, which add $\Box A \rightarrow \Box\Box A$ and $\Diamond A \rightarrow \Box\Diamond A$ to M, respectively. It's not important for our purposes to delve too deeply into these systems of modal logic. We're not interested in being logicians right now but rather metaphysicians. Nevertheless, what's interesting is the idea that adding or removing axioms (which basically structure our accessibility relations) can model features of the domain in which we're focused. For instance, temporal logics might model the axioms of K but add

---

[28] If you're worried about where 'possibly' went, 'necessary' and 'possibly' are duals of one another, so they're interdefinable.

something that captures the asymmetry of temporal points or 'time's arrow' such as 'if A, then it will always be the case that A' and 'if A, then it was always the case that it will be A'. Your axiomatisation might change depending on your temporal metaphysics, that is, block universe versus a tense logic or presentism. In this way, you can think of temporal logic as an axiomatisation of temporal possibility. Similarly, you can think of deontic logic as an axiomatisation of moral possibility (or moral obligation and permissibility). Epistemic logic models epistemic possibility or knowledge and so on. For linguistic possibility, I think we can stick with a system like S5 and add sui generis axioms where necessary. So we can keep the logic but let our metaphysics amend the picture in accordance with some of the properties identified in the discussion so far. In order to do so, we need to make use of an important topological metric in both modal logic and modal metaphysics, namely, *closeness*.

If we return to Cyril Ramaphosa and Hilary Clinton for a moment, the scenario I sketched above concerning the former winning the US elections and the latter winning the South African seems to have a flavour of the far out. Unlike Clinton winning the US elections, which didn't happen but *could* have, her becoming president of South Africa seems like a more remote possibility. Another way of saying 'remote' is not close. In possible world semantics, some worlds aren't just possible or accessible to others but closer and further away from them. As Berto & Jago (2019) write with relation to counterfactuals:

Closeness between worlds is understood as involving (contextually determined) similarity in the relevant respects. So evaluating a counterfactual will typically involve the *minimal change* (with respect to the world of evaluation) required to verify the antecedent. (p. 20)

Two things to note about the above intuitive idea. Firstly, closeness is determined with relation to the actual world (which is usually the world of evaluation). Closeness is also defined in terms of 'minimal change'. A world in which the dodo still exists is closer than a world in which unicorns do. This is due to the fact that dodos actually existed relatively recently in our world while unicorns never did, which might be due to an unstable/unlikely evolutionary or biological form.

With these tools in hand, let's put the positive account together. The first step is to start thinking of possible languages in terms of possible worlds. The actual world contains all the particular languages that ever existed. For us, a possible language is a possible state in which or *way language could have been*. But from the discussion in this chapter, we're not interested in the set of all possible languages (*L*) but only the natural ones. *L* could contain LPA, the language of set theory, and programming languages. Recall that we described naturalness as involving both acquirability by a human infant (within the critical period) and usability as a primary communicative tool in a community. These two concepts seem to fit together well. Thus, let's add an axiom to our system:

- **Naturalness axiom:** Necessarily, if a language is acquirable then it can be used as a primary mode of communication within a linguistic community.

This axiom, where the antecedent means something like 'acquirable by a human infant during the critical period' and the consequent ensures that the language can be used as a primary method of communication, should give us a union of the set of all actual languages ($L^{@}$) and the set of possible *natural* languages. In other words, it should restrict our domain of quantification such that the set of formal languages is excluded. What this means already is that there's no possible language that isn't both acquirable and usable as a primary means of communication by a linguistic community. At this juncture, you might worry that Latin is acquirable since it's been acquired by millions of speakers in the past but not usable as a primary mode of communication since it died. This is a contingent fact, however. If a community of speakers wished to revivify Latin, they could do so, as has been done with Biblical Hebrew. In fact, the modal force of the axiom tracks the dynamics of acquisition. As we know from the case of Genie, the feral child who suffered serious abuse and neglect, without a linguistic community or primary communicative medium, acquisition is impossible (Curtiss *et al.* 1974). Acquisition presupposes a community in which a language is used as the primary means of communication. On the other hand, our axiom does allow counterfactual worlds in which there are languages that are usable as primary communicative devices but aren't acquirable by children during the critical period (since the consequent of a conditional can be true even if the antecedent is false). Pidgins would qualify as possible languages on this view.[29] Pidgins are communication systems that are developed primarily in exigent circumstances such as migrant labour or slavery in which populations of different speakers are forced to find common linguistic ground. They often lack complex syntax or morphology and borrow liberally from the structure and lexicon of the established languages in contact with one another. They cannot be acquired by definition despite often acting as the primary means of communication. Once they're passed on to a second generation, the process of creolisation grammaticalises the original pidgin, resulting in a different language, a creole.

Statistical universals give us some details on what the set $L^{@}$ looks like. But they don't tell us exactly which languages are possible viewed from the actual set. This is where linguistic theory comes in! It organises and restricts the topology of linguistic possibility. For instance, we know from Shieber

---

[29] Allowing pidgins as possible languages is a departure from Szabó's intentions.

(1985) that natural language syntax isn't context-free. Most linguists assume it lies somewhere between context-free and context-sensitive, namely, the mildly context-sensitive.[30] If the actual world/language is mildly context-sensitive, then both context-free and context-sensitive languages are possibly natural or human. But the former is closer than the latter given that for the latter to be true of natural language, humans would need much more cognitive processing power than they have at present. This might in turn require alterations in brain chemistry. In fact, the more processing power required, the more impossibility looms (similar to the Superman scenario).

We now have enough resources to develop the account a bit further. A possible language is one that respects our naturalness axiom. All actual languages are possible languages. Closeness is then determined by properties associated with human language given to us by theoretical linguistics. I've already provided an example of one closeness metric above: computational complexity (in the Chomsky Hierarchy). Others include effability, intertranslatability, productivity, and recursive structure.[31] Let's consider the last one since it connects to Moro's experiments on impossible languages.

Moro's claim is that the actual world is such that all actual languages are recursive in structure. But does this mean that all possible languages are recursive? I think we've reason to doubt this further modal claim. Recall, Moro's central assumption is that impossible languages rely on linear rules. His experiment showed that these rules were learnable but they didn't activate the right areas of the brain during processing. But he only tested his hypothesis on languages he knew or assumed had recursion, or rather structure dependence, in the first place.

Above, I concluded that at best, Moro gives us a local notion of impossibility. In fact, he seems to have merely identified a distant possibility given his assumptions. But perhaps it isn't so distant after all if these assumptions are reconsidered. David Gil's work on the structure and nature of Riau Indonesian gives us a clue as to the true possibility of the languages Moro identifies as impossible. Gil states:

Riau Indonesian is the variety of colloquial Indonesian used in informal every-day contexts as a lingua franca for interethnic and increasingly also intraethnic communication by residents of the eponymous region. (1999, p. 4)

---

[30] A set of languages (L) is mildly context-sensitive iff (1) L contains all the context-free languages, (2) L can describe the copy language and certain cross-serial dependencies of that sort (like in Swiss-German, cf. Shieber 1985), (3) L is parsable in polynomial time, and (4) L has the constant growth property.

[31] Evolvability is another interesting constraint on the set of possible human languages. Only certain kinds of languages have emerged both structurally and in terms of usability within linguistic communities. An adequate theory of this emergence would narrow the linguistically possible down even further. I thank Giosué Baggio for this suggestion.

Gil makes a number of startling observations about Riau. He claims that it's an Isolating-Monocategorial-Associational (IMA) language. The 'isolating' here refers to morphologically isolating, meaning 'no word-internal morphological structure', the 'monocategorial' means syntactically monocategorial, which denotes the fact that the language lacks syntactic categories, and lastly, the 'associational' stands for semantically associational, which means 'no distinct construction-specific rules of semantic interpretation' (Gil 2005, p. 347). Gil states that this language combines a simplified version of grammaticality with a certain stylistic felicity, resulting in a highly developed idiomaticity or the property of alternative expression of grammatical structure. The details aren't very important to our discussion. What's important is what a language like this would mean for linguistic possibility in Moro's terms. In order to characterise languages like Riau Indonesian, Jackendoff (2017) defines the concept of a linear grammar as one in which some combination of the following properties holds:

1. No parts of speech, but only semantic features which distinguish objects, actions or properties.
2. No phrases (or nonterminals) but possibly linear order and prosody.
3. No recursion or subordination (unless it's semantic).
4. Semantic roles based on linear order such as 'Agent precedes Patient', 'Focus Last', 'Modifier follows Modified', etc.
5. Morphological structure builds from semantics not syntax.

He believes that the languages that go with this grammar already live among us. Here, he specifically mentions Gil 2005 work on Riau Indonesian, which he agrees has 'virtually no syntax' and 'definitely no recursion'. In Chapter 3, we'll return to the possibility of language without syntax and the issue of linear grammar for different purposes. But for now, we can appreciate that Jackendoff is making a case for a linear rule-based grammar for languages like Riau Indonesian. Thus, if this is correct, then these rules, grammars, and languages cannot be impossible.

Again, you might be concerned that Riau Indonesian isn't a natural language in the sense of our definition. It's certainly used as a primary means of communication by the speakers of the community. But is it acquirable? Are there native first-language speakers? Gil (2005) answers all of these questions and more in the affirmative. From our perspective, notwithstanding Gil's convincing defence, it doesn't matter if Riau is really characterisable by a linear grammar or not. What seems very clear is that it possibly is. Moro himself admits that linear rules are learnable; Gil merely shows that they're more than that. Riau is clearly a possible language since it might be an actual one.[32]

---

[32] From the axioms of S5, we know that $\Diamond A \rightarrow \Box \Diamond A$, so languages like Riau are necessarily possible in our system. Which means Riau is a possible language in all possible worlds (from our perspective).

I can now make good on the promise to explain why Moro's impossible languages are at best locally impossible but more likely possible, as shown above. If linear rules and grammars are possible, then which languages are truly impossible? Unrestricted impossibility as a topic has been receiving increased philosophical interest lately.[33]

For our purposes, impossible natural languages are those from which there is no bridge to our actual languages. We've already encountered some examples. LPA is an impossible natural language since it's neither acquirable as a first language nor usable as a primary means of communication. Actual and possible languages share other characteristics that distinguish them from impossible languages. For one thing, they're consistent pairings of features or properties (perhaps even maximally consistent). Impossible languages are then inconsistent or incoherent combinations of linguistic properties. A language cannot be both pro-drop and non-pro-drop. It cannot be completely agglutinating and completely isolating at once. Of course, these aren't the most interesting properties.[34] A more interesting claim, which dovetails with Moro and generativists, is that a natural language cannot be merely a list of sentences. In algorithmic information theoretic terms, this means that a natural language needs to be characterisable by a compression algorithm, or grammar in this case. An arbitrary long list of expressions with no means of generating new ones (productivity) or finding patterns in the initial set is unacquirable and unusable as a primary mode of communication.

Therefore, we have two forms of impossible languages from the perspective of actual languages. Formal languages like LPA or first-order logic are impossible natural languages. The next form of impossible languages are the natural languages with incompatible features. Some ways of representing syntax, semantics, and phonology are incompatible with one another. Natural languages, like formal languages with logically incompatible properties, cannot possess these properties at one time. Further than this, closeness or modal distance can be mistaken for possibility and impossibility given certain assumptions about the actual world or actual languages. Moro and most generativists, for instance, would reject the naturalness axiom. Of course, the space of possibilities would be different with a different set of assumptions about linguistic possibility, as with the temporal logic case. A linguistic platonist like Katz (1981) or Postal (2009) would equally reject naturalness and argue for more of a correspondence with formal languages. I hope to have motivated the best of all worlds with the present approach. At the very least, I hope to have sketched a *possibly* plausible account.

---

[33] See Berto & Jago (2019).

[34] The principles and parameters framework provides some insight into the possible combinatorics of natural languages. However, many of the proposed parametric settings allow for multiple or optional parameters.

2.5   Summary

Of course, our job isn't done. Theoretical linguistics, and its subdisciplines, houses many more insights into the nature and structure of natural languages and in so doing sheds further light on possibilities within human languages. The rest of the book is devoted to exploring the philosophical depths of the theories and models of various frameworks across subfields and their intersections. This chapter had two aims: one was the motivation of a general modal framework for divining linguistic possibility, and the other pushed a specific picture of that possibility in terms of learnability and usability.

Further Reading

We've covered a number of intersecting topics in this chapter. The following texts are advanced introductions or discussions to separate literatures. Surprisingly, there's little work on what possible languages are as we've approached the question. There are the traditional debates on the ontology of language itself, though.

- Jerold Katz (1981) *Languages and Other Abstract Objects* (Rowman & Littlefield) remains one of the most controversial philosophical works on the ontology of natural language. Katz proffers a platonist understanding of human languages as nonspatiotemporal abstract objects. He introduces a trichotomy of ontological positions including Platonism, Conceptualism (Mentalism), and Nominalism that shaped debate for decades to come.
- For an edited volume with various angles on the issue of recursion, Harry van der Hulst 2010 *Recursion and Human Languages* (De Gruyter, Mouton) stands out. The Pullum & Scholz article finds a place there as well as Tiede & Stout, both cited in this chapter. Additionally, Langendoen's chapter covers the question of linguistic infinity (and the cardinality of natural language itself), and Karlsson's chapter details empirical instances and reflection on both recursion and its formal cousin iteration.
- Andrea Moro has two books on the topic of impossible languages. The latest, *Impossible Languages* (MIT Press (2016)), is central to the present chapter. But this chapter only focuses on some of the arguments and experiments; the book is much richer than this. Its final chapter on artificial languages and their use in 'bettering' possible languages is a fascinating read in and of itself.
- For an advanced introduction to modal logic, its systems, metatheory, and extensions, Ted Sider 2010 *Logic for Philosophy* (Oxford University Press) is excellent. The presentation is clear and systematic, with exercises and application to issues such as counterfactuals and two-dimensionalism.

- Lastly, Berto & Jago's (2020) *Impossible Worlds* (Oxford University Press) offers a unique take on modal metaphysics from the perspective of unrestricted impossibility. Despite the angle, this work also serves as a clear and thorough introduction to modal metaphysics and possible world semantics in general.

3   Syntactic Metatheory

Syntax has had a central place in the study of natural language since, at least, the Chomskyan paradigm was initiated in the 1950s. Many linguists consider syntactic configuration to be at the genesis of human language (Berwick & Chomsky 2016) or at least that its basic operations are candidates for linguistic universals (Hauser *et al.* 2002; Moro 2016). Before that, the concept played a foundational role in mathematical logic and early theoretical computer science from Turing machines, Post-production systems, and even Gödel's incompleteness proof. Interestingly, contemporary machine learning and natural language processing accounts do not always demarcate a separate syntactic level of representation. Part of the difficulty of neat characterisations of the role of syntax within the history and contemporary practice of logic, linguistics, and artificial intelligence is that the term often has different significance within each field. This latter task would be gargantuan in scope and only have a tangential relevance for linguistic theory.

In this chapter, my focus is more parochial but hopefully no less significant. I aim to chart a path through multiple theories and explanations of the varied groupings of phenomena under the auspices of linguistic syntax. In the tradition of recent work on scientific modelling in the philosophy of science, I plan to approach the question of what syntax is from a bottom-up review of the cross-framework literature. I'll make a case for a general explanatory strategy or scientific project at the core of linguistic syntax. The core idea is that the general scientific strategy is relatively stable across syntactic frameworks. What differs are the kinds of explanatory models at play. For instance, Minimalism can be seen as incorporating a 'unification approach to explanation' (Kitcher 1989) in which the goal is to bring together seemingly disparate phenomena under one explanatory framework. Chomsky (2021) has recently considered the concept of 'genuine explanation' in linguistics as a tug of war between the seemingly opposing constraints of learnability, evolvability, and universality (i.e. crosslinguistic invariance). For him, all of these constraints push us towards simpler structures, specifically Minimalist ones.[1] It is the link between these different aspects of the linguistic system that does the explanatory work of the theory.

Model-theoretic approaches and dependency grammar, by contrast, are more mechanistic (Bechtel & Abrahamsen 2005). They isolate individual structures or mechanisms (in the form of rules and principles) that are responsible for explaining particular phenomena. Construction grammar contains elements of causal explanation theories (Lipton 2004), which do not assume universality and tend to find chunks or linguistic units responsible for individual language-specific patterns, as opposed to universal building blocks. This isn't to say that these models aren't mixed in the various approaches (see LFG below), only that some strains are more dominant in the literature.

In Section 3.1, we'll discuss the 'basic conception' of syntactic explanation within general linguistics. If we amplify these properties, we get a more committed view aligned with Minimalism in contemporary generative linguistics. This is the topic of Section 3.2. In Section 3.3, I question some of the assumptions of the latter view in the hope of retaining the former. Here, we consider languages with 'little to no syntax' and what this possibility could mean. Section 3.4 moves to a discussion of two very different kinds of syntactic explanations: dependency grammar and model-theoretic grammar, respectively. Both of these 'alternatives', I suggest, speak the same language as the basic conception from the first Section. Finally, in Section 3.5, I attempt to dislodge the basic conception of syntax by considering construction grammar and its radical counterpart. Here, things get more tricky and finding the basic structure in these accounts requires some syntactic translation. What remains isn't a literal translation but hopefully one that's still in the spirit of the original.

Since the overall aim of this chapter is to identify the core of syntactic explanation in theoretical linguistics, and to trace this conception across distinct approaches, I should say something brief about what we'll take explanation itself to be going forward. In the following, we'll be assuming an equation common to the discipline (and others). The quality of an explanation will be determined by two main factors: (1) the empirical adequacy/coverage of the theory or depth of the explanandum, and (2) the extant theoretical posits used in the explanans.[2] It's a bit of a balancing act between coverage and machinery. As we'll see, there's been a definite shift towards simpler explanations (and posits) across syntactic theory. However, what 'simple' means in each instance is no simple matter as one linguist's parsimony is another's profusion.

[1] In a recent reflection, he attributes the connection between explanation and simplicity to Goodman in which 'the simplicity of a theory provides a measure of its explanatory success' (Chomsky 2021, p. 5).

[2] Another way of describing (2) is as the complexity of the explanans. For example, highly idealised models tend to simplify the assumed mechanisms at their base; see Weisberg (2013) for a developed account.

3.1   The Basic Conception

What exactly is syntax? According to most linguistics textbooks on the subject, syntax describes the rules that govern the ways in which words combine to form phrases, clauses, and sentences, or as Tallerman puts it, '"[s]yntax" means "sentence construction": how words group together to make phrases and sentences' (1998, p. 1). It's a structural enterprise interested in how elements of language are put together given certain formal or structural features. From a disciplinary perspective, the study of syntax is captured by Chomsky in the following way:

> Syntax is the study of the principles and processes by which sentences are constructed in particular languages. Syntactic investigation of a given language has as its goal the construction of a grammar; that can be viewed as a device of some sort for producing the sentences of the language under analysis. (1957, p. 11)

For instance, when we describe the syntactic features of declarative sentences like *Maria kicked the cat*, we're not interested in how the sentence sounds or what it means but rather how it combines components like a verb *kicked* with the noun phrase *the cat* to generate a verb phrase (VP) *kicked the cat*. We can abstract away from the individual words to talk about categories. In this case, a VP is in a nonterminal category, which just means it doesn't immediately terminate in a lexical item or word, that is, there are branches and nodes in between. Visually, this looks like Figure 3.1.

The simplified tree in Figure 3.1 evinces one aspect of the study of syntax. It involves the study of rules of combination based purely on structural or formal features, which basically means the shape linguistic items take. Items form *constituents*, which are the basic syntactic units or building blocks of syntax. They can be fronted, moved around, and replaced with pronouns in some cases. These constituents in turn are often shown in terms of being hierarchically organised into tree structures (as we'll see in the next section). From this basic picture, we can already derive the following property of syntax:

[**RULE-BOUND**]: Natural language syntax is explained by rules for the formation of compound units or constituents.

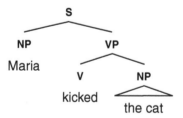

Figure 3.1 Tree for *Maria kicked the cat*

In a sense, this is to say that syntax is describable by a grammar, as Chomsky states above, that's just a set of rules for either transforming one kind of sentence into another or stating the conditions upon which a particular construction achieves grammatical status. A similar sentiment can be found in Smith & Wilson (1991, p. 326):

With modern linguistic theory, to claim that a language is rule-governed is to claim that it can be described in terms of a grammar. A grammar is conceived of as a set of rules ... They separate grammatical from ungrammatical sentences, this making explicit claims about what is 'in the language' and what is not.

The view alluded to above suggests that a language is a set of sentences generated by the rules of a grammar. The basic view of syntax that I want to outline similarly provides a procedure that usually involves some combination of the following three general claims: (1) syntax is rule-governed (as we've seen), (2) syntax is explanatorily autonomous from other linguistic systems such as semantics and phonology, and (3) some form of recursion is necessary to explain certain constructions in natural language syntax.[3] We'll briefly discuss the last two concepts (as the first gestured at above is relatively uncontroversial) before turning to more committed views on the nature of syntax in the next section.

The autonomy of syntax is usually captured by the following type of claim:

[AoS]: Syntactic properties are independent and autonomous of other linguistic properties.

Basically, Chomsky (1957) proposed an architectural picture for the study of language that saw syntax as irreducible to statistical approximation and semantic interpretation (so-called interpretive semantics). Put in a slightly different way, syntax is the generative engine of the language faculty. This means that grammaticality, seen as a property of syntax, is independent of interpretability and other concepts (such as stochastic processes). It creates the forms that receive semantic and phonological overlay at later stages of output.

Let's look at this idea in practice. The rules of grammar allow for potentially indefinite centre-embeddings, or constructions that allow for two nonadjacent elements that may contain further instances of the same construction between them, such as in (1).

1. The cat that the dog that the mouse heard bit ran.

---

[3] Many contemporary generative theories also adhere to mentalism or the idea that studying syntax is a way of studying the mind-brain (see Chomsky 1965, 2000; Poole 2002; Hornstein 2009; and many more). But this is less about modelling and more about ontological commitments.

Sentences like (1) are rare and thus not likely to be found in corpora or predicted by word-by-word Markov chains. Yet, if a grammar encompasses a rule that licenses (2), it should license (1) in principle.[4]

2. A dog that a cat bit just barked.[5]

Any difficulty one might have in processing (1) is argued, on this picture at least, to be related to short-term memory limitations or the principle of dependency-length minimisation in language production (Futrell *et al.* 2015). Similarly, the famous sentence *Colourless green ideas sleep furiously* was meant to show that a perfectly grammatical sentence can have little to no meaning or sense attached to it. More specifically, consider the following minimal pair:

3a. Colourless green ideas sleep furiously.
 b. *Colourless green ideas sleeps furiously.

The sentences above seem to fail on interpretability equally but differ in terms of grammaticality. Adger claims that '[t]he difference in acceptability between the two examples here cannot be tied down to "significance" or meaningfulness in any obvious sense. It follows that we cannot identify the notion of grammatical sentence with that of significant sequence' (2018, p. 160). Some linguists, such as Jackendoff (2002), have dubbed the version of the autonomy of syntax discussed here 'syntacto-centricism' and even deemed it a scientific mistake. Jackendoff particularly takes issue with the idea, maintained in later iterations of generative grammar such as Minimalism, that syntax is the only generative system in the language faculty. Of course, automony doesn't entail only one generative system, as Jackendoff's Parallel Architecture (PA) shows (see below).

Similarly, functionalists and cognitive linguists alike have objected to the claim of syntactic autonomy.

> Syntax is not autonomous from semantics or pragmatics ... the rejection of autonomy derives from the observation that the use of particular grammatical forms is strongly linked, even deterministically linked, to the presence of particular semantic or pragmatic functions in discourse. (Tomlin 1990, quoted by Newmeyer 1991, p. 4)

This might indeed be the case, but it's unclear whether it's in fact incompatible with the original generative claim in Chomsky (1957). Nevertheless, suffice to say that the claim of autonomy at this stage is one of *explanatory* autonomy. In other words, syntactic rules cannot be reduced to semantic, pragmatic,

---

[4] Chomsky (1956, p. 109) claimed that sentences like (1) with arbitrary depth of recursion are grammatical in English, in support of his argument that English cannot be a regular language (or generated by a regular/finite-state grammar). See Karlsson (2007) for more discussion of centre-embedding. We'll see more of this kind of reasoning in Section 5.2.
[5] If these examples seem unnatural in English, they're widely attested to in Dutch, German, and other languages.

or phonetic ones. Let's modify the initial statement in order to highlight the explanatory aspect of the claim as this claim will form the crux of the forthcoming discussion:

[AoS]*: Syntactic representation is independent and not reducible to other linguistic representations.

The next element of the standard view involves the ubiquitous claim that syntax creates or 'generates infinite output via finite means'.[6] We've discussed some aspects of this claim in Chapter 2. For our explanatory purposes, we don't really need to endorse or debate the issue of an actual linguistic infinity or linguistic ontology here. We just need to maintain that something in addition to [RULE-BOUND] is required to explain or model certain kinds of common linguistic constructions, namely a recursive, rule system:

[RECURSION]: In order to explain linguistic competence, some element of recursion is necessary in the grammar.

As we've seen, a central explanandum of contemporary generative linguistics is how language users take a finite device (like the human brain or cognitive system) and put it to infinite use (generating all the possible sentences or expressions of a language). This is the linguistic infinity postulate.

Native speakers of a given language L have mastered rules for L that allow them to generate an unbounded number of tokens of L (i.e. sentences, phrases, etc.). Rules are required because the tokens of L are for all practical purposes infinite and thus cannot possibly be stored individually in a finite organism. (Hornstein 2009, p. 1)

Notice, Hornstein is hedging here. 'Unbounded' doesn't entail infinite. For instance, Hockett (1968) argued that the rules of baseball allow for an unbounded score in that the game could always have been longer and the score higher. 'Unbounded' here means 'no obvious upper bound'. But, of course, no baseball score could be infinite. Rules generate the unboundedness but you don't need recursive rules to do so, only additive ones.

Another related rationale for the infinity postulate often found in the literature is based on the 'No Maximal Length' (NML) argument, challenged in Pullum & Scholz (2010). The idea is that there seems to be no longest sentence in languages like English, so no maximally complex linguistic structure and presto–infinity![7] These kinds of claims are specifically related to the view that syntax is closed under certain rule structures; for example, for every

---

[6] Usually attributed to the linguist Wilhelm von Humboldt in the literature.
[7] Langendoen & Postal (1984) run with this idea and produce a proof as to the nondenumerable infinity of natural languages.

grammatical sentence that contains a 'very', another equally grammatical sentence can be generated by means of additional uses of this word. This in turn means that 'the tokens of L are for all practical purposes infinite' since I can keep adding modifiers ad infinitum. Again, practical purposes are likely to run out way before infinity kicks in. But one has to be careful here. Speakers do not, and cannot, generate infinite sets. What Chomsky initially claimed was that limiting the grammar would be arbitrary, that is, there is no nonarbitrary point at which we can stop and say 'this is no longer a sentence of English'. However, natural limitations abound, such as the claim that centre-self-embedding can happen at most three levels deep. There are such limitations since our brains cannot process more then four or five embeddings. Nor can we process sentences with more than 10,000 words. Assuming the same argument for the size of words, languages will be finite but huge in reality (see Müller 2020 for more detailed arguments to this effect).

Either way, [RULE-BOUND] by itself won't explain a practical or potential infinity or even, more neutrally, an unbounded output. Rather, rules of a special nature are needed for this purpose, that is, recursive rules.[8] The argument goes that something like [RECURSION] is necessary stems from the ubiquitous use of constructions such as centre-embedding (shown above), unbounded adverbial modification (all the uses of 'very'), and even reported or indirect speech in which iteration can go on as long as a situation requires with no obvious upper bound. This is the usual motivation, at least.

Mallory (2023) argues strongly against the picture of recursive grammars as a requirement for capturing the unboundedness of natural language expressions, that is, the infinitude claim. He traces the orginal motivation for recursion to Harris and early Chomsky, and makes a case that a metalanguage with recursive rules (supplied by grammatical theory) is not explanatorily adequate since it requires interpretation itself. Rather, he claims that the original reason for linking recursive grammars to linguistic competence (or knowledge) was to provide an analysis of 'what an "intelligent interpreter" brought to understanding a language' (Mallory 2023, p. 3), one that didn't presuppose a language in the first place. Despite the divergence, Mallory insists that [RECURSION] is necessary for the explanation of our linguistic knowledge.

Thus, to recap, the basic conception comprises three central claims:

[BASIC] $=_{def}$ [AoS]* + [RULE-BOUND] + [RECURSION]

---

[8] The original insight allegedly came from mathematical logic (and especially the work of Emil Post) in which it was shown that a finite-rule system could yield infinite well-formed formula, much like a system of natural deduction. Chomsky (2000) claims that the explanation of natural language creativity only became available with the advent of computability theory in the twentieth century (and before then seemed like a contradictory property) (see Lobina 2017 and Nefdt 2019 for more on infinity, recursion, and linguistics).

For our purpose, there's an implicit ranking between them. [AoS]* is the most important explanatory claim or the idea that there's an autonomous or independent level of syntactic description or explanation. Then, specific aspects of this system are usually characterised by means of [RULE-BOUND] and [RECURSION]. In contrast, formal semantic explanation usually also involves some form of [RULE-BOUND] and [RECURSION]. But instead of [AoS]*, compositionality (or [COMP]) is explanatorily central. Compositionality is in some ways the antithesis of autonomy since it insists on a marriage or interface between syntax and semantics.[9] In the next section, we'll briefly consider some extensions of the basic picture in linguistics towards a backdoor to Minimalism.

3.2   Minimalist Syntax

One can derive a more sophisticated scientific view from the basic conception above. To do this, we basically need to take all of the tenets of [BASIC] and amplify them in certain ways. As I mentioned above, amendments to the basic picture have a number of motivations. One such motivation within the Minimalist Program (MP) is that linguistic theory carries a heavier epistemic burden than [BASIC] can accommodate. Not only does syntax need to cover observational data (corpus forms), descriptive data (judgements elicited from native speakers), and explanatory data (data collected or sensitive to how young children learn language) but also explanations of how language evolved. In order to take on this mammoth task, [BASIC] needs a suit of armour.

The first modification is naturally to [RULE-BOUND]. In this version, the claim becomes one about specific aspects of rule systems, especially hierarchical ones.

[RULE-BOUND]′: Natural language syntax specifies rules for the formation of hierarchically ordered constituents.

This might seem like a benign adjustment, but it immediately limits syntax to versions of what's known as phrase structure grammar. It suggests that hierarchy is constitutive of syntax. Explanatory adequacy or acquisition data is pushing this epistemic move. As we've seen (in Chapter 2), children's production is sensitive to structure beyond linear order. You could argue that descriptive adequacy already suggests hierarchy. How else would we explain Wh-movement (or movement in general) when a particular linguistic item leaves its position to occupy a higher (or lower) position in

---

[9] In some sense, we could even hold that [RULE-BOUND] and [RECURSION] are inherited from syntax and its assets before the marriage (see the next chapter for more details). Chomsky's position exemplifies this possibility by considering semantic explanation to be syntax (or 'logical syntax') in disguise.

a tree? At this stage, this is a suggestion with a number of assumptions and, in Section 3.4, we'll encounter formalisms that can do the trick from a sedentary position. Furthermore, Kubota & Levine (2020) insist that hierarchical representation isn't theoretically motivated but historically contingent on a tradition dating back to Boas & Bloomfield's immediate constituency theory.

One consequence of the move to [RULE-BOUND]′ is that we have to admit nonterminals into the syntactic ontology. This requirement is brought out in the motivation for X-bar theory. As Poole describes it:

> [W]e discovered that your language faculty appears to structure phrases into three levels: the maximal projections or *XP* level, the intermediate *X′* level, and the head or *X*. (2002, p. 50)

'Discovered' might be a bit strong ('hypothesised' might be more *la mot juste*). The three-levelled approach means that there's a lot going on below the surface of syntax. Indeed, many linguists posit covert material that doesn't get pronounced (like the PRO subject of infinitives) and pronounced elements that don't mean anything (like expletives such as 'it' in *It is raining*). Which is to say that a lot is assumed to be happening below the surface. In most of these cases, the positing of such objects is motivated by explanation since we literally cannot see these elements in the syntax. But, since their positing creates an imbalance in our equation, because we have more posits, some linguists have been compelled to find their existence in reality. In search of the reality of this layered system in the human mind, neuroscientists interested in language have attempted to locate structural hierarchy in brain structures. This task is made especially difficult since the elements of the hierarchy are unpronounced and unmarked in language production. For example, Ding *et al.* (2015) attempt to cortically track hierarchical structures such as phrases in speech production. First, they attempted to isolate any prosodic interference. Cortical activity was tracked by means of MEG. What they discovered was that 'given that the phrasal- and sentential-rate rhythms were not conveyed by acoustic fluctuations at the corresponding frequencies, cortical responses at the phrasal and sentential rates must be a consequence of internal online structure building processes' (Ding *et al.* 2015, p. 159). Commitment to [RECURSION]′ forces one's hand on this issue towards the hierarchical interpretation.[10] In Section 3.4, I'll present an argument that suggests hierarchy might not be necessary for the basic concept of syntax.

The transformation of [AoS]* is also found in the literature. This becomes a claim about the centrality or uniqueness of syntax within the language system. Many such views take syntax to be 'the heart of language' while semantics, phonology, and pragmatics are epiphenomenal aspects at the periphery. The

---

[10]   Hierarchy isn't identical to the X-bar schemata or intermediate levels. For instance, Minimalism since Chomsky (1995a) eschewed intermediate bar levels.

stronger explanatory claim view amounts to something of the following sort:

[AoS]′: All other linguistic systems supervene on syntax.

Just like physics or physical explanation is basic or the supervenience base in most naturalistic metaphysics, so syntax or syntactic explanation is basic in language. You can see some subtle adherence to a view similar to this in work on the evolution of language that takes as a central explanandum questions of how complex syntactic configuration evolved (see Bickerton 2014b; Berwick & Chomsky 2016). Consider the claim from Hauser *et al.* (2002) that combines [Recursion] with [AoS]* to yield something more substantial:

All approaches agree that a core property of FLN is recursion, attributed to narrow syntax in the conception … This capacity of FLN yields discrete infinity (a property that also characterizes the natural numbers). (Hauser *et al.* 2002, p. 1571)

FLN, or 'the faculty of language narrowly construed', is more or less the syntactic or computational component of the language faculty. On the cognitive side, such claims take the form of arguments to the effect that syntax is domain-specific while the other linguistic systems are domain-general or shared by other cognitive systems.

Lastly, as already indicated by the Hauser *et al.* (2002) quote above, [Recursion] can also be modified to reveal a stronger claim. This claim amounts to the view that recursion is a strong linguistic universal. What this essentially means is that every human language is recursive in its syntax. As Yang (2006, p. 104) puts it, '[r]ecursion pops up all over language: many have argued that the property of recursive infinity is perhaps the defining feature of our gift for language'. Thus, we have:

[Recursion]′: Natural language syntax is recursive by definition.

In other words, syntactic explanation without explicit reference to recursion is empty. In later versions of generative grammar, the Merge postulate took the role that recursion had played in previous phrase-structure accounts.

Within syntax, the consensus opinion is that recursion is the province of the phrase structure component of the grammar … Minimalist accounts return to an earlier view of phrase structure. Phrase structure rules are replaced by a Merge operation … Observe that [Merge] is recursive. There is no upper bound on how many distinct elements the operation can assemble into a set. (Hornstein 2009, pp. 53–55)

Again, Merge is a universal property of language on this view. The Minimalist Program, constrained by evolutionary theory, is interested in the virtually conceptually necessary elements of language for the purpose of 'the reduction of the computational load in carrying out a derivation' (Langendoen 2003, p. 307). The operation of Merge, which takes two items and creates a labelled set containing both of these, is supposed to be the minimal requirement for the productive capabilities of the language faculty. Technically, Merge comes in two flavours. External Merge takes two distinct syntactic objects and derives a labelled (or projected) amalgam of the two. Internal Merge applies to its own output resulting in recursive structure or embedding. Let's briefly look at an example of Merge at work in syntactic explanation.

Consider the following sentence:

3. The driver will speed recklessly.

In a bottom-up fashion, *speed* and *recklessly* will merge to form a VP; thereafter, this union will merge with the auxiliary *will* to form a TP, or Tense Phrase. Merge will independently take *the* and *driver* and create an NP that'll merge to form the final TP to deliver (3) above (the T is the label projected for the entire syntactic object). Freidin (2012, p. 911) notes, channelling Hornstein above, that '[t]his last step merges two independent phrases in essentially the same way that generalized transformations operated in the earliest transformational grammars'.

Lastly, there is a core epistemic principle underlying the Minimalist framework, known as the 'Strong Minimalist Thesis' (Chomsky 1995a, 2001), that plays an essential role in the more committed view of syntax. Merge as a mechanism is part of what is known as 'bare phrase structure', a bottom-up reversal of the top-down X-bar theory of early frameworks. Basically, unlike earlier versions of generative grammar where you had deep structures from which you derive or transform surface structures like questions or passives, MP says all you have is a set of lexical items and a bare tree structure ('bare phrase structure'). Then there's a procedure for taking an item from the set to create a subtree (as we've seen in the example above). You then merge that product with another item and project a head creating another tree and so on until you derive sentences ready for pronunciation/interpretation, that is, to be sent off to the interfaces. 'The system linking these interfaces is the *minimal* system that satisfies "legibility" constraints or conditions imposed by both the [perceptual/articulatory] system and the [conceptual/intentional] system' (Ludlow 2011, p. 36). In fact, MP goes one step further to say that the system is perfectly designed not as a result of messy evolutionary biological processes but rather driven by 'virtual conceptual necessity'. This is what SMT or the Strong Minimalist Thesis amounts to, in that it states that language is the optimal matching between sound and meaning as per the demands of the phonetic and semantic interfaces. Moreover, 'the SMT holds that the merge function, along with a general cognitive requirement for efficient computation and minimal search for agreement and labelling operations, suffices to account for much of human language syntax' (Friederici *et al.* 2017, p. 714).

Thus, Minimalist syntax is a more committed view in that each element of [BASIC] is amended or amplified. However, in another sense, it's less committing than other views of syntax, such as Government and Binding (Chomsky 1981), in that it attempts to posit the least machinery towards the most comprehensive goals. As we'll see with other frameworks below, MP is more ambitious than most other frameworks, perhaps with the exception of the Parallel Architecture. To reiterate:

$$[\textsc{min}] =_{def} [\textsc{AoS}]' + [\textsc{Rule-bound}]' + [\textsc{Recursion}]'$$

In the next few sections, I want to challenge the picture of syntactic explanation so far developed. In Section 3.3, we'll look at an argument based on a framework that reduces the role of syntactic explanation and, in so doing, admits some very intriguing theoretical possibilities. In Section 3.4, we'll look at two different families of formalism that challenge constituency and hierarchy and the proof-theoretic foundations of syntax, respectively. Lastly, in Section 3.5, we look at accounts that disrupt the idea of a separable level of syntactic explanation for any description of natural language whatsoever. The first argument draws inspiration from cognitive science, the second from formal language theory and logic, and the last from a particular brand of cognitive linguistics.

3.3 Multiple Syntaxes and Syntactic Gaps

In this section, I describe a controversial consequence of an influential view of syntax that challenges [MIN]. Specifically, I'll discuss an argument based on an alternative cognitive architecture that allows for the possibility of certain, rare, languages to have no need for a distinctive syntactic level of representation or explanation. Both [MIN] and [BASIC] presuppose that the *sine qua non* of linguistic analysis is syntactic explanation to different degrees. But if some languages can be completely described without recourse to these conceptions, then these latter views are in serious need of revision. So let's see how far we can go in the opposite direction, even if only to test the tensile strength of syntactic explanation.

What's interesting about some accounts that diverge from generative grammar, in my view, is that despite sharing some similarity in their critiques of [BASIC] and [MIN] above, they often make use of different understandings of syntax to make their points.

Over the years, Ray Jackendoff has challenged mainstream linguistic theory in a number of ways. In terms of our discussion, his Parallel Architecture (PA) (Jackendoff 2002) has been especially critical of [AoS]'. Not only does he not adhere to the idea that syntax is the sole generative engine of the language faculty but he also advocates separate but parallel generative components in terms of phonology, morphology, and semantics. What links these components are

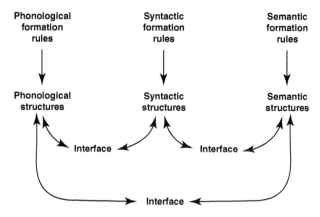

Figure 3.2 The Parallel Architecture

interface principles. He describes the project as follows (graphically represented in Figure 3.2):

The alternative to be pursued here is that language comprises a number of independent combinatorial systems, which are aligned with each other by means of a collection of interface systems. Syntax is among the combinatorial systems, but far from the only one. (Jackendoff 2002, p. 111)

We can see from the above statement that the PA does not endorse [AoS]'. What interests us here isn't, however, the PA itself but rather one consequence Jackendoff (2017) thinks it has for [RULE-BOUND]' and especially [RECURSION]'. The idea goes something like this: if the language faculty is truly composed of independent combinatorial systems linked by interface rules, one linking phonology to syntax and syntax to conceptual semantics, then in principle, there could be a link directly between phonology and semantics that bypasses syntax altogether. In local cases, idioms partly operate this way. They have meaning and phonetic output (or, in a broader sense, phonology in the case of sign languages) but they don't undergo syntactic variation.[11] In fact, the suggestion here is stronger than partial freezing of syntactic constructions, which can be explained in other ways. The idea is that the PA leaves room for the possibility of entire natural languages without syntax, that is, a syntax-free language, a feat that 'would be impossible in a traditional generative grammar, in which everything comes from syntax' (Jackendoff 2017, p. 202).

Above, I stated the claim in terms of [RULE-BOUND]' and [RECURSION]'. However, Jackendoff technically pitches his argument at [RULE-BOUND] and

---

[11] Well, as we'll see below, construction grammarians and those who advocate the PA suggest a continuum from partial idioms to fully frozen ones in which syntax and morphology intervene to different degrees. More on this in Section 3.5

[RECURSION]. To see this, we need to go back to his idea of 'linear grammar' that we encountered in the previous chapter.

Let's look again at what a linear grammar is and what a language that's characterised by one looks like for Jackendoff. A linear grammar has some combination of these five components:

1. No parts of speech, but only semantic features that distinguish objects, actions, or properties.
2. No phrases (or nonterminals) but possibly linear order and prosody.
3. No recursion or subordination (unless it's semantic).
4. Semantic roles based on linear order such as 'Agent precedes Patient', 'Focus Last', 'Modifier follows Modified', and so on.
5. Morphological structure builds from semantics not syntax.

He considers certain cases to be evidence of languages that are characterised by it, such as Riau Indonesian, which has 'no parts of speech, almost no function words ... virtually no syntactic structure or morphology' (Jackendoff 2017, p. 203). But beyond this language, which played such a role in our possible language argument, he also suggests that pidgins qualify as 'unsyntactic' but possess phonology and semantics. Second-language learners' initial stage of development (or 'Basic Variety') and evidence from the early development of certain sign languages are cited as well. Lastly, he considers subsystems of English that exhibit the aforementioned properties of linear grammar.

We can see the cases of underdeveloped languages such as pidgins, early stages of sign languages, and initial stages of the linguistic development of second-language learners as *local* restrictions on [BASIC] (and a fortiori [MIN]). It's the same for the case of subsystems of languages that themselves clearly have syntax. The *global* claim is what interests me here. The reason is that the possibility of a genuinely syntax-free linguistic description truly challenges the basic syntactic scientific project I'm hoping to identify, not necessarily the possible syntactic gaps on the road to linguistic competence or creole formation.[12]

So the relevant cases are the whole, mature languages that exhibit no syntax and are describable by means of linear grammar. As we've already seen, Jackendoff references Gil's 2005 work on Riau Indonesian but admits that it has 'virtually no syntax' and 'definitely no recursion'. Perhaps a more prominent, albeit infamous, example of a candidate for a language with only parataxis and no recursion is the indigenous Mura language of the Amazonas, Pirahã (which Jackendoff mentions in a footnote). Everett 2005 research on this language has met with scepticism (and vitriol) within the linguistic community, and it's not

---

[12] Many of these examples are developed in more detail in Jackendoff & Wittenberg (2014), in which a hierarchy of syntactic complexity is proposed, but my general point remains.

my purpose here to enter into the polemic over whether or not he was correct in his analysis. Rather, I want to draw from a recent study as to the best grammar formalism (read: scientific explanation or model) for such a language if it did in fact exhibit no form of recursion. In addition, I think it would be a better candidate for the claims concerning linear grammar that Jackendoff is making with Riau.

In Futrell *et al.* (2016), a corpus study on Pirahã was conducted 'to investigate the formal complexity of Pirahã syntax by searching for evidence of syntactic embedding' (p. 1). The researchers searched for any form of recursive structure such as conjunction, adverbial modification, sentential complements, centre-embedding, and so on. They found no obvious evidence of the existence of any such structures in the language and concluded that '[t]he corpus is consistent with the hypothesis that Pirahã is a regular language' (Futrell, 2016, p. 17). This is, in turn, consistent with Jackendoff's claim about linear grammars since Pirahã, on this analysis at least, allegedly fulfils all five properties he specifies.[13]

Jackendoff's claim amounts to the idea that [Rule-bound] and [Recursion] are not explanatorily necessary for certain languages. In so doing, he casts doubt on whether syntax is involved in their generation (a move allowed by the PA). If syntax is indeed not involved, then [AoS]* is also naturally questioned since we don't have a case of independent syntactic analysis, even of the explanatory kind. I think that if we dig a little deeper, we can see that there are two notions of 'syntax' at play in his framework.

In the first, he presupposes something like [Rule-bound]′, which aligns syntax with hierarchical structure. I'll argue below, in Section 3.4, that this isn't necessary from a formal language theory perspective, and, in Section 3.5, that it isn't necessary from a cognitive scientific perspective either. Nevertheless, if we believe Futrell *et al.*, then indeed Pirahã (and maybe Riau) seem to lack this form of syntax.

The second sense of syntax goes in the opposite direction. Rather than thinking that the PA endorses the idea that some natural languages express 'little to no syntax', it can actually be interpreted as the opposite kind of view from a theoretical perspective. Specifically, as mentioned above, Jackendoff's view endorses the claim that phonology, morphology, semantics, and syntax are all generative systems. Trivially, this view incorporates [AoS]* since not only syntactic but semantic and phonological explanations are explanatorily autonomous. In other words, in so far as these systems are 'separate' and hence in 'parallel', they're autonomous representations of sorts. There's something structural going on here. Each linguistic system is a combinatorial rule system

---

[13] Everett thinks that the Pirahã are capable of recursion (for instance, in their story-telling behaviour) just not syntactic recursion, which suggests Jackendoff's condition 3 or purely semantic recursion. See Everett (2017) for more details.

for creating well-formed representations at that level. This means that all of these systems respect [RULE-BOUND]. In addition, since [RECURSION] in [BASIC] isn't limited to syntactic recursion – semantic or musical recursion could count too – we have it applying tout court as well.

Therefore, the PA can be considered to posit multiple syntaxes in a broader sense of the word. This broad sense isn't irrelevant to the discussion here precisely because it clearly respects [BASIC]. And if [BASIC] is just what syntactic scientific explanation amounts to, then the PA is even more 'syntactocentric' than [MIN]![14]

Therefore, Jackendoff's full theory might, instead of being taken to allow for the possibility of syntax-free languages, be considered a theory with multiple syntaxes. Indeed, the kind of picture presented by [MIN] is rejected, but the logical limits of [BASIC] are pushed rather than abandoned.

For now, let's consider the formal language theory perspective and the alternative picture of syntax that it uncovers.

3.4   Dependencies, LFG, and Model Theory

In this section, I want to expand the syntactic horizons in two different directions. In some sense, these explorations will offer alternative syntactic strategies to Jackendoff's claims about linear grammar from two related but distinct perspectives. The first is based on an alternative conception of syntax to the mainstream phrase-structure syntax, with a rich history in Continental Europe, called dependency grammar. The second is based on a broader notion of syntax in terms of formal first-order logic and model theory resulting in what is often called model-theoretic syntax (Pullum 2013).

In the previous section, in accordance with Jackendoff's data (and the PA), we split syntax into a broader notion that respects [BASIC] and a narrower notion that challenges [MIN]. The question that wasn't really dealt with is whether or not linear grammar is the only way of accounting for the data. In science, theory is usually underdetermined by data. This case is no exception. Furthermore, I think appreciating alternatives can illuminate the syntactic explanatory project in useful ways. For this, we need a soupçon of formal language theory and a dash of formal logic to truly appreciate the cocktail on offer here. Let's start with the former.

There's a class of grammars, lurking in the work of continental grammarians and, more recently, natural language processing (NLP) researchers, that exhibits many of the properties mentioned by Jackendoff and are expressively equivalent (or 'weakly equivalent' in formal language theoretic terms) to context-free

---

[14] The word 'syntactocentric' is often considered a slur against Chomskyan 'interpretivist' theories.

grammars. These are known as dependency grammars.[15] As we'll see, despite some major diversions from phrase structure and constituency-based syntactic explanations, dependency grammars are compatible with [RULE-BOUND], [AOS]*, and [RECURSION]. In the following, I'll briefly describe what this framework looks like and how it adheres to [BASIC].[16]

Dependency grammar is a family of grammatical formalisms that has received renewed interest in linguistics as well as in applied linguistic settings such as NLP, psycholinguistics, and neuroscience. It's based on a notion of *dependencies* that are binary, asymmetric governance relations that hold between words. If word A dominates or governs word B, then word B depends on word A. In standard terminology, word A is called a *head* and word B a *dependent*. These relations are labelled in dependency trees, which are rooted, directed acyclic graphs. One node acts as a root from which arrows (relations) emanate to other nodes in the structure. Importantly, nodes are in a one-to-one mapping with words. So dependency grammar has just one layer of representation or 'flat structure' as opposed to the kinds of hierarchical structures of phrase-structure grammars (so no [RULE-BOUND]') with nonterminal elements. The analysis looks something like Figure 3.3.

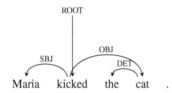

Figure 3.3 Dependency graph for *Maria kicked the cat*

Dependency grammars, like regular grammars, are easy to parse, and, like Jackendoff's linear grammars, reflect argument structure and semantics more clearly since they use functional labels as well as don't contain phrases or recursion explicitly. But they're equivalent formally to phrase-structure grammars, or rather context-free grammars (see footnote 15); thus, they have many of

---

[15] Well, technically, projective dependency grammar is weakly equivalent to CFGs (or can be induced by lexicalised CFGs), a result proven by Hays (1964). However, parsing in unconstrained non-projective dependency grammar is an NP-hard problem, thought to require $O(n^2)$ time to parse a sentence (n is the length of the input in words), that's similar in complexity to parsing with context-sensitive grammars. See Debusmann & Kuhlmann (2010) for the claim that certain dependency grammars are mildly context-sensitive.

[16] Futrell *et al.* are open to the journey we're on:

We do not claim that this grammar is the best grammar for the corpus; it might be that a simpler grammar would have recursive embedding, for some definition of 'simple'. We hope that the data we are currently releasing will make it possible to find the best grammar. Currently, we only claim that the grammar above is consistent with the corpus. (2015, p. 18)

the expressive capabilities of more complex formal languages. At first glance, the notion of head-dependent unit seems incompatible with [RULE-BOUND] since the structural units captured by phrase-structure grammars are movable, elidable, pronoun-replaceable, frontable constituents. The relationship between a head and its dependents hops around the sentence with the only proviso that the lines don't cross (just like in *Ghostbusters*)! A simple ordered pair of words is not a constituent in the traditional grammatical sense. I think this is the reason that finer-grained groupings have been proposed across the dependency literature. In word grammar (Hudson 1990), variously coordinated elements, like conjuncts, are represented by means of square brackets, demarcating word strings. Kahane 1997 bubble tree formalism allows dependency relations to hold between sets of nodes.[17]

Some dependency theorists have even put forward a new notion, that of *catenae* (O'Grady 1998; Osborne 2005; Osborne *et al.* 2012). A *catena* is defined as a word or a combination of words continuous with respect to dominance. Basically, a subtree in graph theory. But the words in a catena don't need to be contiguous in the linear ordering, which means that constituents can be thought of as special cases of catenae, where subtrees are complete. One prominent contemporary dependency grammarian even advocates the idea above its rival:

The catena unit is much more flexible than the constituent, and the argument has therefore been put forward that the catena is better suited to serve as the basic unit of syntactic (and morphosyntactic) analysis than the constituent. (Osborne 2014, p. 620)

To me, this shows that practitioners in the field are sensitive to the core explanatory role of [RULE-BOUND] and have found innovative means of retaining it within their scientific work.

[RECURSION] is another matter. Dependency grammars don't posit special recursive rules. Nor are there special phrases organised hierarchically as in [RECURSION]'. In fact, in his famous proof, Hays (1961) considered the capability of licensing an infinite set or allowing recursive categories (a '[phrase-structure] system of infinite degree', in his terminology) to be a separating factor between dependency grammar and phrase-structure grammar.[18] This offers us a nice point to pause and appreciate an important distinction. The distinction is between theory and data. Recursive rules fall clearly on the theoretical side of the divide. The data, on the other hand, which includes centre-embedding, coordinate conjunction, subordination, and so on, is susceptible to various theoretical explanations. Dependency grammar can model some of this data. In terms of explanatory coverage or empirical adequacy as per our aforementioned

---

[17] Other older approaches, including Mel'cuk (1988) and Garde (1977), introduced 'fragments' and 'significant elements', respectively, to capture constituent-like units.
[18] He also considered that this departure would have little linguistic application.

equation, it's more than sufficient. In some sense, what's lost with the added nodes or nonterminals is gained in terms of parsability and structure. Again, Osborne is explicit in this regard:

> The number of nodes in dependency-based structures tends to be approximately half that of constituency-based structures. The greatly reduced number of nodes means a greatly reduced amount of syntactic structure in general. The minimalism of these reduced structures then permeates the entire theoretical apparatus. Most DGs draw attention to this fact, and, in so doing, they are appealing to Occam's Razor: the simpler theory is the better theory, other things being equal. (2014, p. 624)

I warned you that 'simplicity' is polysemous in syntax. If you still aren't satisfied, then we can play the expressive equivalence card again. Phrase-structure grammars, at least the context-free versions, are expressively equivalent to dependency grammars. This means that they generate the same sets of strings (or expressions) syntactically. Furthermore, there are many algorithms for converting dependency grammars into context-free grammars by translating the rule systems that show that dependency grammar is compatible with [RECURSION] (and even [RECURSION]') (Debusmann 2000).

Lastly, and thankfully, we get [AoS]* for free. Dependency grammars generally separate syntactic information from other linguistic systems in their representation as is required by [AoS]* as a matter of course. The variants that don't are often called 'multistratal' dependency grammar (Sgall *et al.* 1986). Notwithstanding these cases, the majority of explanatory work in this framework isolates syntax.

Many of its practitioners claim that these grammars are more useful than phrase-structure grammars in dealing with free-word-order languages and long-distance dependencies (Osborne 2014; de Marneffe & Nivre 2019). I'm not endorsing these claims here.[19] Rather, what I'm suggesting is that dependencies offer a way of explaining the cases Jackendoff and Futrell *et al.* describe without requiring us to claim that these languages lack syntax in the narrower sense. Thus, their arguments are best understood as challenging syntax in terms of [MIN], but not [BASIC].[20]

In one interesting direction, which we will briefly consider here, if we add some aspects of [MIN] to dependency grammar, we get lexical-functional grammar (LFG). There are many similarities between these explanatory projects.

[19] For an overview of and comparison between dependency grammar and constituency-based grammars, see Rambow & Joshi (1997) and Nefdt & Baggio (2023).

[20] I've focused on equivalence here, but flat structure and dependencies seem to be required for nonconfigurational languages (which involve free word order, discontinuous expressions, and null anaphora) that, unlike Pirahã, are highly complex and have notoriously caused problems for phrase-structure grammar. So much so that one classical generativist treatment, Hale (1983), of Australian Warlpiri proffered a 'dual structure' approach in which the projection principle is optional for certain structures (via a parametric setting), thus allowing for a separation between constituency and functional representation, or, in other words, between dependency and phrase structure.

LFG was initially proposed as a means of capturing aspects of a broader class of language families and a wider range of morphosyntactic phenomena, such as free-word-order languages and agglutination (Austin & Bresnan 1996). Additionally, LFG was established on a platform of psycholinguistic plausibility (Bresnan 1982) and is considered a 'deep approach' to NLP since it aims to provide a tractable computational framework that's inspired by theoretical linguistics (Forst 2011). However, it's generally not pitched at the level of individual theory, similarly to [MIN].

[T]he formal model of LFG is not a syntactic theory in the linguistic sense. Rather, it is an architecture for syntactic theory. Within this architecture, there is a wide range of possible syntactic theories and subtheories, some of which closely resemble syntactic theories within alternative architectures, and others of which differ radically from familiar approaches. (Bresnan *et al.* 2016, p. 39)

The most profound connection might be LFG's take on the alleged notational variance of phrase structure and functional structure. LFG maintains that syntax comprises multiple interconnected levels of linguistic information. The most prominently articulated levels have been f-structure (functional), c-structure (constituent and category), and a-structure (argument). But LFG also contains p-structure (phonology and prosody), i-structure (information), s-structure (syntax–semantics interface), and m-structure (morphology) (Börjars 2020). I'll focus on f-structure and c-structure here since they map well on to the relationship between dependency and phrase structure.

F-structure represents the grammatical functions, such as subject and object, and is supposed to be invariant between languages. The standard means of representing f-structure is as an attribute–value matrix (AVM) or an unordered set of feature–value pairs, for example, TENSE=FUTURE and so on. Lexical items, such as nouns and verbs, also have a PRED feature with a unique semantic value. F-structure comes with a host of conditions such as the 'uniqueness condition', or the requirement that every feature has exactly one value, and the 'coherence condition', which mandates that all argument functions occur in the value of a local PRED feature and that all functions with a PRED feature also have a θ-role (thematic role).

C-structure is familiar from phrase-structure grammar and is, in fact, a modified version of X-bar theory. However, as Börjars notes, 'in comparison to other frameworks, LFG's approach to X-bar syntax is unorthodox in that, for instance, nonbinary branching as well as exocentric categories is permitted' (2020, p. 157) and 'that all nodes, including preterminal and head nodes, are optional' (p. 159). Unlike f-structure, c-structure can and does vary cross linguistically. One of the guiding motivations for LFG was to account for nonconfigurational languages like Warlpiri in which word order is much more flexible and the phrase structure appears to be more 'flat', as in dependency analysis. Multiple c-structures can map on to the same f-structure.

Essentially, LFG rejects the idea that the phrase structure and dependency graphs are notational variants or the same syntactic explanation under different mathematical guises. In fact, it motivates their union via interface principles. Much like dependency grammar, LFG is a lexicalised formalism because 'every partial tree licensed by a grammar rule contains a lexical element" (Müller 2018, p. 392). The similarities between f-structure and dependency grammar already trivially establish a correspondence between LFG and [Basic]. The further incorporation of c-structure pushes [Basic] towards a [Min] kind of project, with the caveat that the overall architecture is not similarly minimalistic. Specifically, LFG hasn't really been subjected to the evolvability constraint of Chomsky and its architecture remains highly modular and complex.[21]

The PA is a multiple derivational theory of language modelled on the singularly derivational syntax of generative grammar. This means that it's in the business of explaining how and why certain well-formed expressions are generated or derived by a particular grammar or model. Dependency grammar is a nonderivational theory of syntax even though it can be translated into a derivational theory. LFG seems to occupy a hybrid position. Consideration of these departures from mainstream generative grammar opens the door to alternative frameworks such as those that derive from the other side of logic. Under those conceptions, syntax is more related to formal languages in the model-theoretic sense as opposed to the proof theory that inspired much of early generative linguistics (see Pullum 2011). Pullum (2013) takes this to be at the heart of what he calls 'syntactic metatheory' or the metascientific study of frameworks for natural language syntax.

The question I regard as most central, in that it arises at a level more abstract than any comparison between rival theories, concerns the choice between two ways of conceptualizing grammars. One has its roots in the mathematicization of logical proof as string manipulation in the early 20th century, and the other springs from a somewhat later development in logic, namely model theory. (p. 492)

Model-theoretic syntax replaces the centrality of that proof-theoretic notion of syntax with a more logical syntax drawing from first-order logic and model theory.[22] Grammar formalisms such as generalized phrase structure grammar (Gazdar *et al.* 1985) and head-driven phrase structure grammar (HPSG) (Pollard & Sag 1994) are prominent examples of this approach. They're also contrasted with the derivational approach of generative grammar. Simplistically, instead of a grammar generating the well-formed formulas of

---

[21] In Chapter 8, I challenge this interpretation of explanation from evolution in such a way that complexity is no longer an obvious nonstarter.

[22] In a sense, 'formal language' is polysemous in referring to a meaningless or uninterpreted calculus akin to its use in the Hilbert programme and a component of a compositional logical language assumed in the work of Frege and Russell. See van Heijenoort (1967) on the history of the different views.

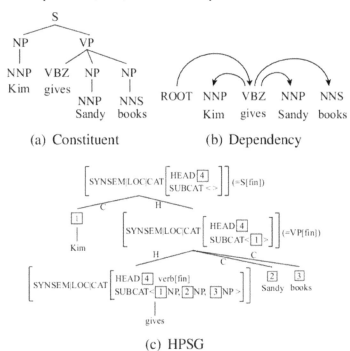

Figure 3.4 Formalism comparison: (a) Constituent; (b) Dependency; (c) HPSG (from Zhou & Hai 2019)

a language, a grammar models the rules of that language via constraints. 'An MTS [model-theoretic syntax] grammar does not recursively define a set of expressions; it merely states necessary conditions on the syntactic structures of individual expressions" (Pullum & Scholz 2001, p. 19). In this sense, a sentence or expression is well formed iff it's a model of the grammar (defined in terms of constraints that act as the axioms of the formalism). To be a model of the grammar is to be an expression that satisfies the grammar or meets the constraints.

It's not hard to see that model-theoretic grammars respect [Basic]. To see how they adhere to [Rule-bound], [AoS]*, and [Recursion], let's briefly look at a particular model-theoretic grammar: HPSG. HPSG is a phrase-structure grammar that shares features with LFG and dependency grammar. Compare the graphical representations for the ditransitive sentence *Kim gives Sandy books* in Figure 3.4. Structurally, (a) and (c) are similar in branching since they're both phrase-structure grammars (although contemporary phrase-structure grammars are exclusively binary). However, like the dependency graph in (b), HPSG maps features and is highly lexicalised. There's similarly no movement or covert operations in HPSG. It uses similar AVMs to LFG. Following de Saussure, strings of the grammar are modelled as combinations of signs where a feature structure of a sign represents its phonological, syntactic, and semantic properties or information. The information is organised in terms of inheritance hierarchy of types where a given word such as 'gives' in the above examples would fall under the types *word* and *verb*.[23]

HPSG is perhaps an extreme example of [AoS]* at work. The syntactic information contained in the average tree is highly precise and specific. Instead of multiple representations for modelling the relationships between functional elements and phrasal structure (as in LFG), the formalism contains very large structures with multiple subrepresentations related to each other by constraints. This is part of the reason the analysis can look very daunting (see Figure 3.4). But the precision is also part of the reason HPSG has actually played well with computational implementation and modelling (Borsley 1991).

HPSG is also radically rule-bound. It contains principles, grammar rules, and a rich set of lexical rules. Phrases and words both belong to the subtype *expression* since the framework's lexicalism ensures that the lexicon is as structured as the phrasal units. The *expression* type models the feature structures that form the units of the grammar or constituents and is itself a subtype of SYNSEM, which has as one of its primary functions the encoding of grammatical information for constituency. All the components of the grammar are composed by rules for morphological alterations (like pluralisation) and phrase construction like the head feature principle (or HFP) that makes sure that the value of the head is the same for headed phrases (like VP) and the head-daughter (the V in this instance). In effect, there are rules all the way up and down in HPSG!

To see how [RECURSION] can be captured, we need to consider the central operation of HPSG, namely, unification. I'll keep it brief and simple for the sake of illustration. Unification takes two AVMs and combines them into an AVM with information from both. Of course, this procedure presupposes that the information is compatible. There's no question over whether HPSG can handle embedding data in natural language. All the theories we've dealt with so far can do so. But with unification, recursive rules can be incorporated into the grammatical structures directly. The labelling of feature structures already provide us with a clue as they allow for something called 'cyclic structures' in which 'one ends up going in a circle if one follows a particular path [that] can be potentially repeated an infinite number of times' (Müller 2018, p. 211). This just means that a given feature structure can be labelled ' 1 ' and contain another feature structure that references it as a value. In fact, even when a given feature structure doesn't include a cycle, unification can result in them. Nevertheless, like LFG and dependency grammar – and unlike [MIN] – HPSG is a so-called surface-oriented grammar, which means that it specialises in characterising

---

[23] This basically means that if a feature falls under type t_2 and t_2 is a subtype of t_1, then t_1 inherits that feature.

surface forms of sentences. This means that when you use the formalism, you're unlikely to need cycles for linguistic purposes.

We've been very formal and abstract in this chapter so far. Perhaps so much so that a concern could be raised that since [BASIC] is derived from formal theory, its application to it is rather unsurprising. Therefore, in the next section, we'll move well beyond the bounds of formalism and formal language theory generally to cognitive linguistics and a special radical case thereof. I hope to show that aspects of the [BASIC] picture can be resurrected even in this diametrically opposed conception of syntax.

3.5 Constructions and the Rejection of Syntax

Cognitive linguistics is a broad research programme that covers a number of distinct frameworks. The general idea involves bringing the study of language closer to the scientific results and theories of cognitive neuroscience. Lakoff (1991) calls this the 'cognitive commitment' or the idea that one should 'make one's account of human language accord with what is generally known about the mind and brain from disciplines other than linguistics' (p. 54). Aspects of generative syntax such as [AoS]* and domain specificity are thus often eschewed in most of these accounts. The field itself emerged in the 1970s as a response to the formalist and computationalist approach of generative grammar. Its theoretical inspiration drew from the Gestalt theory, nonmodular views in the philosophy of mind, and work on concepts such as prototype theory, among other things. The linguistic framework fits well into the 'second-generation cognitive science' with its focus on embodiment and situated cognition as opposed to the more abstract mentalist tradition of formal linguistics (Sinha 2010).[24] However, instead of surveying the broad research programme, which would take us too far afield, I'll focus on one particularly radical departure from mainstream linguistics and its notion of syntax, namely, radical construction grammar, or RCG (Croft 2001). I believe that this view showcases the limits of the alternative conception of syntax embodied in the general cognitive linguistic theoretical stance.

The first way in which RCG breaks with traditional syntax is by claiming that all grammatical categories are language- and construction-specific. Thus, RCG assumes no formal syntactic structure whatsoever, except the part-whole structure of constructions, which are themselves chunks or units not decomposable into further atomic units as assumed in standard syntax (and presumably by [RULE-BOUND]).[25]

---

[24] Johnson & Lakoff (2002) argue quite strongly that syntax, semantics, and pragmatics *require* some form of embodied realism.

[25] Jackendoff's 2002 take on idioms is inspired by standard construction grammar of the nonradical variety.

Croft's theory rejects [AoS]* wholly. For him, there are no universal syntactic categories, such as NP, VP, or PP, but only language-specific categories derived from constructions. The important aspect of his view for current purposes is the framework's rejection of a style of syntactic argumentation that Croft calls 'distributional analysis'. 'In distributional analysis, a hypothesis about the proper analysis of a syntactic unit is formed by examining the occurrence or nonoccurrence of that unit in a range of syntactic structures' (Croft 2013, p. 2). The distributional analysis rests on a 'building block model of grammar' or the claim that

> Grammar is seen as being made up of minimal units (words or morphemes) belonging to grammatical categories, and constructions are defined as structured combinations of these units. The purpose of the distributional method, therefore, is to identify the grammatical categories that are the building blocks, and the units that belong to those categories. (Croft 2013, p. 3)

To the contrary, Croft claims that distributional patterns don't match within and across languages. This causes tension for the building block model according to him since specific language constructions seem to define distinct categories (e.g. Absolutive–Ergative is not identical to Subject–Object, etc.). The radical step is to jettison universal categories entirely and acknowledge that the building blocks differ for each language and are perhaps more interesting for each construction of individual languages.

What exactly are constructions? Well, these are usually taken to be pairings of form and meaning such that there are 'slots' for saturation of individual constructions, as in the following (adapted from Hoffmann & Trousdale 2013):

a. idiom construction: for example, *X takes Y for granted* – 'X doesn't value Y'
b. comparative construction: for example, *John is taller than you* – 'X is more Adj than Y'
c. resultative construction: for example, *She rocks the baby to sleep* [X V Y Z] – 'X causes Y to become Z by V-ing'

This situation leaves us with a conflicting account to the standard framework suggested by [BASIC] (and a fortiori that suggested by [MIN]). Constructions are complex entities taken to be basic units of grammar. For instance, [RULE-BOUND] standardly operates on the opposite assumption that basic units are words or lexemes, and via rules (and [RECURSION]), more complex entities are generated. Goldberg (2015) mounts a version of this argument against the principle of compositionality (assumed in formal semantics) that, equally to [AoS]*, adheres to the building block model of grammar. Constructions, she argues, are ubiquitous in natural language and a failure to acknowledge this can lead to untoward consequences, such as infinitely many verb senses if the projection principle of generative grammar is true (see Goldberg 2015, p. 6 for more).

As it stands, the view can be seen as a radical rejection of both [Basic] and [Min]. But just how radical is RCG really? Specifically, I want to argue here that some aspects of the view can be reconciled with the core syntactic project identified in [Basic], perhaps at a more local level.

The first thing to show is that construction grammar of the standard variety is compatible with the building block model of grammar (or [Rule-bound] + [Recursion]). Then, we will be in a better position to adjudicate what RCG adds and whether or not these additions indeed rule out the possible compatibility with [Basic].

The acceptance of semi-fixed constructions in grammar, as assumed by construction grammar, is not tantamount to rejecting the building block model by itself. For instance, one could assume that grammatical constructions are on a scale from completely decomposable (or flexible) to less so (e.g. from novel structures to fixed idioms). Jackendoff (2002) assumes such a continuum. All that's required, following classical cognitivist treatments of constructions (such as Fillmore *et al.* 1988), is to distinguish between syntactic configurations in terms of 'schematicity', with the more schematic involving more syntactic and morphological variation. Idioms are less schematic on this picture since many of their parts do not undergo morphological inflection and so on, such as *kick the bucket* in which only the verb is grammatically flexible. A syntactic rule is interpreted as entirely schematic on this account. Furthermore, it's constructions all the way down. Not only syntactic rules but also lexical items can be reinterpreted as constructions (albeit less schematic ones).

Given this, [Rule-bound] is clearly compatible with the presence of constructions. Perhaps less schematic constructions limit its application but it still applies when grammatical flexibility is present in other cases. In addition, other frameworks also have to accommodate fixed structures like idioms. Even if we adopt the methodology of the general framework, which reverses the order of the theory such that what were complex derived structures are now complex primitive structures, the degree to which a given construction admits flexibility licenses the application of [Rule-bound]. In fact, according to sign-based construction grammar (Sag 2012), an offshoot of HPSG, constructions are rules. That framework goes further to show that construction grammar is basically a form of phrase-structure grammar.[26]

Similarly, the argument for [Recursion] is straightforward. If a given construction is schematic enough to allow other constructions to be embedded within its environment, then it can be considered recursive in the minimal sense. Consider the construction 'either … or' and conditional constructions below. There's no obvious limit to the embedding in these cases.

4. Either$_1$ you think that if$_2$ it is raining then$_2$ either$_3$ it is cold or$_3$ it is wet or$_1$ you think that it is not raining.

---

[26] See Müller (2021) for more comparisons between construction grammar and other approaches.

Müller makes a very similar point when he admits that construction grammar seems incompatible with recursion at first glance given its surface orientation.

For example, one often talks of a [Sbj TrVerb Obj] construction. However, the grammars in question also become recursive as soon as they contain a sentence embedding or relative clause construction. A sentence embedding construction could have the form [Sbj that-Verb that-S], where a that-Verb is one that can take a sentential complement and that-S stands for the respective complement. A that-clause can then be inserted into the that-S slot. (2018, p. 555)

Lastly, construction grammar of the standard variety does not assume a clear distinction between syntactic form and semantic function, as generative grammar does, for instance. But, importantly, it 'allows for constructions which have formal values but no semantic value' (Fillmore 1999, as cited in Croft 2005, p. 276) even though its basic units are generally amalgams of these. By admitting such cases into the model, enough leeway is created for the explanatory autonomy of syntactic characterisation in terms of [AoS]*, at least in principle. This is part of the reason Jackendoff can endorse both construction grammar and [AoS]* in his PA.

So if construction grammar simpliciter is not directly or wholly incompatible with [Basic], then what does RCG add that might introduce this incompatibility, if anything?

Croft calls the combination of the features above (and some others)[27] 'vanilla construction grammar'. He distinguishes his view in the following way:

Radical Construction Grammar adds the following three theses to vanilla construction grammar as described above–perhaps they should be thought of as anti-theses. First, constructions, in particular complex syntactic units, are the primitive elements of syntactic representation; grammatical categories as such are derived from constructions. That is, there are no formal syntactic categories such as 'noun', 'verb', 'subject' or 'object' per se ... Second, the formal representation of constructions consists only of a (complex) construction and its component parts. That is, there are no syntactic relations at all. Third, there are no universal constructions (e.g. a universal passive). That is, all constructions are language-specific. In other words, virtually all formal grammatical structure is language-specific and construction-specific. This is to say: what I have described as vanilla construction grammar is all that is universal in formal syntactic representation. Vanilla construction grammar, with no toppings, is Radical Construction Grammar. (Croft 2005, p. 277)

---

[27] For instance, Goldberg (2013) also emphasises the 'network' aspect of the approach in which '[p]hrasal constructions, words, and partially filled words (aka morphemes) are related in a network in which nodes are related by inheritance links' (p. 1). Network and inheritance hierarchies are also utilised in formal frameworks such as Word Grammar (Hudson 1990), HPSG (Sag *et al.* 2003), and sign-based construction grammar (Boas & Sag 2012). She additionally claims that construction grammar explicitly rejects the kind of thinking involved in [Rule-bound]' that postulates hidden layers of syntactic analysis (such as nonterminals).

Some of these features we've already seen above. I'll focus here on the features that I think are the best candidates for being inconsistent with [BASIC]. There are two: (i) the complete rejection of major parts of speech, and (ii) a mereological claim about the composition of constructions.

In terms of the rejection of syntactic categories such as 'noun', 'verb', 'subject', and so on, Croft uses crosslinguistic arguments against distributional analysis. In fact, RCG adopts what Croft calls the 'Semantic Map Connectivity Hypothesis' or the view that 'any relevant language-specific and construction-specific category should map onto a CONNECTED REGION in conceptual space' (2001, p. 96). Nevertheless, one answer to the worry about (i) involves treating it as a division of labour argument that merely reassigns tasks from the syntax to the semantics (similar to the 'simpler syntax hypothesis' of Culicover & Jackendoff 2005). In which case, its scope is local and limited and thus it doesn't affect other aspects of a purely syntactic representation of natural language suggested by [BASIC] and [AoS]*; (ii), if true, is a much more serious problem for [BASIC].

Essentially, RCG takes the mereological structure of language to be part-whole with no formal relations. I think stretching [RULE-BOUND] to the composition rules of any mereological ordering would be a step too far, notwithstanding the overt rejection of [AoS]*. To see how this view might be reconciled with [BASIC], another short detour into formal modelling is required.

RCG is a 'nonreductionist' theory of syntactic representation. Unlike most other accounts discussed in this chapter that reduce larger complex structures to smaller simple or atomic ones (whether they're derivational or not), RCG follows theories like the Gestalt theory of perception in distinguishing the parts from the whole ontologically.

To see how such a radical account might be reconciled with a more standard one, consider the following procedure. Associate every construction, from more schematic to less, with a *treelet*, where a treelet is a clipped section of a syntactic tree. Then, allow certain variable nodes ($N \downarrow$) on the treelets upon which other treelets can be attached or adjoined, as seen in Figure 3.5.

The new structure immediately respects the minimal conception of syntax in that it allows for [RULE-BOUND] via the composition rules of substitution on trees, [RECURSION] by allowing subtrees or treelets qua constructions to be inserted within trees, that is, adjunction, and finally [AoS]* by representing the syntax independently from other aspects of the grammar. It also respects aspects of RCG in that it takes constructions (viewed as treelets) to be primitive, complex structures, not reducible or derivable from simpler parts. There are also no production rules in this formalism. Thus, the mereological spirit of RCG remains intact. Nor is there any need to assume that these structures are universal and not language-specific. Each language can be seen as its own syntactic ecosystem with its own indigenous treelets.

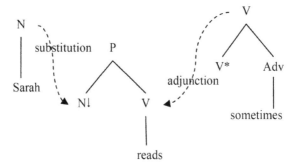

Figure 3.5 Tree operations

For the syntactically knowledgeable reader, this basic formalism is already well known in the literature, namely, tree-adjoining grammar (TAG) (see Joshi 1987; Joshi & Schabes 1997). Furthermore, TAGs are formally equivalent to phrase-structure grammars that clearly respect [BASIC]. Additionally, there are various means of adding semantic information to this kind of formalism such as the feature structures found in unification-based grammars like HPSG and sign-based construction grammar. Or, more in the spirit of RCG, Shieber & Schabes (1990) specifically modify TAGs as synchronous tree-adjoining grammar in order to move beyond syntax to semantics and effectively take the insights of the formalism to model form-meaning pairings as is fundamental to construction grammar.[28]

Thus, the crux of RCG doesn't seem to be pitted directly against [BASIC] and the scientific project it embodies, despite claims to the contrary. In so far as it's a construction grammar, it's amenable to the kind of treatment I suggest above. Moreover, even some of its radical departures can be captured formally while respecting [BASIC]. This isn't to reduce RCG to traditional grammar but rather to offer a way of reconciling certain elements of its proposal with a core view of the scientific syntactic project I've explored in this chapter.

3.6   Summary

This chapter has been an exercise in metasyntax quite distinct from most others on the market. For one thing, I haven't really made too many theoretical comparisons. There's no talk of poverty of stimulus, innateness, or language learning. Instead, there's a rather high-level (but with some stepping ladders) comparison of how structures are built in syntax across multiple frameworks. I maintained throughout that there's a basic scientific project at the heart of syntactic theory, one that focuses on rules in creating structural units, captures

---

[28] Lichte & Kallmeyer (2017) explicitly make a case for a tree-based constructionist framework based on TAGs.

recursive phenomena, and, most importantly, treats syntactic information as explanatorily autonomous. In other words, this chapter can be best seen as an attempt at the philosophy of scientific modelling in syntax. We'll return to issues of learnability and evolution in later chapters.

Further Reading

There are a number of excellent books on syntax. The problem is that actual syntax and syntactic metatheory aren't always clearly distinguished.

- Without a doubt, the most comprehensive and detailed compendium on syntactic theory in existence is Stefan Müller's (2018) *Grammatical Theory* (Language Sciences Press). The first volume provides detailed analyses of everything from Minimalism to HPSG to dependency grammar to categorial grammar and LFG. The second volume focuses on comparative metatheory and covers numerous concepts like recursion and language acquisition.
- For an introduction to the theoretical foundations and methodological implications of Minimalist Syntax specifically, I recommend Cedric Boeckx (2006) *Linguistic Minimalism* (Oxford University Press). It's pitched less as a guide to Minimalist analysis and more as a treatise on the philosophy of science that underlies it.
- Jackendoff's (2002) classic *The Foundations of Language* (Oxford University Press) is an essential read for a comprehensive account of language pitted directly against mainstream generative linguistics.
- If Jackendoff's magnum opus is on the reading list, then Chomsky's (1995a) astronomically influential *The Minimalist Program* (MIT Press) should be there as well. Chomsky's text not only sets up a future research programme in linguistics (and syntax specifically) but it details the nature of previous epochs in generative grammar and how the theory changed to shed considerable structure and, perhaps more importantly, why it did.
- Thomas Hoffmann's (2022) *Construction Grammar: The Structure of English* (Cambridge University Press) provides detailed analysis of almost every aspect of various versions of the framework. It's in the spirit of the formal tradition with which I've tried to wrestle in this chapter.

4   The Science of Semantics

The previous chapter investigated the philosophy of syntax by surveying a number of theoretical frameworks and finding a common underlying scientific strategy. In this chapter, we shift gears to the scientific study of meaning. To many, a language can be considered to be a pairing of form and meaning (Lewis 1975; Chomsky 1986). This view suggests there is an intimate connection between syntax and semantics. Syntax is often seen as a springboard for semantics, with some within the Chomskyan tradition arguing for a more central role for the latter and a purely parasitic role for the former (so-called interpretative semantics). Model-theoretic semantics, too, starts from syntactic structure. Despite this trend, I also plan to discuss the science of meaning in its own right as a unique subdiscipline beyond its connection to syntax.

In Section 4.1, I lay the groundwork by specifying what's meant by 'metasemantics' and thus what the nature of the present inquiry entails. I distinguish between two projects under this label and argue that the more fruitful of the two is the one that comes with a metascientific, as opposed to a priori metaphysical, viewpoint. In Section 4.2, I discuss the 'default' position in Montagovian model-theoretic semantics and the adherence to the polemical principle of compositionality (PoC) it entails. I present a case for the principle at two levels, one semantic and the other metasemantic. I show that certain problems for the principle evaporate upon ascension. Section 4.3 introduces what I'll call 'formal context' to semantic theory. I paint a picture of the connections (or cline) between formal, dynamic, and distributional approaches to semantics in terms of how much formal context is incorporated. In Sections 4.4 and 4.5, I discuss what happens when semantics 'goes rogue'. Here, I consider semantic theory applied beneath the sentence level (lexical semantics), underspecification (semantic explanation not bound directly by syntax), and supersemantics, or semantics applied beyond language.

4.1   Two Senses of 'Metasemantics'

The term 'metasemantics' picks out a broad, relatively recent collection of philosophical views directed at the cross-disciplinary study of meaning. In some sense, it acts as an offshoot of the many theories of meaning traditionally investigated under the auspices of the philosophy of language. In another, it aims its reflections at the science of meaning, that is, formal semantics. Sometimes, the two trends are mixed together. Theorists themselves use the term loosely, even perhaps inconsistently.

Thus, in this section, I'm not planning to make an exegetical or rather descriptive case. Rather, I want to engage in some light *conceptual engineering* (Burgess *et al.* 2020; Isaac *et al.* 2022). This means that instead of describing how a term is used or a discipline operates, a normative claim is made about how a particular domain *should* operate, how a term *ought* to be used. Specifically, I see two broad projects that both aspire to the label 'metasemantics'. The first is a largely metaphysical pursuit, germane to the philosophy of language, that attempts to uncover the nonsemantic properties that underlie semantic facts. In this sense, it works a bit like metaethics in which various candidate accounts rival one another for an explanation of what makes a fact moral (to be distinguished from the ethical question of what makes an action right). The second is a more naturalistic approach to understanding the study of meaning. It's an exercise in metascience more than it is metaphysics. In reality, these pursuits can overlap, of course. However, I think conceptual hygiene dictates some separation. Furthermore, I maintain that metasemantics guided by the philosophy of science offers more insight into theoretical linguistics, the interface between semantics and syntax, pragmatics, and general cognition. The metaphysical mode is much less helpful in this sense. I'll refer to the first approach as metasemantics$_1$ and the second metasemantics$_2$, before shedding the subscripts in subsequent sections when we adopt the latter as our strict domain of inquiry.

So what is metasemantics$_1$? Essentially, it's a grounding project. Stalnaker (1997), for instance, considers the remit of 'foundational semantics' to be an inquiry into the systems that underlie language such that 'descriptive semantics' is possible. A similar distinction is made by Kaplan (1989) with a linguistically porcine example:

There are several interesting issues concerning what belongs to semantics. The fact that a word or phrase has a certain meaning clearly belongs to semantics. On the other hand, a claim about the *basis* for ascribing a certain meaning to a word or phrase does not belong to semantics. 'Ohsnay' means *snow* in Pig-Latin. That's a semantic fact about Pig-Latin. The reason why 'ohsnay' means *snow* is not a semantic fact; it is some kind of historical or sociological fact about Pig-Latin. Perhaps, because it relates to how the language is *used*, it should be categorized as part of the *pragmatics* of Pig-Latin (though I am not really comfortable with this nomenclature), or perhaps, because it is a fact *about* semantics, as part of the *Metasemantics* of Pig-Latin (or perhaps, for those who prefer working from below to working from above, as part of the *Foundations of semantics* of Pig-Latin). (pp. 573–4)

So, from this, we get a distinction between the fact that a word like 'ohsnay' means something in Pig-Latin and *how* or *why* it comes to mean what it does (whatever that is). In other words, in virtue of what nonsemantic fact does this semantic fact pertain? This isn't the same thing as giving truth conditions for a sentence, which is a semantic-level procedure. David Lewis famously stated 'semantics with no treatment of truth conditions is not semantics' (1970, p. 18). By this, he meant that the meaning of declarative sentences, for instance, is intimately connected to the conditions under which those sentences are true (also called 'propositionalism', as we'll see in Section 4.3). We'll get to how such a project is to be realised on the semantic level in the next section. But here, it's important to note that a metasemantic inquiry would go beyond this process to ask how and why meaning is connected to truth conditions, if indeed it is. For example, if the meaning of a sentence is determined by factors inside the heads of speakers (as internalists would have it), then reference to external circumstances of evaluation might not be appropriately semantic at all. Although internalists can resurrect some aspects of the truth-conditional framework with some sort of internalised mental model theory, where a mental model is 'an internal model of the state of affairs that the premises describe' (Johnson-Laird & Byrne 1991, p. 35). However, this thought does get us slightly closer to the metalevel. Internalists about semantics hold that what makes an expression meaningful supervenes on internal factors in the mind/brain of the language user. Externalists allow external factors into the mix. Of course, some, like Putnam (1973), claimed meanings just ain't in the head at all. Others, such as public language theorists or inferentialists, insist that what *grounds* meaning is something about social communal communicative practice. It seems as though the external allows for more options than the internal.

So far, it might sound like we're dealing with a neat dichotomy: semantics is about what words, phrases, and sentences mean while metasemantics is about how they get their meanings via linguistic convention or other *externalia*, mental competence, or some hybrid cocktail. But we need to apply scalpel-like precision going forward as the lines between semantics and metasemantics can be sinewy at best. For example, the concept of semantic value is essential to the enterprise of semantics. Semantic values are like the output of the semantic machinery that takes syntactic objects as input. Give the machine a name of a person and it assigns a semantic value like $<e>$ for entity to it. That's a semantic type. This assignment value is a placeholder for whatever object corresponds to the linguistic item. But turning a semantic value into a variable doesn't automatically make it a metasemantic value. It does mark a level above the specific semantic value, which can vary between semantic theories. To get to metasemantics$_1$, we can talk about semantic value in terms of the role it's meant to be playing. In this case, we wouldn't need to specify if it's a truth value, context-change potential, or distributional vector. Stanley & Szabó (2000) make a similar point with relation to context dependence:

That is, the foundational problem of context dependence for an expression e relative to a context c is specifying what it is about the context in virtue of which certain entities (be they objects, properties, or propositions) play the role they do in the interpretation of an occurrence of e. (p. 223)

They help themselves to Stalnaker's earlier distinction between descriptive and foundational semantics. More recently, Nowak & Michaelson (2022) advocate a metasemantic pluralism to answer such questions. They discuss how the meaning of a context-sensitive expression, like a demonstrative, is determined. They worry that trying to establish a fixed or unitary account to explain all such phenomena is fruitless. Their argument presupposes that metasemantic disputes turn on two central *explananda*: (1) that highly context-sensitive (or ambiguous) terms rely on speakers' 'privileged access' for resolution, and (2) speakers can be wrong about what they said. They focus on demonstratives as a case study and show that externalist accounts tend to do well on prong (2) but not as well on (1), while the internalist accounts suffer from the opposite problem. Hybrid accounts, they claim, fare slightly better but only on pain of weakening one of the explananda. The problem they point to with their pluralism is precisely the one I have with the metasemantics₁ mode of metasemantics in general. It leads to precious few resolutions or conclusions. Before we get into this, let's review a recent exposition of metasemantics₁ courtesy of Burgess & Sherman (2014) for maximum perspicuity.

They differentiate between three different submeanings for metasemantics under the auspices of metaphysics. The first is what they call 'basic semantics', which 'aspires to uncover non-semantic facts in virtue of which such semantic facts obtain' (p. 10). The second, or 'the theory of meaning' follows traditional a priori philosophy of language in that it 'looks for a real definition of the meaning relation: an account of its nature or essence' (p. 10). Lastly, 'the metaphysics of semantic values queries the intrinsic natures of meanings themselves'. These come together in the following way:

In sum, insofar as any semantic fact can be regimented as [E means M], the metaphysics of semantic values will target 'M,' the theory of meaning will target 'means,' and basic semantics will target the grounds of the fact as a whole. (Burgess & Sherman 2014, p. 12)

The problem, as I see it, isn't necessarily with the remit of these subprojects or metasemantics₁ itself but with the methodology it presupposes. As Burgess & Sherman state, 'the central modes of explanation in metasemantics [are] *metaphysical*' (2014, p. 3). Metaphysics mode, however, is a fraught philosophical endeavour often characterised by its lack of clear resolutions, vague appeals to the 'intuitiveness' of arguments (or counterintuitiveness of alternatives), and general neglect of developments in the relevant sciences (in this case, linguistics). In a controversial book, Ladyman & Ross (2007) take aim at a priori or analytic metaphysics for precisely these reasons (and many more).

> Our core complaint is that during the decades since the fall of logical empiricism, much of what is regarded as 'the metaphysics literature' has proceeded without proper regard for science. The picture is complicated, however, by the fact that much activity in what is classified as philosophy of science is also metaphysics, and most of this work is scientifically well informed. This book is an exercise in metaphysics done as naturalistic philosophy of science because we think that no other sort of metaphysics counts as inquiry into the objective nature of the world. (p. 7)

Their aim is to resurrect metaphysics on the basis of legitimate philosophy of science to serve a unifying explanatory role.[1] Although I don't agree with all their arguments (see Dorr 2010), they do make a strong case for a naturalistic or scientific metaphysics as an alternative. Naturalistic metaphysics takes the science (whichever science) as prior to any logical or philosophical reasoning from so-called first principles. Metaphysics has a role to play only in so far as it investigates the repercussions of scientific theory. If you want to know about the furniture of the universe, consult physics. If you want to know about the meaning of linguistic expressions, consult a semanticist. But if you want to know about what makes semantics (or physics) work the way it does or what it's *about*, the philosophy of science is your best option.

This brings us to metasemantics$_2$, the metascientific study of the science of meaning, or, as Ball & Rabern (2018) describe it, 'metatheory of the science of meaning' or 'semantic metatheory'. It is a higher-order philosophical reflection on first-order semantics. Despite the reduction in remit, there's still a lot of real estate left for metasemantics under the banner of the philosophy of science. There are methodological issues such as whether semantic value is best modelled as truth conditions, dynamic context-change potentials, or numerical vectors representing collocational data, questions about the interface between syntactic structure and semantic interpretation, and the distinction between semantic and pragmatic information. All of these topics (and more) will be covered in this chapter and the next.

The main reason I think metasemantics$_2$ trumps a direct metaphysical approach relates to the central aims of the book. Those aims are all directed at the illumination of theoretical linguistics as a science. Even when we entertained some mild modal metaphysics in Chapter 2, it was informed by posits and claims of theory. On the other hand, attempting to settle

---

[1] See Nefdt (2023a), for a similarly inspired treatment of the philosophy of linguistics.

the internalism–externalism debate or the precise nature of reference are unattainable goals. This isn't to say that there are no notable accounts of these issues or phenomena but rather that there don't seem to be any clear resolutions, or even the hope of them on the horizon.[2] Moreover, part of the project of understanding theoretical linguistics will not only involve finding out how different subdisciplines relate to one another but also how linguistics relates to other disciplines such as cognitive science, physics, and biology. Chomsky, contra analytic philosophy of language, has emphasised 'methodological naturalism' or the view that language and mind should 'be studied by ordinary methods of empirical inquiry' (2000, p. 106) as the foundation for the field. Jackendoff (2007) produced a comprehensive framework for integrating linguistics with the cognitive sciences, including cognitive linguistics (see Chapter 3). Baggio (2018) goes further to marry formal semantics to cognitive neuroscience along internalist lines.

By adopting the metascientific perspective, we can hope to attain some necessary clarity as to the metatheory of semantics and understanding the science that studies human meaning at its core. Henceforth, the term 'metasemantics' will solely refer to the practice of metascience based on semantic theory in linguistics. Before we pursue the topic in more depth, we need to understand the target of the standard approach, also known as formal semantics, and the centrality of the concept of compositionality within it.

4.2   Formal Semantics and Compositionality

The methodology of formal semantics has been well established in various standard textbooks on the subject from the Davidsonian Larson & Segal (1995) to the more generative linguistics–inspired Heim & Kratzer (1998) and the more theory-neutral GAMUT (1991). I'll follow an exposition (and terminology) adapted from Nefdt (2020a) and Nefdt (2020b), inspired by all of them. The common apparatus of formal semantic theories is familiar from logic, type theory, and lambda calculus. These theories are usually built up from the denotation of individual morphemes or words, the terminal elements of syntactic trees, to complex elements conjoined semantically through functional application. As Dever (2012) puts it,

There is no precise delineation of what counts as formal semantics. Roughly, though, formal semantics is the attempt to give precise accounts of the relation between syntactic

---

[2] There might be deeper concerns about the 'metaphysical mode', as discussed in Ladyman & Ross (2007), relating to the role intuitions play in argumentation or the misinterpretation of science. But I don't want to enter into those polemics here.

Figure 4.1 Tree 1

structures and semantic values, typically while making use of tools from mathematics and logic. (p. 49)[3]

Two basic insights characterise the field, namely, that the meaning of an expression is provided by the conditions under which it is true (at least for declarative sentences) and that meanings are composed according to the principle of compositionality (PoC), a version of which is presented below.

Let's first describe the basic functional methodology of formal model-theoretic semantics with an example. Thereafter, I'll discuss the underlying PoC, some issues with it, and how to possibly evade them from a metasemantic point of view. For the purposes of exposition, I'll simplify matters by sticking to an extensional truth-conditional semantics for the example.[4] Let's start with a basic intransitive sentence, *Richard drives*, represented in a tree in Figure 4.1.

Proper names and other physical objects are represented by the type e for entity and intransitive verbs are functions from entities to truth values $\langle e, t \rangle$ where the semantic value of a sentence is t. Following Heim & Kratzer (1998, p. 17), the semantic value of the nonterminal V or N node is inherited from the semantic value of its terminal counterpart. The interesting part of the analysis occurs at the nonterminal nodes that mark syntactic composition, in this case, the S-node of the tree. By means of Fregean insight, the corresponding semantic rule is provided by functional application where the semantic value of *Richard* (indicated by the double-line delimiters) is applied to the semantic value of *drives*.

- $\llbracket Richard\ drives \rrbracket = \llbracket drives \rrbracket (\llbracket Richard \rrbracket)$

The entire sentence then has a semantic value t while the intransitive construction has a value represented by a function from objects to truth values, or $\langle e, t \rangle$. This means that the semantic value of a sentence is a truth value and the semantic values of its parts are contributions to the truth value. Let's add a

---

[3] For Cann (1993, p. 2), 'this theory is a formal theory of semantics and is distinguished from general linguistic semantics by its greater use of mathematical techniques and reliance on logical precision'.

[4] The mathematics involved in the intensional variant is very much the same as the extensional theory with the exception of the possible-world type s and functions involving it.

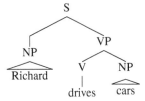

Figure 4.2 Tree 2

further level of complication by considering a transitive extension of the sample sentence. Consider the tree in Figure 4.2.

The set-theoretic object associated with this tree involves two levels of functional application. The semantic value of a transitive verb has the type $\langle e, \langle e, t \rangle \rangle$, or functions from entities to functions from entities to truth values, represented below in two steps of functional application:

- $[\![\textit{drives cars}]\!] = [\![\textit{drives}]\!]([\![\textit{cars}]\!])$
- $[\![\textit{Richard drives cars}]\!] = [\![\textit{drives}]\!]([\![\textit{cars}]\!])([\![\textit{Richard}]\!])$

The verb *drive* is ambiguous between a transitive and intransitive construction (or optionally selects for direct objects). Modelling transitive verbs sometimes seems to require that we use more than just functional application; we might also use the technique commonly known as *currying* a function in mathematics (Heim & Kratzer prefer the term 'Schönfinkelization'). Currying a function involves taking a function with multiple arguments or a domain of ordered n-tuples and turning it into a sequence of functions (or complex functions), taking each argument individually. For instance, in the case of a ditransitive verb like *give*, instead of taking it to involve the Cartesian product of three entities to a truth value (or $\langle e \times e \times e, t \rangle$), we take each in turn, as in $\langle e, \langle e, \langle e, t \rangle \rangle \rangle$. Currying, or Schönfinkelization, however, might not just be artifacts of the modelling. If we take semantic values as aspects of the target system and certain kinds of functions to represent these in our models, we could allow for the possibility that semantic values qua functions come pre-'curried' to a certain extent.

Technically, transitive constructions can be handled within the bounds of functional application. What does pose a problem for strict functional application are phenomena such as object-position quantifiers, as in the examples below.

1. Judy likes every politician.
2. Tony met some people.

The problem is that there's no straightforward way to apply functional application in this case since the semantic value of a transitive expression is type $\langle e, \langle e, t \rangle \rangle$ and the quantifier expression is of type $\langle \langle e, t \rangle, t \rangle$. One way in which to account for such data is by positing quantifier-raising or movement rules. In essence, *every politician* or *some people* move to a higher node in the tree and leave a trace behind, thereby allowing the semantic values to be computed as before (*as if* the quantifiers were in the higher position). Of course, this analysis does require something akin to logical form (LF) for surface forms to map on to. We'll return to the issue of syntactic reinterpretation based on semantic considerations in the forthcoming sections. For now, however, the point is that unappended functional application is not enough to account for every syntactic combination.

Lastly, before concluding the present sketch, we need to mention that the use of λ-notation is ubiquitous in formal semantics. We've already seen that in the process of mapping syntactic structures on to set-theoretic objects, we encountered complex functional notation, and with the inclusion of quantifiers, reflexives, and traces, the notational complexity only grows. In order to limit confusion and name various set-theoretic objects, we introduce λ-notation with variables from formal logic. Thus, a simple sentence like *Barbara works* becomes $\lambda x(x$ works$)$(Barbara), where we replace the name *Barbara* with a variable x, add the name as an argument, and attach the λ-operator to bind the variable, with the result that the λ-formula now represents a truth-conditional function. The formula for lambda abstraction used by semanticists is the schema '$\lambda \alpha : \beta . \gamma$', where α is a variable place reserved for the argument, β specifies the domain of the function, and γ assigns a value for the argument α. The example in Heim & Kratzer (1998, p. 34) represents the successor function in arithmetic:

- $F_{+1} := [\lambda x : x \in \mathbb{N} . x + 1]$

The above definition can be read as the function that maps every x such that x is in $\mathbb{N}$ to $x + 1$. This notation proves extremely useful in denoting various complex set-theoretic objects corresponding to the semantic values that in turn represent syntactic objects and their composition. With the tools of functional application, type theory, and λ-calculus, formal semantics can represent the semantic values of a range of syntactic objects, both simple and complex.

What connects these tools to genuine semantic explanation is the PoC. It's meant to explain how language users do some remarkable things. For instance, when you encounter a completely novel sentence, you somehow have the cognitive resources to interpret it. Not only this fact but the idea that these resources are finite and what we learn and express seem to be beyond this limit. Davidson characterised these features as key explananda for a theory of meaning:

When we can regard the meaning of each sentence as a function of a finite number of features of the sentence, we have an insight not only into what there is to be learned; we also understand how an infinite aptitude can be encompassed by finite accomplishments. (1965, p. 8)

The answer? The PoC.[5] The modern idea of the principle can be found in Montague (1974) and Partee (2014), among others, and it usually takes the form of the following type of statement:

PoC: The meaning of a complex expression is determined by the meaning of its component parts and the way in which they are combined.

In the methodology of logic and computer science, it's been considered the standard way of interpreting formal or programming languages (although alternatives do exist). Tarski 1933 definition of truth for formal languages has a natural compositional interpretation (Janssen 2012). Davidson (1967) used what he called Tarski's T-schema as a basis for a compositional semantics for natural language. In the twentieth century, the principle was widely adopted in the philosophy of language and logic, by Carnap, Quine, Davidson, and various others. Now, it's become an essential part of most linguistic theories including generative approaches such the seminal Heim & Kratzer (1998).

   Unfortunately, the statement as it stands is vague and in need of clarification. The problem is that there doesn't seem to be a neutral way of going about this clarification. Let's start with the term 'complex expression', which will be characterised as a syntactic object built up from simple (and perhaps other complex) expressions, as will its subcomponents. We'll remain characteristically reticent about meanings and what is exactly meant by 'meaning' for the moment.

   'Determined by' is usually interpreted functionally, which suggests that given a syntactic object as an input, a semantic object or value is returned as an output. One might worry that this suggests a unique semantic output for every syntactic expression, but in natural language, this tends to overgenerate as there are distinct expressions that arguably should be assigned the same meanings. That would be a very strong constraint on meaning. However, such a scenario isn't an issue for compositionality. Consider the sentences below:

1. Zoltan threw the ball.
2. The ball was thrown by Zoltan.

---

[5] The genesis of the PoC has been linked with the writings of Gottlob Frege, hence the term 'Frege's principle' (sometimes used synonymously). In 'Sinn und Bedeutung' (1892), Frege challenged a simple notion of compositional meaning in terms of co-reference (due to Mill) by testing the latter view on the so-called substitution thesis, often erroneously assumed to be equivalent to the PoC (see Szabó 2000). Yet, his distinction between sense (*Sinn*) and reference (*Bedeutung*) did aim to rescue a compositional account of meaning in some other form, as the compositionality of sense. Janssen (2012) argues that Frege was not the source (nor an adherent) of the PoC. In fact, he argues that Frege subscribed to a quite different principle for natural language semantics. Its true origins can actually be traced further back than Frege to Lotze, Wundt, and Trendelenburg, according to Janssen.

These sentences both seem to express the same meaning but consist of different lexical items, such as the preposition *by*, as well as different methods of combination (active vs passive). It's quite apparent from the literature that if the term 'function of' (when used to interpret 'determined by') is to be conceived of in its strict mathematical sense, it doesn't involve an injective function.

A stronger interpretation has it that we start from atomic elements and assign a meaning to each of those, then define a semantic rule for every syntactic rule. In this way, we have a compositional semantic procedure that parallels every syntactic one (this is in essence Montague's homomorphism definition), also called 'parellelism'. This approach doesn't overgenerate since the rules that combine (1) and (2) may be different but, along with the meaning of the words, they could produce the same meaning for the expressions. The functions sqrt and cbrt will both produce the number 2 when the input is 4 or 8, respectively.[6]

Lastly, what's meant by 'component' as it's used here? The convention in the literature is to take this to mean *constituent*. In linguistics, this is a loaded term. Usually, it refers to sets of linguistic items that act as structural units in given expressions. In terms of representation, constituents are the groupings of items that appear in the hierarchical tree diagrams of phrase-structure grammar. Consider sentence (3):

3. The host speaks to the caterer after the ceremony.

This sentence can be separated into distinct constituents. One can follow phrase-structure syntax, in which roughly the NP – the host – the VP – the host speaks – and the PP – to the caterer – would be constituents. Alternatively, the verb phrase, or predicate, *speaks to* and its two arguments *the host* (subject) and *the caterer* (complement) could be considered constituents. This latter strategy is common to formalisms such as dependency grammar. Items such as *after the ceremony* are 'adjuncts' that can float independently of the other constituents (as opposed to complements, which are obligatory).

Above is a sketch of how formal semantics operates at the first-order level and the general methodological principle that governs it. But over the years, the PoC has amassed a large counterculture of counterexamples. I won't go into the catalogue here. They generally fall into three categories: (1) constructions, such as certain conditionals or adjectives, that seem to present the same syntactic structure but different semantics (Travis 1994; Kay & Michaelis 2012); (2) constructions, such as idioms, that seem to indicate that the semantic value of the parts do not constitute the semantic value of the whole, as the mereology of compositionality would have it (Goldberg 2015); and (3) expressions that

---

[6] Paralellism has other weaknesses, though. For instance, it strongly suggests a building metaphor of a step-by-step procedure mapping syntactic combination with semantic interpretation. Possible-world semantics does not respect this constraint, nor do semantic formalisms with intermediary representations like Montague's original account.

require more context than combinatorics to interpret their meanings (Recanati 2004). To each set of counterexamples, certain strategies have been developed. For (1), we often see the employment of some impressive logical casuistry such as alternative syntactic derivations (Montague's strategy) or underspecification (Section 4.4). For (2), we see everything from the dismissal of the data to the concession that certain linguistic objects are stored wholesale and not piecemeal outside of the bounds of the PoC. The treatment for (3) often involves some of the strategies we'll see in the next section, an incorporation of formal contextual parameters in the spirit of retaining the PoC, or simply relegation to pragmatics (see Chapter 5).

Given the pushback from various quadrants, one might question the veracity or applicability of the PoC. As an inference to the best explanation (Szabó 2011), it fares well on particularly well-behaved data, much like model-theoretic semantics in general. Again, we might wonder whether this principle, inherited from formal logic and model theory, serves to capture the semantics of the formal segment of natural language and *only that*. We'll investigate the role of context in the next section and various semantic responses to the counterexamples to the PoC in Section 4.4. But for now, I think there's an alternative metasemantic interpretation of the PoC that evades many of these concerns, courtesy of Dowty (2007):

To put the focus and scope of research in the right place, the first thing to do is to employ our terminology differently. I propose that we let the term natural language compositionality refer to *whatever strategies and principles we discover that natural languages actually do employ to derive the meanings of sentences, on the basis of whatever aspects of syntax and whatever additional information (if any) research shows that they do in fact depend on.* Since we don't know what all those are, we don't at this point know what 'natural language compositionality' is really like; it's our goal to figure that out by linguistic investigation. Under this revised terminology, there can be no such things as 'counterexamples to compositionality', but there will surely be counterexamples to many particular hypotheses we contemplate as to the form that it takes. (p. 12)

On this view, the PoC, as we've described it, is only one possible interpretation of the general idea. The idea is that natural language is compositional but the best account of compositionality or how it is to be expressed in first-order theory is still a matter of debate. The principle itself is a metasemantic principle.[7] It's a claim about the explanandum of semantic theory, not about its first-order procedures directly. In fact, even if we move beyond truth-

---

[7] Linnebo (2008) assumes this level for the principle, similarly, when he argues for the compatibility between Frege's two principles: the context principle, which says the meaning of a term can only be determined in the context of a sentence or whole expression, and the PoC, which seems to push in a different direction.

conditional or model-theoretic semantics, the principle can still guide our practice, as we'll see.

4.3   Formal, Dynamic, and Distributional Approaches

Life would be greatly simplified if semantics merely involved assigning syntactic objects a model-theoretic companion and then functionally applying oneself up a syntactic tree. However, things are rarely this simple outside of stipulated formal languages. In this section, we'll investigate the ubiquitous feature of the natural language meaning that holds up the simple semantic process, namely, context sensitivity, or context dependence.[8] In fact, I'll characterise a context dependence continuum that starts at the extreme of 'semantic minimalism', moves to dynamic semantics, and finally ends with distributional approaches to semantics.

The Montague grammar that inspired much of the early work in formal semantics can be considered 'static' in a particular way. As mentioned before, semantics is in the business of assigning semantic value or truth values to sentences. In other words, meaning is modelled in terms of truth conditions. These values are assigned relative to certain things. For instance, in the model-theoretic semantics we've been considering so far, truth is relative to a model M and assignment function g that provide values to variables (we can add possible worlds in the intensional variant). Whatever determines the truth conditions of expressions is thus defined in terms of parameters in the models.

However, if we move to modelling linguistic items such as demonstratives and indexicals (sentences involving 'this', 'that', 'here', 'now', 'I', etc.), we find that more parameters are needed, in particular, a contextual parameter c. Static accounts cannot accommodate such phenomena without it. What they can do is specify a variable that assigns the compositional meaning of terms relative to a particular context, or 'at certain points the semantics inserts a variable or a context-dependent function term, which will be evaluated after all the semantics is done' (Partee 2009, p. 3).

There are two well-known formal treatments of context in the formal semantic literature: Kaplan (1989) and Lewis (1980). They offer two related but distinct accounts. Both authors differentiate between context and index. For Kaplan, context generates content and indices (such as time, person, etc.) that provide points of evaluation. Procedurally, this involves two steps. Lewis streamlines this approach and suggests instead a one-step procedure of evaluation at both a context and an index. The difference is that on the latter view, the

---

[8] This notion is to be distinguished from the complexity designation of formal languages in the Chomsky Hierarchy mentioned in Chapter 3.

semantic value of sentences is invariable across contexts while on the former, it isn't.[9]

On this end of the spectrum, the machinery stays relatively stable. The relevance of truth conditions as meanings of sentences, the technique of functional application, and the general procedure of assigning model-theoretic objects to syntactic objects compositionally all remain. The metasemantics implied is compatible with what Cappelen & Lepore (2005) call *semantic minimalism*. Semantic minimalists tend to assume a level of semantic invariance for expressions in that much of the context sensitivity characteristic of natural language is projected on to the realm of pragmatics. They recognise only a few truly context-sensitive expressions, such as indexicals like 'I' and 'today' or pronouns like 'he', 'she' and 'it'. So, for instance, Cappelen & Lepore (2005, p. 2) state the position in the following way:

The most salient feature of Semantic Minimalism is that it recognizes few context sensitive expressions, and, hence, acknowledges a very limited effect of the context of utterance on the semantic content of an utterance.

This is another way of saying that most expressions have literal semantic content (determined by formal semantics) that isn't altered or determined by the contexts in which they're uttered. That happens after the fact, as Partee suggests. Thus, there's some propositional content that's fixed by the semantics of the language. Semantic minimalists claim that 'what's said' by an expression (its propositional content) is related to the conventional meaning of the linguistic expressions of which it is composed. This process can in turn be characterised by compositionality, with contextual parameters of the Lewisian or Kaplanian variety added for flavour.

Of course, although aligned with the static view, semantic minimalism isn't entailed by it. One could adopt an 'index theory' in which you have to specify all the features of the context of utterance that are relevant to determining extensions (or intensions). This would be cumbersome. As Szabó (2009) notes, Lewis himself adopted a 8-tuple account of indices that specified possible worlds, times, place, person, and so on. Eventually, Lewis abandoned this means of representing context as even the indices he modelled were clearly not up to the gargantuan task of representing all the required parameters.

Philosophically, the static view in semantics is aligned with *propositionalism*. This is the idea that the meanings of natural language expressions or utterances express propositions, which are themselves identical to the conditions under which they're true (or else determine those truth conditions). It represents the

---

[9] However, '[Lewis] emphasises the fact that mathematically there is not a genuine difference between these two options' (Ball & Rabern 2018, p. 4).

world as being a certain way.[10] Propositions, understood in this way, play a number of important roles in linguistic theory. They're meant to not only explain what's asserted by my utterance of a particular expression but also what my interlocutor comes to believe, namely, the proposition that *p*. The static, propositional, view also has a natural pairing with a neo-Gricean picture of communication. If what's said or the content is determined by a proposition aka truth conditions, then how the proposition is used in a context can be calculated pragmatically. The paradigmatic examples are implicatures that manipulate the literal content of expressions to generate pragmatic inferences. For instance, a job reference letter that only mentions penmanship is likely to generate the implicature that the candidate has few relevant qualities to mention, despite the literal content.

From the above, we can extrapolate three major components of the static view: (1) the meaning of a sentence or utterance is a proposition given in terms of truth conditions; (2) following the lead of mainstream syntax, the nexus of meaning is found at the sentential level; and (3) context shapes meaning after or independently of the literal content, generated by the compositional semantics (á la semantic minimalism). In the rest of this section, I want to populate our continuum in terms of departures from each of these components. We'll start with the middle point of the cline where, I believe, dynamic semantics is located.

Dynamic semantics is an umbrella term for a number of specific accounts, such as dynamic predicate logic (Groenendijk & Stokhof 1991), file-change semantics (Heim 1982), discourse representation theory (DRT) (Kamp 1981), and update semantics (Veltman 1996). I cannot describe them all in detail here but, thankfully, they do share in a few characteristics that set them apart from static accounts. There are two general types of argument pushed by proponents of dynamic semantics: (a) arguments in favour of extending the boundary of semantic interpretation beyond the sentence towards the discourse, and (b) arguments concerning constructions (such as modals) that allegedly outstrip truth-conditional propositionalism. Both of these topics essentially motivate a view of semantic value in terms of its power to change the context. Let's start with (a). Consider the following pairs of sentences:

4. A linguist entered the classroom *and* we sat down.
5. We sat down *and* a linguist entered the classroom.

---

[10] Propositions are generally associated with truth conditions across possible worlds or *intensions*. Interestingly, there have been a number of metasemantic arguments to the effect that truth conditions play little role in explanations of semantic phenomena. For example, Napoletano (2019) argues this point based on work on gradable adjectives and degree modifiers by Kennedy & McNally (2005). Pietroski's (2018) seminal work similarly eschews truth conditions as an important aspect of natural language semantics.

In classical logic, as well as static semantics, 'and' is commutative like '+'. In dynamic semantics, there's a sequential procedure involving first updating with the first conjunct, then the second. This process seems to track the perceived difference in meaning between the two sentences, such as the distinctive causative flavour to (4) that (5) seems to lack. The same phenomenon occurs across the sentence boundary, as in (6a,b) and (7a,b) (adapted from Lewis (2014, p. 234):

6a. Hans graded ten papers and passed all of them, except for one.
 b. It is probably very bad in quality.
7a. Hans graded ten papers and passed only nine of them.
 b. ?? It is probably very bad in quality.

There are a few things to note. Firstly, truth conditionally, the pairs are equivalent. Where they differ is with the structures they license since '[6a] licenses a singular pronoun (but not a plural one) and [7a] licenses a plural pronoun (but not a singular one)' (Lewis 2014, p. 234). Dynamic semanticists insist that the first sentence in each pair changes the context in different ways. In fact, they go one step further in claiming that this potential to change the context is the essence of meaning or a context-change potential (CCP).[11] To understand the full picture, we need to appreciate why propositionalism fails more generally for them.

Basically, dynamic semanticists place context at the centre of the semantic machinery. Truth conditions qua semantic values are ill-fit for the job, according to them. Take modal vocabulary and conditionals, for instance. Statements involving modals such as 'might' can at first glance be treated as expressing propositions (Kratzer 1977, 1981). The idea is presented in Stojnić (2017):

An utterance of 'It might be raining' is true in a world and a context, just in case there is at least one world in the (contextually restricted) domain of quantification of the modal 'might' in which it is raining. The utterance expresses the proposition corresponding to the set of worlds in which it is true. (p. 396)

But there are serious problems with this proposal, as various philosophers and linguists have shown (Veltman 1996; Yalcin 2007; Yalcin & Knobe 2014). These phenomena point to a problem with deriving propositional content from modal statements in context, such as examples of contexts in which 'might'

---

[11] DRT is another form of dynamic semantics (Kamp 1981). Notice, in (6), the pronoun 'it' seems to get its value from 'one' but *one* is not a referring term and also cannot bind pronouns. In DRT, 'it' is a 'discourse referent' representing the objects or entities to which the discourse refers. The discourse representation structures (DRSs), central to DRT's semantic representation, are ordered pairs containing a set of discourse referents and a set of formulas over these. The theory is classically motivated by anaphora, especially a special brand called 'donkey anaphora' that cannot be explained by the standard accounts of variable binding or coreference.

is licensed despite marked departure from truth conditions. To adumbrate an example from Yalcin & Knobe (2014), a convincing murder scene is staged by a known criminal and an expert deduces from the copious evidence that said criminal 'might be dead'. Participants in a study were reluctant to say that the modal statement was false and seemed inclined to agree it was true. But how can such a statement be true if the criminal is known to be alive?

In one prominent account, *update semantics*, the role of a modal is not to express truth-conditional content but to perform a check (?) on the context. Semantic content of a sentence, on this view, is not a truth value but the effect that the utterance has on the context. This is measured by comparing the context before and after the utterance and evaluating how it has changed. In nonmodal cases, there's little discernible difference between this view and static accounts. But in the modal cases, the departure is more stark. The test checks if the context is compatible with the modal and returns it as if it is. If not, the context is reduced to the empty set.[12]

Dynamic semantics differs from static semantics in a number of ways. As Kamp *et al.* (2011) put it,

> The focus on context dependence has led to an important shift in paradigm, away from the 'classical' conception of formal semantics which sees semantic theory as primarily concerned with reference and truth and towards a perspective in which the central concept is not that of truth but of information. (p. 125)

What's interesting from the purview of this 'paradigm shift' is that once semantics moves into the territory of pragmatics, it has some pretty big shoes to fill. All kinds of context-sensitive behaviour now fall under the remit of semantic theory. Take implicatures again. These phenomena are generated from literal propositional content. It's unclear how one would make the semantics–pragmatics distinction without some compositional static or literal content. In fact, dynamic semantics wants to live in both worlds, hence its occupation of the midpoint on our continuum. Dynamic semanticists maintain adherence to compositionality, functional application, and even the model-theoretic methodology of assigning mathematical entities to syntactic objects.[13] Ball & Rabern (2018, p. 22), echoing Yalcin (2012), claim that 'there is a clear continuity between the kind of dynamic views that we are focusing on and standard Montagovian,

---

[12] From the perspective of updates, the existential quantifier in dynamic predicate logic has a particularly interesting interpretation. An existentially quantified sentence can change the assignment parameters such that the parameters of the output context can differ from those of the input context: $\|\exists x_1 \phi\| = \lambda c\{\langle g, w\rangle : \exists h.\langle h, w\rangle \in c$ and $g[1]h$ and $\langle g, w\rangle \in \phi\}$ where $g[1]h$ means something like g different from h in, at most, what it assigns to 1.

[13] Some have worried that DRT was originally not pitched as a compositional account. Zeevat (1989) showed that it could be reconceived of compositionally. Again, on the metasemantic interpretation of the principle, even the original variant can be thought of as compositional.

model-theoretic approaches to semantics" in that they both assign entities as semantic values and build these values up compositionally.[14]

The last position on the continuum is the final step in linking meaning with context, not as the potential to change contexts compositionally but literally as collections or rather collocations of contexts. Distributional semantics is a computational approach to meaning that adheres to what is known as the 'distributional hypothesis' (DH). Lenci (2008, p. 3) characterises it in the following way:

The degree of semantic similarity between two linguistic expressions A and B is a function of the similarity of the linguistic contexts in which A and B can appear.[15]

In distributional semantics, context determines meaning based on the idea that semantic similarity is measurable in terms of similarity in context. On one prominent account, vector-space semantics, word meaning is represented as a vector or list of numbers acting like a coordinate system on a multidimensional space. Given that these views are usage-based theories, they don't formally or functionally stipulate the nature of semantic value but rather extract it from corpora. You can think of a word's vector as an abstraction over all of its contexts of use. So how does the process work? Basically, words are collections of points along a number of dimensions. Similar words, like *shoe* and *sneaker*, will have similar vectors, that is, similar values across various dimensions. What's more is that 'the collection of units in a distributional model constitutes a vector space or semantic space, in which semantic relations can be modeled as geometric relations' (Boleda 2020, p. 3). One such relation is measured by the cosine of the angle of two vectors in which closeness of vectors is indicated by largeness of cosine similarity (which ranges from 0 to 1).

Note the stark contrast with 'static' formal semantics. Under those accounts, meaning is an invariant output of a compositional process that starts with syntax. Context is added post facto as a parameter of the model that can track things like person and time of utterance. In distributional semantics, context is paramount. Meaning is extracted from patterns in corpora that stand as proxies for real-life language. It's clear that this approach should be at the context end of any semantic spectrum. But why should it be related to the other approaches? The methodology is statistical and continuous whereas both formal and dynamic semantics are discrete and logical. Nevertheless, despite the focus on usage, empiricism, and corpus data, distributional approaches, even the lexical ones, have to contend with compound words and phrases. Once compounds, like

---

[14] There are notable views that depart from this model, including Davidsonian approaches that focus on T-schema disquotational translations (Davidson 1967) and proof-theoretic semantics that build semantic value in accordance with proofs (Francez & Dyckhoff 2010).

[15] Firth is credited with saying 'you'll know the meaning of a word by the company it keeps', which is a slightly more colloquial version of DH.

'cut cost' or 'trick shot', are represented, composition naturally follows. In fact, even though the market place is flooded with sophisticated tools, Boleda (2020) maintains that simple vector addition has proven highly successful:[16]

Compositional distributional methods build representations for phrases out of the representations of their parts, and the corresponding meaning is expected to emerge as a result of the composition. (p. 9)

In a sense, we can witness a similar picture of formal (and dynamic) semantics at play here. Semantic values of phrases (and larger linguistic units) are built from the semantic values of their constituent parts. Meanings are mathematical objects, in this case, vectors. On another note, unlike dynamic semantics, which extends the semantic boundaries beyond the sentential level, distributional approaches tend to focus on the lexical level – compositionality from the bottom up as opposed to the top down. Traditionally, they have also had difficulty with capturing long-distance dependencies like anaphora and agreement (see Chapter 7 for more).

The main difference between static and distributional accounts is that context, and operations on context, exhausts the semantic resources and plays an even more significant role than it does in dynamic semantics. But again, as is the case with dynamic semantics, when context becomes so central to semantic value, a clear notion of pragmatics suffers. For instance, Westera & Boleda (2019) argue that distributional semantics can account for expression meaning (or literal meaning) but not what Grice (1989) calls 'speaker meaning'. Traditionally, speaker meaning is generated by a rational process involving communicative intentions of participants in a conversational setting. These processes might be invisible to standard distributional accounts.

Of course, the diminished or shifted role of pragmatic explanation isn't a knockdown argument against either distributional or dynamic approaches. However, if, as both Stojnić (2017) and Lewis (2014) advocate in the case of dynamic semantics, the data can be accounted for by means of formal semantics buttressed with a richer pragmatic component, then this body of work might merely point to the need for a more robust division of labour.[17] We'll cover pragmatics in more detail in the next chapter. For now, let's sum up the semantic context continuum in a table that shows both the similarities and differences (mostly in terms of the role of context as semantic value) of each approach to semantics (Table 4.1).

---

[16] We'll return to some of these tools, such as artificial neural networks, in Chapter 7.
[17] In the debates that characterised the philosophy of language in the early 2000s, this picture was associated with semantic minimalism and speech act pluralism over its radical contextualist rival (Borg 2004; Recanati 2004; Cappelen & Lepore 2005).

Table 4.1. *Formal context continuum*

	Continuum		
Approach	Composition	Level of analysis	Semantic value
1. Formal semantics	Functional	Sentential	Invariant functional type
2. Dynamic semantics	Functional	Cross-sentential	Context-change potential
3. Distr. semantics	Additive	Lexical	Contextual vector

Lastly, one might worry that these are all distinct scientific projects with distinct targets. It's a bit like comparing apples to oranges.[18] I'm sympathetic to this concern. However, I think context is like a fruit salad, and within this setting, apples and oranges can be legitimately compared. Somewhat less cryptically, semantic theories target a heterogeneous domain. Sometimes, different theories are needed to approach such a task. In the philosophy of science, this is called 'multiple models idealisation' (Weisberg 2013; Nefdt 2023a). In my view, the connection point between the different theories is the role assigned to context and its degree of incorporation.

4.4   Rogue Semantics

In this section, I want to address what happens when semantics 'goes rogue'. What do I mean by 'rogue' in this context? Basically, rogue semantics involves violations of a particular interpretation of compositionality or the syntax–semantics interface. The standard interpretation assumes a neat correspondence between syntactic objects and semantic value. We'll approach the topic from two angles. The first starts below the word level and the second departs from the assumed connection between syntax and semantics to establish a further level of semantic representation somewhat independent of syntax.

Formal semantic compositionality generally starts from the terminal elements in trees (words) and assigns meaning to each constituent on their way up to the final S node via functional application. We covered some aspects of this process in Section 4.2. What's assumed in much of the formal semantic work that stems from this launching pad is that words are semantically basic in some sense. The meaning of 'house', 'John', and 'cow' are *house'*, *John'*, and *cow'*, respectively, denoting intensions. In fact, there's an old semantics joke that when the mother of formal semantics, Barbara Partee, was asked by a

---

[18] Louise McNally expressed this worry to me through personal communication. But she also suggested the strategy for addressing this problem.

philosophically minded student what the meaning of life is, she walked over to the chalkboard and simple wrote '*Life'*'.

This view presupposes that there's nothing of interest to semantic theory emanating from beneath the word level, a claim Asher (2012) rejects strongly. His argument for why compositional formal semantics should pay more attention to the lexical meanings of open-class linguistic items involves the notion of *binder rules* in discourse semantics. All versions of the discourse semantic theories we've seen so far incorporate 'an operation *b* that takes a text meaning, combines it with a sentence meaning and returns a new text meaning that can be integrated with further text meanings' (Asher 2012, p. 230). For instance, in dynamic predicate logic (Groenendijk & Stokhof 1991), *b* is a relational composition since meaning is determined by an input assignment and an output assignment. In DRT, it's a merge over DRSs (see Footnote 11). Asher argues that this binder rule can be affected or depends on the meanings of open-class words like verbs. The types assigned to the meanings of verbs ($<e, t>$ or $<e<e, t>>$) are just not fine-grained enough to capture the semantic differences that the verb phrases in the following sentences produce:

8. Nicholas fell. He slipped.
9. Nicolas fell. He got hurt.
10. Nicholas fell. He landed hard on the floor.

In each case, the verb phrase adds a layer of meaning absent from other cases. In (8), the link is causative or explanatory, in (9) it's resultative, and in (10) it elaborates. Asher's conclusion is that in order to identify the binder rules of various theories, a lexical theory of words and how they interact with predication is necessary.

Asher, of course, is already assuming an extrasentential view of formal semantics generally found in dynamic approaches. However, there is reason to seek compositional structures below the word level, even on a more static account. Wunderlich (2012) suggests that '[u]nder a more sophisticated view [of semantics] even simple lexical items could be seen as internally complex, consisting of more atomic pieces of meaning' (p. 307). The need for this kind of view can already be witnessed in derivational morphology in which the meanings of complex words like *decompositional* is built up from the meanings of individual morphemes such as 'de', 'compose', and 'tional' (which can be divided further). But lexical decomposition is not limited to derivational morphology. Simple words can hide deeply complex semantic concepts. I'll briefly discuss two prominent accounts of lexical semantics before moving on to challenges to the PoC from underspecification techniques. The accounts are Jackendoff's (1990, 2002) *conceptual semantics* and Pustejovsky's (1991, 1995) *generative lexicon*.

Both of these theories are quite comprehensive and technical. Since I cannot do full justice to these vicissitudes here, I'll focus on the aspects of the theories that touch on the internal structure of words. Let's start with Jackendoff's account. Jackendoff starts with a mentalist or internalist perspective on meaning, that is, meaning is in the heads of speakers not in the external world, or rather, 'it is a combinatorial structure in a speaker's mind that can be shared with other speakers via acoustic or visual signals' (Jackendoff 2019, p. 87). But Jackendoff adds some more familiar model-theoretic commitments as well, like compositionality and fixed-utterance meaning.[19] The framework proposes six basic conceptual categories: EVENT, STATE, ACTION, PLACE, PATH, PROPERTY, and AMOUNT. Formation rules combine these categories together. A lexical item is then interpreted by a conceptual structure that's built with these rules. The lexical decomposition of a word like *drink* is similar in meaning to 'cause a liquid to go into one's mouth' (Jackendoff 1990, p. 53). The proposed semantic structure for such a simple surface form is quite complex on this view: $[\![drink]\!] = [_{event}CAUSE([_{thing}]_i, [_{event}GO([_{thing}LIQUID]_j, [_{path}TO([_{place}IN([_{thing}MOUTH OF([thing]_i)])])])])]$. For him, the learnability condition on semantics, which involves explaining how humans learn an unlimited variety of meanings, forces the view 'that word meanings are composite, built up in terms of a generative system from a finite stock of primitives and principles of combination' (Jackendoff 2019, p. 87). This sounds a lot like the argument for sentential compositionality common in the formal semantics literature. The atomic treatment of word meaning would ignore the important semantic effects the internal structures of words have on the entire semantic process.[20]

Pustejovsky (1991, 1995) is more concerned with polysemy or 'the multiplicity of word meanings'. He proposes a sort of generative syntax for lexical meaning in which multiple senses of words are not characterised by enumerations or lists but a rich balance between generation and context. Given the focus on contextual effects, his work is very friendly to NLP and computational linguistics. By way of example, Pustejovsky (1995, p. 122) formalises two different readings of the verb *bake*. He shows how different senses emerge or are generated by the lexical interaction of the verb and different nouns, as in the change of state in *James baked a potato* generated by mass nouns vs the creation sense of *James baked the cake* generated by artifacts. Pustejovksy,

---

[19] Zwarts & Verkuyl (1994) argue that conceptual semantics can be safely translated into a model-theoretic framework for maximum applicability.

[20] Conceptual semantics has considerably loftier goals than just lexical decomposition. It's markedly generative and combinatorial (as a component of the Parallel Architecture we met in Chapter 3), includes pragmatics, and connects semantics with cognition. Jackendoff (2019, p. 92) claims his 'central hypothesis' is that conceptual structure is a level of mental representation 'which instantiates sentence meanings and serves as the formal basis for inference and for connection with world knowledge and perception'.

similar to Jackendoff, posits that lexical items are decomposed into four kinds of templates: argument structure, event structure, qualia structure, and lexical inheritance structure. Generative devices connect to the levels by type coercion, selective binding, and co-composition. Co-compositionality is an interesting concept. It emerges when unexpected or nonstandard meanings are generated in traditional semantics. Standard accounts, inherited from Fregean notions of saturation, incorporate a predicate-argument view of semantic composition while co-compositionality models composition in terms of both the predicate and argument having influence on or *coercing* each other. Pustejovsky considers co-compositionality to be an extension of the standard PoC. Thus, the subsentential properties of lexical semantics can be used to identify entirely novel semantic structure, including possible extensions of principles assumed in formal semantics.[21]

I've described lexical compositional semantics as rogue since it undercuts syntactic structure in applying semantic decomposition below the word level. In another sense, lexical compositional semantics is very conformist. In fact, it's compositionality all the way down! The last consideration of this section involves more ostensible detachment between syntax and semantics.

So far, I've painted a picture of complex lexical semantics as a level of compositional semantics below the word and sentence level. Standard interpretations of formal semantics either abstract away from this information or ignore it entirely. Semantics, however, can go rogue in other ways beyond the sentence level. Many theories assume a tight connection between syntax and semantics. For example, Jacobson's (2012) *direct compositionality* entails that syntax and semantics work so closely together that no syntactic structure is left without a semantic correspondent. A related notion, what Szabó (2000) calls 'strong principle of parallelism', involves the idea that syntactic and semantic processes operate in parallel to one another. This means that the meanings of complex expressions must themselves be complex. Szabó shows that this notion is stronger than compositionality but a weaker version entails it. In any case, most standard accounts of compositionality assume that semantics is directly built off syntactic structure. This means that in order to account for the classic scope ambiguity issues such as the two readings of *Every linguist loves a derivation* (denoting one specific derivation or multiple respective derivations), resolution must produce distinct syntactic structures or trees.

---

[21] Pustejovsky's general account has played well with distributional and computational approaches to semantics. Pustejovsky & Jezek (2008) make a case for an extension of DH based on sensitivity to lexical architectures. Pustejovsky *et al.* (2014) provide a novel model, based on the generative lexicon, for automatic text annotation in corpora called 'Generative Lexicon Mark-Up Language'. The idea is to capture compositional structure lying beneath the surface relationships usually captured by annotation systems in corpus linguistics.

Semantic underspecification takes a different route. It involves an intentional omission of linguistic information from semantic description. The underlying idea is to postpone semantic analysis until it can be executed in such a way that various ambiguities can be resolved. This is accomplished by producing a single representation capable of representing multiple realisations. In other words:

> The key idea of underspecification is to devise a formalism which allows to represent all logical readings of a sentence in a single compact structure. Such a formalism allows one to preserve compositionality without artfully casting pure semantic ambiguities into syntactic ones. (Lesmo & Robaldo 2006, p. 550)

This process amounts to a type of storage of interpretations without immediately checking for consistency. At a later stage, these interpretations are pulled out or extracted and interpreted in parallel. A given semantic representation can be underspecified in one of two ways:

1. Atomic subexpressions (constants and variables) may be ambiguous, that is, do not have a single value specified as their denotation but a range of possible values.
2. The way in which subexpressions are combined by means of constructions may not be fully specified. (Bunt 2007, p. 60)

These paths specify constraints on representations of meaning and are often viewed as meta-representations, which display all the representations that satisfy the set of constraints, that is, all the possible readings of an expression. For example, Cooper storage is one well-known way of resolving scope ambiguities (Cooper 1983). This method assumes a single, surface-syntactic structure from which multiple semantic representations can be produced. Each expression of natural language is assigned an ordered pair of a semantic value (or type) and a quantifier store (typed according to its compositional value). Now, quantifiers, which generate the scope ambiguities, can either be interpreted in their current position or *stored* for later application. Retrieval occurs at the sentence node in which stored quantifiers can be reinserted and applied to the content. This usually involves moving the quantifier to a higher position in the tree. It's a bit like trying to figure out a jigsaw puzzle. Some pieces might not quite make sense in the positions you initially assign them. But if you remove them, fill in more of the puzzle, and place them in at a later stage, you might finally be able to see the all-important image of the kitten with a ball of yarn.

Where do underspecification and storage techniques leave compositionality? It seems, as with the case of co-compositionality, we need to extend and amend the concept. One way in which to do this is by separating it into two distinct notions, one involving compositionality in denotations and the other trading in semantic representations. Cooper storage, and some other underspecification techniques, don't seem to meet the former condition since the denotation of the whole is not determined by the denotation of its constituents. However, the semantic representation of a complex expression does seem to be determined by that of its parts or constituents in Cooper storage.[22] If direct compositionality involves a one-to-one mapping between syntactic objects and semantic values, then storage and underspecification is *indirectly* compositionality by comparison.

In some ways, all of the above considerations leave the principle or concept at the level it should be, namely, the metasemantic. Assuming a particular, strict, functional, one-to-one mapping between syntax and semantics will rule out the rich semantically compositional structure of the lexicon as well as relegate techniques such as underspecification uncompositional by fiat. There's at least one lesson to be learned from rogue semantics, as I've called it: *much formal compositional semantic structure lives beneath and beyond the syntax–semantics interface.*

4.5   On the Possibility of a *Super*semantics

In the previous section, we delved into the formal semantics of words and the indirectly compositional techniques of meaning storage and retrieval. The aim was to apply formal semantic methodology outside of its usual linguistic domain. Nonetheless, this expansion was somewhat conservative in that it only really shifted us to other linguistically relevant areas, such as lexical semantics. In this final section, we'll briefly consider a more radical application, one that utilises formal semantic machinery outside the bounds of linguistic phenomena entirely. This is a rapidly and recently emerging research area, so it would be unfair of me to characterise or criticise it as a finished product. Thus, I'll limit myself to some cautionary comments, after a very brief overview of the idea. My comments will mostly pertain to the methodological trajectory 'supersemantics' is currently on in light of the arguments and claims of the chapter so far. In other words, I'll argue that for supersemantics to be a successful project in the extension of semantic methodology beyond language, it needs to apply much more than traditional static, model-theoretic techniques that have failed to sufficiently characterise natural language meaning in its full splendour.

The emerging supersemantics literature is ambitious in coverage to say the least. Proposals on music semantics, dance semantics, primate grammar, gesture, and many others abound. For manifesto-level introductions, see Schlenker (2018) and Patel-Grosz *et al.* (2023). Let's evaluate what supersemantics is and

---

[22] See Nefdt (2020a) for a further extension of compositionality to address whether deep learning NLP systems are compositional.

why we need it. In essence, supersemantics is a call for the extension of formal semantics to nonlinguistic phenomena or 'nontraditional objects'. As Schlenker (2018, p. 366) puts it,

It is striking that the project [of formal semantics] could in principle apply beyond sentences: for any representational form R, one could posit that 'to know the meaning of R is (at least) to know under what conditions it is true'. R could for instance be a visual or an acoustic representation.

This 'striking' fact coupled with the claim of the alleged 'extraordinary fruitful' nature of the enterprise over the past fifty years is what motivates the creation of this novel field of inquiry. So the basic idea is that many of the objects traditionally studied by semiotics could benefit from formal semantic treatment. Schlenker offers two initial arguments in favour of the extension. The first is linguistic in nature. He argues that iconicity or the phenomenon of semantic reference connecting with iconic form (like an elongated vowel reflecting quantity in words like 'huuuge') are necessary inclusions in formal semantics. The idea is that formal semantics without a treatment of iconicity is impoverished and incomplete. Gesture, speech, sign language, and even emoji communication apparently all evince the need for this inclusion. The other argument is typological or perhaps phylogenetic. Meaning phenomena are not exhausted by the linguistic. Pictures, animal calls, and music all display semantic properties to varying degrees. A unified account of meaning in the wild, if you will, would open up channels of comparative study and possible fruitful collaboration.[23]

These are no doubt notable pursuits. But they make a number of controversial assumptions in setting up this new research programme. The first is that they might overstate the success of formal semantics. As we saw in Chapter 2, static formal semantics looks successful from the perspective of a very small fragment of natural language. In this chapter, we've argued that natural language semantics must contend with the pervasiveness of contextual factors, something formal semantics hasn't always been adequate at managing. Stanton (2020) goes one step further to suggest that model-theoretic semantics is unlikely to survive the emergence of more sophisticated distributional vector-space models.[24] The present chapter could certainly be read as a disquisition on the limitations of standard model-theoretic semantics.

One could argue that these aforementioned observations merely point to a broader conception of formal semantics and thus a broader application of it

---

[23] One issue with the extension is that something like compositionality has been motivated precisely due to features of natural languages like productivity, systematicity, and infinity in front of the backdrop of our limited cognitive capacities. These same arguments would need to be analogously applied to these other domains for a legitimate comparative project.

[24] See Erk (2020) for a discussion and review of literature on how they could possibly coexist.

to nonstandard objects. The worry with this response is that the supersemantics project is already quite expansive. To include dynamic semantics, distributional approaches, and lexical decomposition is going to render the programme infeasible. Of course, practical issues such as what could possibly constitute a context in a musical score or how the distributional hypothesis could apply to corpora of pictures or signs beset the project from the onset. Patel-Grosz *et al.* (2023) seem to push in the direction of supercharging supersemantics to include formal syntax and pragmatics. The problem with super-duper-semantics is that it doesn't really fix the foundational issues of the original programme but pushes them down the line for later resolution. This might not, in itself, be unreasonable given the inchoate nature of the field.

A further theoretical response to the concern over the linguistic limitations of formal semantics in general can perhaps be mounted on the basis of the nature of the nonstandard objects in question. Specifically, the fragment of natural language that seems most amenable to truth-conditional, model-theoretic treatment is the referential part. Pictures certainly have this property; so too does the 'language' of emojis. Nevertheless, even if this case can be made for those particular objects, it's not clear that the same can be said of others. Dance and music are less obviously referential, if at all.[25] In any case, it might be unwise for supersemanticists to hang their hats on the referential bandwagon exclusively. Semantic internalists have long argued that reference is not a proper part of meaning (Chomsky 2000; Pietroski 2018).

None of my above ruminations are proposed as knockdown arguments against a promising new extension of semantics. They're only meant as cautions and considerations, not kryptonite. Another way of putting this point might be that if supersemantics is to succeed, it needs to develop a super-metasemantics to go along with the technical results.

4.6   Summary

In this chapter, we've explored the scientific theory of natural language meaning from a multitude of perspectives, accounts, and approaches. Starting with a plea for scientific metasemantics as opposed to a more metaphysical approach, we covered the connections (and divergences) between a number of prominent frameworks and offered novel ways of understanding the role of context and formalism. We've also discussed the limitations and extensions of the basic machinery beneath the word level, at the extrasentential discourse level, and out in the nonlinguistic world. Despite the ambition of the journey, we're not quite done with meaning yet. In the next chapter, meaning and use take centre stage.

---

[25] I thank Louise McNally for useful discussion of some of these issues.

Further Reading

Metasemantics has become a prominent field of inquiry in the past few years. Thus, there are a number of books on the topic. I'll mention just a few here that discuss or expand on the topics in this chapter.

- There are a number of classical introductions to formal semantics on the market (many already mentioned in the text). Thus, for a more philosophical approach to the formal study of meaning, I recommend Zoltán Szabó and Richmond Thomason's (2019) *The Philosophy of Language* (Cambridge University Press). Despite the name, the book is actually concerned with the historical development and philosophy of semantics and pragmatics. It covers a number of foundational topics in some detail, ranging from compositionality, reference, tense, and modality to externalism vs internalism, and vagueness.
- The first volume that motivates a similar picture of metasemantics to the one promoted at the beginning of this chapter is Derek Ball & Brian Rabern's (2018) *The Science of Meaning: Essays on the Metatheory of Natural Language Semantics* (Oxford Univerity Press). The book contains a number of excellent chapters written by some of the most prominent and influential figures in semantics such as Barbara Partee, Robert Stalnaker, Michael Glanzberg, and Frank Veltman. Stalnaker's chapter covers the nature of formal context within semantics with a focus on Lewis' view. The last chapter of the book, written by Derek Ball, offers a fascinating measure-theoretic analysis of the nature of formal semantic explanation, one that dovetails well with my continuum of context in Section 4.3.
- For a book on dynamic semantics that specifically covers different accounts of anaphora, modals, and information updates, I recommend Paul Dekker's (2012) *Dynamic Semantics* (Springer Verlag). It presents contemporary dynamic predicate logic, update semantics, and DRT-style theorising and analysis.
- Nicholas Asher (2011) provides a sophisticated account of lexical semantics in his *Lexical Meaning in Context: A Web of Words* (Cambridge University Press). Asher develops a rich compositional system of types for words in order to explain a complicated set of phenomena including category mistakes (semantic mismatches), copredication, and coercion. This book is extremely technical but rewarding nonetheless.
- For a very different-style volume on both the foundational texts and contemporary reflections, see Louise McNally and Zoltán Szabó (2022) *A Reader's Guide to Classic Papers in Formal Semantics* (Springer Verlag). The book contains twenty-one chapters, each written by a prominent linguist or philosopher, discussing a seminal paper in semantics. This isn't only an essential resource for advanced students but a refreshing perspective on highly influential texts in semantics.

5   Context and Pragmatics

Defining the boundaries of pragmatics isn't an easy task. Even just saying what pragmatics is *about* is surprisingly challenging at the onset. One reason for this is that for many years, theorists treated pragmatics like a convenient box to put all the recalcitrant data that didn't quite fit into semantics or other areas into – the so-called wastebasket of linguistic theory. Unfortunately, over time, any wastebasket starts to overflow and some recycling system is required. What's clear is that pragmatics is related to meaning and context in significant ways. The systematic answer to the 'how' question is the main issue. In some sense, this chapter is a continuation of the previous one. Specifically, we'll have to address what I'll call 'the demarcation problem of meaning'. This philosophical difficulty, similar to the original conundrum in the philosophy of science, involves finding where to draw the line between semantic information/phenomena/analysis and the pragmatic counterpart. Thus, philosophers have been vying for decades for accounts of how to separate semantic from pragmatic meaning phenomena and where exactly to draw the line(s) between them. Alongside these sometimes verbal disputes and immovable debates, pragmatics has emerged as a viable scientific pursuit within linguistics. For better or worse, this has happened often in the history of science: while philosophers argue about where the best place for the artisanal café is, scientists have already set up shop and started brewing. In this chapter, my goal won't be to rehash the voluminous work on the semantics–pragmatics divide that's dominated the late-twentieth-century philosophy of language. There have been many books on that subject (see the *Further Reading* section for some references). Instead, my plan is to attempt a connection between the philosophy and the linguistics of pragmatics.

In Section 5.1, I'll describe three classical and influential ideas on the nature of pragmatics courtesy of Grice (1975), Stalnaker (1978), and Lewis (1979). Next, in Section 5.2, I present three general philosophical frameworks for separating semantic from pragmatic processes and analyses that have roots in the aforementioned triumvirate: (P1) the indexical conception, (P2) the cognitivist conception, and (P3) social-inferential conception. In Section 5.3, I look at three linguistic theories of pragmatics: (L1) optimality-theoretic pragmatics,

(L2) game-theoretic pragmatics, and (L3) Bayesian pragmatics. I won't pretend to have exhausted the different formal or scientific treatments of pragmatics. I will, however, show how each of these prominent frameworks exploits the philosophical demarcations (P1–P3) presented in Section 5.2. Finally, I suggest that appreciating this correspondence can provide useful clues as to how to unify the study of pragmatic phenomena under different empirical and theoretical guises.

5.1 The Intimation Game

The late 1970s were strong with formal pragmatic frameworks. Paul Grice, Robert Stalnaker, and David Lewis all contributed significantly to the understanding of the logic behind using language for communicative purposes. They also inspired different views of what pragmatics involves. Griceans and neo-Griceans alike have emphasised a distinction between 'what is said' and 'what is meant' (in a context) to distinguish between semantic content and pragmatic inference. Stalnaker, on the other hand, marshalled in a movement towards modelling an ever-changing, dynamic conversational context, one that led in no small way to the later flourishing of dynamic semantic theories. Lewis takes this theoretical framework a step further by capturing how to keep conversational score, game-theoretically. For all of these philosophers, the conversation is key to accessing pragmatics. Let's start with Grice and the underlying logic he unearthed.[1]

Grice's picture of pragmatics starts with the notion of literal content or what's said by a speaker in uttering a particular expression. Specifically, Grice (1967) states that this content is 'closely related to the conventional meaning of the words (the sentence) he has uttered' (p. 25) and that it relies on 'the elements of [the sentence], their order, and their syntactic character' (p. 87). This might sound like a commitment to truth-conditional semantics (or propositionalism) but Szabó (2009) notes that it's actually unclear, from his writings, whether Grice held any such view. What's clear is the distinction between speaker meaning, or what the speaker intends or means by the use of an expression, and sentence meaning, or what the sentence conventionally means by the rules of the grammar. The central idea is that what's meant can go beyond what's said in systematic and predictable ways due to context. This simple idea brought forth one of the most interesting and productive areas in the philosophy of language and pragmatics alike, *the theory of implicature.*

---

[1] Dynamic syntacticians have also realised the importance of dialogue data in modelling syntactic and semantic processes. See Cann *et al.* (2012) for an overview of the framework and Eshghi *et al.* (2012) for a focused discussion on the role of conversational dialogue.

I'll provide some brief remarks here as the framework is quite well known. Basically, Grice gives us a recipe for understanding the logic of conversational and communicative spaces under the assumption of rational discourse. This assumption is encoded in the *Cooperative Principle*. The principle states that conversational participants 'make [their] conversational contribution such as is required, at the stage at which it occurs, by the accepted purpose or direction of the talk exchange in which [they] are engaged' (Grice 1975, p. 26). With this assumption in place, conversations become like interpretation games in which hearers attempt to infer the meaning of an utterance by the speaker that doesn't seem to fit the principle or its injunctions. How this principle is cashed out in conversational logic is by means of certain 'implicature'-generating phenomena such as *respecting*, *flouting*, or *cancelling* the four maxims of conversation.[2] I'll illustrate one of these processes by means of different maxims. Consider the following examples:

1. **A:** How many books has Larry published? **B:** Larry has published three books.
2. **A:** What's the time? **B:** The sun just came up.
3. **A:** Is Craige a good linguist? **B:** She has excellent handwriting ... which isn't to say that she isn't also an excellent linguist!

In (1), the maxim of quality, or the demand to make your contribution a truthful one, is observed or respected. One can make a case for the maxim of quantity applying here too. That maxim requires contributions to be as informative as is necessary, no more and no less. In fact, multiple implicatures can be generated simultaneously. (2) involves flouting a maxim, quantity in this case. If you're expected to be as informative as is necessary and your interlocutor perceives that you have violated this maxim, then they're likely to assume that your utterance has a hidden meaning. In this case, they might assume that your utterance is asking them to make an inference, such as the current time is correlated with the sunrise. In dialogue (3), the implication that Craige isn't a good linguist generated by the violation of the maxim of relation ('be relevant') is cancelled by the clause after the ellipsis. This latter feature also distinguishes cases of pragmatic inference from semantic entailment.

It's no surprise that many of the examples one encounters in the pragmatics literature involve dialogue. Understanding pragmatics seems to require the perspective of rational discourse. Compare the concept of conversational implicature to that of conventional implicatures for a moment. Conventional

---

[2] Thomas (2012) discusses other options such as 'infringing', in which a nonnative speaker could generate implicatures unknowingly. In what follows, I'll idealise away from these phenomena for simplicity's sake.

implicatures, according to Grice, are generated either by syntactically encoded information or the conventional meanings of individual words. For instance:

4. Even Tom published a paper.

The conventionally implicated content of (4) is something that involves the fact that Tom isn't a likely person to publish his work, probably due to its poor quality. Other proposed differences between these kinds of implicatures involve the lack of cancellability for the conventional variant and detachability, which is the idea that changing the words while retaining the content (what is said) preserves the implicature. This is apparently true for conversational implicatures but not conventional ones, which makes intuitive sense since the latter are meant to be triggered by the lexicon and syntax.[3]

Lastly, Grice distinguishes between *generalised* and *particularised* conversational implicatures. On this topic, he states:

[P]articularized conversational implicatures [are] cases in which an implicature is carried by saying that p on a particular occasion in virtue of special features of the context, cases in which there is no room for the idea that an implicature is normally carried by saying that p. But there are cases of generalized conversational implicature. Sometimes one can say that the use of a certain form of words in an utterance would normally (in the absence of special circumstances) carry such-and-such an implicature or type of implicature. (Grice 1975, p. 37)

Unlike the distinction between conversational and conventional implicatures, both of these kinds of implicatures are triggered by the context. What's different in these cases is the type of context at play. I think this is very interesting from a semantic point of view. It basically suggests that there are pragmatic phenomena that are invariant across contexts. In most (or all) contexts, an utterance like *Paul walked into a house yesterday* implicates that the house in question isn't his. It does so conventionally. Of course, this implicature can be cancelled but the default situation is one in which it's generated. By contrast, conversational implicatures are ad hoc and extemporaneous. This is what makes them fascinating. A decent command of the conventions of language will suffice for decoding conventional implicatures, but conversational implicatures require a rich mixture of appreciating the Cooperative Principle, tacitly identifying the subtle action with relation to the maxims, and understanding how the context is being exploited by the speaker to achieve their ends.

Various aspects of the basic Gricean picture have been altered by later adherents. Neo-Griceans, like Horn (2004) and Levinson (2000), have sought to streamline the maxims so as to avoid potential clashes (a serious problem for the maintenance of the Cooperative Principle). Horn manages to reduce Quantity,

---

[3] None of the features are without exceptions. See Blome-Tillmann (2013) for more.

Relevance, and Manner to the *Q Principle*, to 'say as much as you can', and the *R Principle*, to 'say no more than you must'. Levinson adds an *M Principle*, resembling Manner, which advocates the introduction of 'marked expressions' in nonstandard or nonstereotypical cases. We'll discuss one particular neo-Gricean theory in relevance theory below. Before we do so, let's move on to Stalnaker's slightly different take on the dynamics of pragmatics.

Whereas Grice's picture is one of individuals decoding each other's intentions from a mixture of the literal meaning of sentences and the context of utterance in a kind of theory of mind way, Stalnaker (1978) is a croupier's call to the game of cocreating a context. The Stalnakerian model of communication starts with the idea that a conversation takes place against a *common ground*.[4] The common ground itself is modelled as the set of propositions (or possible worlds) interlocutors mutually accept for the purposes of that conversation. The context set, or worlds compatible with all the propositions of the common ground, is in turn determined by it.[5] In fact, the body of information taken for granted by participants (or interlocutors), known as the context, is defined both in terms of the common ground and the context set equivalently.

Once the cards are in place and the die is set up, we start the game. The initial state is one in which all possibilities are open in terms of what the world of the conversation looks like. This is the context set. Stalnaker idealises away from 'defective' contexts in which the presuppositions of participants are incompatible (but admits that most real-world cases are probably defective in some ways). Once the players begin their discourse, they gain more information about the world (or the world according to the conversation, which might be intentionally or unintentionally distinct from the real world). With each new datum, the space of possibilities is reduced by intersection. For instance, the effect an assertion has is to rule out worlds in the context set that are incompatible with the proposition expressed by that assertion. This is the 'characteristic effect' of an assertion. If I say 'It's raining', I rule out all the nonrain worlds from the context. At the same time, I'm also adding to the deck of cards, which is the common ground. That's if my interlocutors accept my move. By accepting, we all agree to hold a certain position towards that proposition, that is, we believe it or suppose it or know it depending on the mood in which it was presented. The eventual goal of the conversation is to end up with as few worlds as possible (like *Go Fish*) under the assumption that the game ends when we've reached the actual world.

---

[4] Stalnaker (2002) attributes the term 'common ground' to Grice's William James lectures.
[5] All this talk of possible worlds is not metaphysical for Stalnaker: 'The decision to treat possible worlds, or possible situations, as PRIMITIVE elements in a theory of propositions and propositional attitudes does not require an ontological commitment to possible worlds as basic entities of the universe. Rather, it is a decision to theorize at a certain level of abstraction' (Stalnaker 1978, p. 316).

We already saw some features of this style of modelling with dynamic approaches, such as update semantics, from the previous chapter. However, Stalnaker himself doesn't endorse this picture as a characterisation of the semantic process but rather the pragmatic one. So what's the relationship between semantic content and pragmatic inference on Stalnaker's view? In general, 'assertoric content', or the semantic content of a sentence on a particular occasion, is the same as the content of an utterance itself on that occasion. This is the default situation.[6] But there are cases in which these concepts come apart. Stalnaker considers cases in which the semantic content is either necessarily true or necessarily false across the context set. Take the first disjunct: if asserted content were identical to semantic content in these cases (necessary truths), it would be a strange move to make an assertion that literally has no impact on the context set. On the flip side, necessarily false statements are self-defeating. 'To assert something incompatible with what is presupposed is self-defeating … And to assert something which is already presupposed is to attempt to do something that is already done' (Stalnaker 1978, p. 89). Other cases involve contingent semantic content where 'the semantic content of an utterance is different at different worlds in the context set' (Hawthorne & Magidor 2009, p. 379). In these cases, the participants don't know how to update the context when an assertion is made. This can happen when the semantic content rules out a world in some live options but not others. Consider the following example:

Suppose I know there is only one person in a certain room, but I do not know whether it is Bill or Ben. Someone points to whoever is in the room and asserts 'He is on fire'. Assuming semantic orthodoxy, there is at least one world in the context set where the semantic content is the proposition that Ben is on fire, and at least one world where it is the proposition that Bill is on fire. Prior to the assertion, there are four relevant classes of live options? Ones where Bill is in the room and on fire, ones where Bill is in the room and not on fire, ones where Ben is in the room and on fire, and ones where Ben is in the room and not on fire. If asserted content is semantic content, then three of these classes are ruled out, but while I know two of the three ruled out classes (those where the person in the room – be it Bill or Ben – is not on fire), I do not know which is the third class (the one where Bill is in the room and on fire, or the one where Ben is in the room and on fire). (Hawthorne & Magidor 2009, p. 380)

Stalnaker infamously introduced the mechanism of *diagonalisation* to resolve these sorts of issues. Since these cases are meant to show that standard propositions cannot always be the semantic content, he opts for a novel concept of a diagonal proposition (marked with '†') to capture the content. The diagonal is determined such that for each world w in the context set, the proposition that some sentence S expresses relative to w is true at w. The diagonal, like an implicature, can be generated when participants flout certain principles

---

[6] This assumes some principles of rational discourse similar to the Cooperative Principle.

of rational cooperative discourse in nondefective contexts. For instance, as we've seen, asserting a proposition that's necessarily true or already in the common ground is redundant. If you did so anyway, your interlocutors would be forced to look for a reason for the assertion beyond the literal content of your utterance. These are rather sophisticated pragmatic dynamics and mechanisms of conversations compared to Grice.

Lastly, Stalnaker's framework has undergone some updating of its own. Initially, the common ground was determined by the joint presuppositions of the participants: '[p]resuppositions are what is taken by the speaker to be common ground of the participants in the conversation, what is treated as their common knowledge or mutual knowledge' (Stalnaker 1999, p. 84). Later versions broadened this notion under the banner of 'acceptance' to include 'presupposing, presuming, postulating, positing, assuming and supposing as well as believing' (Stalnaker 1984, p. 79). Like believing, acceptance can be nonfactive. But unlike cognitive states like believing, acceptance is done for particular purposes or the sake of argument. This means that you can accept p in one context and reject it in another. In Stalnaker (2014), he defines the common ground as the set of propositions that participants 'mutually accept' for the purposes of conversation, where mutual acceptance involves an iterated ackowledgement between parties of their respective acceptances (A accepts that B accepts that A accepts that ... and so on, ad infinitum).

All of these components (especially acceptance) buttress my interpretation of Stalnaker's pragmatics as more game-theoretic than Grice's theory of mind model. There's a further 'make-believe' element in the idealised setting with which Stalnaker presents us. The rules of conversation and discourse go beyond the compositional meanings of our terms and sentences. It's a fluid landscape of ever-changing moves and assertions, held together by consensus, ruling sets of possibilities out at every turn until few are left. In the last of the pragmatic frameworks we'll discuss, the game-theoretic element is maintained while some other aspects of the role of context in conversations are emphasised.

Lewis (1979) builds on his earlier game-theoretic take on language and conventions outlined in Lewis (1969). Here, he focuses on a particularly interesting pragmatic phenomenon that he calls 'accommodation'. In order to explain this concept and other semantic dynamics (like quantifier domain restriction), we need to delve into Lewis' metaphor a little bit. For him, the linguistic context is best modelled as a scoreboard in a language game, similar to the same physical device used in a game like baseball. One key difference between conversations and games is that conversations reverse the role of competition towards accommodation via the removal of interpretive obstacles. Basically, the contextual parameters are assigned the values needed to make an utterance true, or as Lewis puts it, 'conversational score does tend to evolve in such a way as is required to make whatever occurs count as correct play'

(1979, p. 346). In this way, the score is a reflection of the events in the conversation like scoreboards record events in a game. But importantly, the score can also have an effect on the game itself; for example, if you're on two strikes, the third is fatal. In other words, context has a bidirectional effect on meaning such that 'contextual factors relevant to determining the truth value of assertions tends to shift (as Lewis says, "ceteris paribus and within limits') so as to make assertions true" (Ball 2018, p. 376).

Presuppositions are paradigmatic instances of accommodation. If you utter the sentence 'Even Eliza can do it', you require a presupposition that Eliza isn't very good at whichever activity is being referred to. However, if that presupposition isn't already in the common ground, the utterance literally creates it. Promises and other performatives are also good examples of accommodation in action. Performatives like 'I now pronounce you husband and wife' can license propositions that go beyond not only the compositional semantic meaning of the utterance but also beyond simply an addition to the Stalnakerian common ground, that is, the proposition that the couple is married. Context can even create the conditions under which utterances are true. Lewis describes it thus:

If at time t something is said that requires component sn, of conversational score to have a value in the range r if what is said is to be true, or otherwise acceptable; and if sn, does not have a value in the range r just before t; and if such-and-such further conditions hold; then at t the score-component sn, takes some value in the range r. (1979, p. 347)

Prima facie, this statement makes it sound like first an assertion is made, then accommodation makes it such that the proposition asserted is true. Ball (2018) disagrees with this interpretation. For him, it amounts not to the claim that assertion is prior to accommodation but rather that whatever proposition is asserted depends on the context or conversational score. Furthermore, the proviso that 'such-and-such further conditions hold' means that accommodation doesn't always take place. One such limiting condition is that your conversational partners explicitly or implicitly agree to accommodate your assertion, that is, no objections from your interlocutors. In the case of the marriage performative, if your audience doesn't believe you have procured the relevant authority, then the act is null and void.

So what does a context or conversational score look like for Lewis? Basically, similar to a score in baseball, it can consist of a set of coordinates or parameters encoding each team's runs, the specific time, the innings, strikes, balls, and outs. In the language case, conversational scores are tuples of abstract set-theoretic entities like the set of presuppositions (Stalnaker's common ground), the interlocutors' respective plans, and the comparative salience of the afore-mentioned abstract entities within the discourse and so on. In an attempt to use Lewis' own logic to decipher what the scoreboard is, Roberts (2015) asks us to figure out what a context of utterance does, how it interacts with the rules of language games to produce interpretations, and then 'find something that does that' (p. 356). The result is a mechanism for interlocutors to cooperatively engage in a mutual linguistic exchange in order to determine not only the common ground but the information at each stage of play relevant to keeping track of mutual goals, directives, and tools for repair and adaptation (like accommodation). Sentences or utterances depend on this scoreboard for their truth and/or acceptability at the stage of the language game in which they occur. Subexpressions and names might also depend on the score for intension/extension. This dependence can take historical record as well as processes like accommodation into account. By including the plans of the participants, Lewis' model goes beyond Stalnaker's towards a game theory of mind that 'depends on the ability to abductively infer what the speaker meant: to reason about the best explanation for her speech act, given its conventional content, in light of *what we already know of her plans and intentions*' (Roberts 2015, p. 358). In other words, based on the score, participants are using inference to the best explanation to decode their interlocutors' moves. This inference is in part based on the compositional semantics of the terms and sentences used but often involves extra-linguistic information and score tracking. The scoreboard itself is determined by constitutive rules of engagement (what Lewis calls 'kinematics') that allow the score to evolve in a particular kind of way. If these kinematics are well-defined, then there's one 'score function' (a function from stages of the conversation to tuples of abstract entities) that represents the 'correct' state of play. Thus, Lewis' model involves a normative dimension of regulative rules that specify correctness that depends on the score. For example, what counts as correct play after two strikes in baseball is different from what counts as correct after one. Similarly, what counts as a correct response after a supposition is different from that after a question or command.

Again, my intention isn't a comprehensive account of Lewis here, or Stalnaker and Grice for that matter. I merely hope to have provided a sample flavouring for later digestive choices. All of these theories, frameworks, and models have been monumentally influential in the philosophy of language and linguistics respectively. In the next section, we explore how they have influenced different answers to what I call the demarcation problem in pragmatics, and, in the section after that, I argue for their sedimentary status in some prominent contemporary linguistic theories of pragmatics.

5.2   The Pragmatic Demarcation Problem

We've already met one important interface in linguistics, namely, the syntax–semantics interface. Many volumes, journal articles, and books have devoted their pages to deciphering the precise nature of the confluence of syntactic and semantic information within natural language data and processing.

Compositionality is one way of capturing the connection. But as we saw in the previous chapter, it's unclear as a particular semantic principle and open as a metasemantic one. Nevertheless, despite the technical difficulties, theorists are generally able to appreciate the difference (intuitive or stipulative) between syntax and semantics, form and meaning, and even the different types of data to which each domain answers. I use 'generally' because, in practice, things are rarely this clear. Theoretically, however, syntax and semantics operate on different structures, and various proposals have been proffered to link the two kinds of linguistic systems.

The major problem with the semantics–pragmatics divide is that this intuitive, or theoretically apparent, distinction is missing. Both fields are clearly concerned with natural language meaning. Both involve context in a content-determining manner. Both play with truth conditions or semantic values of other sorts. Both can be construed dynamically. As McNally notes, '[t]he fact that two separate disciplines have developed for this purpose reflects the complexity of human language as a semiotic system' (2013, p. 285).[7] This situation results in a demarcation problem akin to the infamous puzzle in the mid to late twentieth century within the philosophy of science and epistemology. A quick gloss of the original problem pits science against pseudoscience. Indeed, some philosophers of science might have seen unearthing this latter distinction as their mission. However, a more nuanced appreciation of the puzzle concerns how to distinguish scientific endeavour from nonscientific endeavour. The latter could include pseudoscientific pursuits masquerading as science. But it also includes literature, art, poetry, and other types of human intellectual activity, all of which seem to contribute to human collective knowledge in some way. Interestingly, some similar strategies for demarcation that have been proposed in the original domain were also proposed in our particular one. The argument goes that science, like syntax and semantics, is systematic, formally characterisable, productive, and so on. Nonscience, like pragmatics, is messy, unsystematic, and involves too many real-world variables to be susceptible to neat or formal characterisation. In both cases, this simple demarcation procedure fails. In our case, the previous section has clearly shown that pragmatics is anything but unsystematic or incapable of formal characterisation. So we need more sophisticated options for finding the divide between semantics and pragmatics.

Before we embark on this journey, let's be thorough philosophers and explore the eliminative possibility. Why do we need a semantics–pragmatics divide in the first place? Even Donald Davidson, a pioneer of early semantic theory and as systematic a thinker as you can find, eventually succumbed to sceptical

---

[7] McNally (2013) provides one of the clearest overviews of the semantics–pragmatics divide. Her general idea is that in order to find some sense of uniformity across theories, one has to appreciate the fact that there are multiple, specific ways of dividing semantics and pragmatics depending on one's starting point.

thoughts about language. He questioned whether there was any such object that was characterised by the formal, precise rules of semanticists and other linguists. What seemed to him to be 'real' or attestable were the imprecise communicative devices we use in our everyday lives. These objects were amenable to a 'passing theory' that involved ad hoc rules and contingent characterisations. Static overarching theories, the kinds I've been talking about throughout this book, seem to hold no sway over the messy reality of our everyday linguistic interactions. Not without massive idealisation, of course. In a quixotic paper called 'A nice derangement of epitaphs' (1986), Davidson evocatively references cases of malapropism as extreme examples in which we seemingly seamlessly decode the correct sequence and meaning of expressions based on momentary reflections and fluid rules. Radical contextualists, too, have long decried the existence or need for a systematic, rule-based, theory of meaning. To them, contextual factors are so pervasive that no bedrock procedure explains how meanings are assigned to words independently of the context of utterance or discourse. In other words, there's no semantics, just pragmatics. A fortiori, there's no semantics–pragmatics divide. Fascinatingly, Chomskyans have also rejected the need for a semantic theory of how linguistic items correspond or refer to the external world (albeit for completely different reasons).

It is possible that natural language has only syntax and pragmatics; it has a 'semantics' only in the sense of 'the study of how this instrument, whose formal structure and potentialities of expression are the subject of syntactic investigation, is actually put to use in a speech community' ... In this view, natural language consists of internalist computations and performance systems that access them. (Chomsky 1995c, p. 26)

This kind of view would bypass the entire debate on where the line between semantics and pragmatics of natural language is or should be. All there would need to be is a theory of the internal computational mechanisms of language in the brain and a theory of how these mechanisms are put to use in communication. The syntax–pragmatics divide seems to have a more transparent demarcation procedure.

Opting for either the internalist Chomskyan picture or the radical contextualist one reduces our quandary to nought. There can't be a semantics–pragmatics divide if there's no such thing as 'semantics' to speak of. There are good arguments for both of these positions in the literature. My main concern is that eliminativism of this sort doesn't really get rid of the issue at hand. Whether internalists believe semantic values are computed completely intracranially or radical contextualists believe that meaning is purely contextual, neither seems to deny that linguistic items have individual meanings and these can be determined by their modes of combination in a given context. Even denying the sentences or utterances have a fixed meaning outside of a context doesn't really matter here.

Lewis' (1970, p. 23) dictum is useful to keep in mind: '[i]n order to say what meaning *is*, we may first ask what a meaning *does*, and then find something that does that'. Take the following mundane sentence:

5. The cat is on the mat.

It would be odd to deny that the meaning of (5) can be determined by the meanings of the component parts (words) and how they're combined. Internalists certainly don't deny this. They're mostly claiming that the process is one that concerns *internalia*, not *externalia*. Contextualists seem to be saying that the interpretation of (5) essentially requires context. But they risk giving up a key part of their argument with a radical version of this latter insistence, namely, the fact that this sentence could be used to mean something completely different in a different context. For example, two spies communicating about the position of their target (code name 'the cat') could mean that the target is ready for extraction (or execution). Without a default meaning under the idealisation of a standard context, it's hard to explain how aberrant meanings come to be.[8] Grice, Stalnaker, and Lewis all do a pretty good job of explaining how these kinds of meanings are generated within a context. We don't need 'fixed' meanings either. We just need relatively stable meanings under the usual kinds of scientific idealisation common across the sciences.[9]

   With this in mind, let's move on to some of the options on the table. I'll be considering three 'metapragmatic' possibilities, if you will. The first, exemplified by Lewis' model, is often called the indexicalist view. The second, the cognitivist account, is neo-Gricean and makes particular theoretical use of the relevance maxim. The last view draws from some aspects of Stalnaker's model, especially its possible extension to a social dimension, to argue for a socio-cultural lens on what separates pragmatics from semantics.

   Indexicalism, or the index theory, is inspired by Richard Montague, who saw pragmatics as a formal extension of semantics. He stated the overarching division of labour as follows:

Syntax is concerned solely with relations between linguistic expressions; semantics with relations between expressions and the objects to which they refer; and pragmatics with relations among expressions, the objects to which they refer, and users or contexts of use of the expressions. (Montague 1968, p. 95)

---

[8] There's a stronger argument that sentences like (5) are vastly semantically indeterminate. Putnam's (1981) model-theoretic argument is what I have in mind here. However, Putnam intended this argument to be pitted against metaphysical realism and a particular notion of truth as an intended model, not at formal semantic theory or metasemantics.

[9] See Dupre (2023) for precisely this kind of argument as a middle ground between semantic minimalists and radical contextualists.

What does this mean exactly? In essence, it means that pragmatics takes semantics as a base and extends it to a framework for assignment of truth relative to a model and a context of utterance or use. Another way of describing the view is that pragmatics has a slightly more complex domain of application, natural language with indexicality. But the same basic principles of formal semantics applies; you just have to add the indices to capture all the relevant contextual information. 'Semantics studies something about non-indexical languages and pragmatics studies the same thing about indexical ones' (Szabó 2009, p. 369).

Montague's divide offers a neat solution to our problems of demarcation. On this view, you can hold on to your favourite formal semantic theory and buttress it with something like Lewis' model of scorekeeping in the language game to deal with the indexical parts of natural language. In effect, pragmatics isn't really nonsemantics so the demarcation problem is dissolved.

Unfortunately, there are a host of issues that plague this particular solution. For one thing, a true index theory for every aspect of indexicality in natural language would be deeply infeasible. You'd need a person (both speaker and addressee), time, location, discourse markers, sets of objects (for ostension), and assignment functions at least. Lewis (1970) himself toyed with an 8-tuple monstrosity with all of these parameters and more, before giving up on the index theory altogether. Of course, feasibility issues are secondary to the main problem with this kind of approach to demarcation. As Szabó (2005) notes:

> The main reason for [the index theory's] unpopularity is that it leaves out too much from the domain of pragmatics ... Many phenomena discussed in pragmatics textbooks – presupposition, conversational implicature, rhetorical tropes, etc. – simply do not yield easily to indexical treatment. (p. 371)

Thus, although Lewis' pragmatic theory could be interpreted as an indexical account in the formal characterisation of conversational scores qua tuples of abstract entities and contextual parameters, it would technically outstrip the remit of the Montagovian picture of pragmatics as an extension of semantics. Interestingly, Stalnaker (1970) advocated a similar extension of semantic methodology to one part of pragmatics. As Kepa & Perry (2020) note, however, pragmatics must then be split into 'nearside' and 'far-side' pragmatics. The former can be considered a contextual extension of semantic theory while the latter examines considerably more recalcitrant and sui generis data.[10] Pragmatics seems to be dealing with more than just indexical extensions of semantic phenomena.

---

[10] Szabó's (2009) own take considers the primary pragmatic phenomena to be more concerned with 'problems of utterance interpretation' rather than interpretations of linguistic expressions in context.

Index theory, nearside and nearsighted as it was, had a short shelf life. Neo-Gricean theories tend to dominate the contemporary pragmatic landscape. One of the most influential of these is a cognitivist approach called *relevance theory*. Cognitivists approach the demarcation problem as a cognitive problem: semantic processes reside in one part of the mind and pragmatic processes in another. In this way, it's not the subject matter in which we find the distinction but in the internal processes that govern our linguistic competence. There are many possible interpretations of this approach. The aforementioned Chomskyan internalism is one such approach. Syntax is a mental module that includes semantic interpretation qua logical form (LF) as a proper subset or an interface with other cognitive systems. Pragmatics, on this view, is a separate cognitive mechanism entirely, one that interfaces with the world. Pragmatics puts this internal module to use in performance systems of communication. It does the job of externalist semantics and all the telecommunications work too.

A more dominant approach (within pragmatics) takes a different route. Sperber & Wilson (1994, 1995) (S&W hereafter) draw their lines in terms of the separation between grammar, which is the study of the psychological mechanisms connecting form (or signal) to meaning, and pragmatics, which is the study of the inferential processes that connect internal meaning with contextual information within communication. The resultant theory draws heavily on Grice but also departs from his framework in some significant ways. I'll provide a brief outline of relevance theory here and then (even more briefly) look at an interesting recent application it offers to the practice of philosophy itself. This application helps explain the usefulness of the theory and one of its main pitfalls in accounting for the difference between semantics and pragmatics.

S&W set their view against a historically prominent 'code' model of pragmatics. This model states that a speaker's thoughts are encoded by their utterances such that for a hearer to access them, they would need to decode the hidden message. Simple and intuitive enough. In fact, the problem is the simplicity. Most utterances in need of pragmatic resolution are compatible with a number of different interpretations. The idea that the speaker has one message in mind and the hearer either decodes it or not seems to belie the more complex reality of communication. 'Where indeterminacy is involved, it seems that the most that communication can achieve is to bring about some similarity between the thoughts of the communicator and the audience' (S&W 1994, p. 87). The general problem with codes is that they need keys to decipher. In communication, we don't seem to be provided with such things. If someone asks you how your day was and you respond by gesturing at your dinged car door, you don't access some universal code for 'I'm having a bad day' but the meaning is clear.

Relevance theory assumes communication depends on providing evidence for an intended hypothesis of the intention of the speaker. Successful communication, in turn, rides on whether the evidence is good enough to deduce the intended interpretation from other possible ones. In fact, it's the admission of risk or multiple interpretations that primarily differentiates the 'inferential model' from the code model. In the game of communication, on the former model, we are always forming hypotheses about the intentions of speakers based largely on a kind of inference to the best explanation given the evidence at hand. Here, Grice is the guide. But Grice needs interpretation himself. Only once the precise definitions or accounts of the maxims and their directives are laid out can a complete pragmatic theory ensue.

S&W develop Gricean insights through the study of cognition. Specifically, they home in on one factor in our attention-casting behaviour:

Our suggestion is that humans tend to pay attention to the most relevant phenomena available; that they tend to construct the most relevant possible representations of these phenomena, and to process them in a context that maximises their relevance. (S&W 1994, p. 91)

When we communicate, we're asking for our audience's attention based on the understanding that the information about to be proffered is relevant enough to be worthy of it. When Shakespeare's Marc Anthony says 'Friends, Romans, countrymen, lend me your ears', he's asking for the auricular loan on the promise of relevance to follow. If, instead of discussing Caesar, he described his breakfast that morning, his countrymen might be more guarded with their ears in the future. This idea, that communication is essentially connected to relevant information, is the basis for this particular theory of pragmatics. As for the inferential process, it follows a logic: '[a]n *inferential process* starts from a set of premises and results in a set of conclusions which follow logically from, or are at least warranted by, the premises' (S&W 1986, p. 12). How this works pragmatically is by the idea that contexts can imply other contexts. Take the following example:

6. If it's raining, I'll take an umbrella.
7. It's raining.
8. I'll take an umbrella.

The idea is that (8) requires both the initial bit of information (provided by (6)) and the new information in (7) to be the conclusion of the inferential process. That much we know from basic logic. S&W's take on this trope is that the information provided in (7) is *relevant* in the context of (6). 'Let us say that assumption [6] is the *context* in which the new information [7] is processed, and that [7] *contextually implies* [8] in the context [6]' (S&W 1994, p. 92). From this, we get a definition of relevant information as information with contextual implications (or, more generally, effects); the more such implications, the more relevant.[11] These arguments, and many more, culminate in the 'principle of relevance' (PoR), which S&W hold is more than enough to produce an explanatory account of pragmatics.

PoR: Every act of inferential communication creates an expectation of optimal relevance.

An 'expectation' doesn't guarantee that the hearer will discover an optimally relevant message. The idea is that every utterance can, at least, be shown to have (at most) one interpretation that's consistent with PoR. This means that the utterance needs to achieve a reasonable amount of contextual effects, and that it shouldn't unduly burden the interpreter with processing effort (as per Manner).

So, in this sense, Grice lives on in the call to conversational logic and the theory of mind-style definition of remit. Furthermore, the central concept of relevance, cognitively construed, draws from, and expands on, the maxim of relation in his theory – make your contribution as relevant as is required.[12] So where does relevance theory depart from its Gricean grandfather? Well, in many of the ways we've already seen, for instance, by being more cognitively grounded. In addition, Grice's account left quite a bit unexplained or vague. Relevance theory is more precise. Another advantage is that with a reduced maxim load, conflicts are not generated as frequently.

One major departure is the rejection of the maxim of quality. In Grice's theory, the directive to make one's contribution truthful, or based on one's best evidence, does some heavy lifting. It explains metaphor ('Juliet was never the sun, surely?') and sarcasm ('you couldn't possibly have had a great time playing soccer, if you broke your leg'). The PoR makes no demand on whether an utterance is truthfully believed or believed by the speaker at all. 'According to relevance theory, the speaker guarantees not the truth of her utterance, but merely its optimal relevance' (S&W 1994, p. 101). Irony, sarcasm, and metaphor can be explained by the added cognitive effort required to interpret their inherent indirect messaging. It's this, not mendacity, that generates the implicatures.

Before we see the theory in action, let's briefly reflect on where this leaves the semantics–pragmatics divide. Basically, relevance theory places them in two distinct parts of the mind/brain. When matching acoustic signals to meanings is called for, semantic processing kicks in. When inferences from contextual

---

[11] Other relevance-generating cases involve assumption strengthening and contradicting of assumptions.

[12] Another use of a maxim is when two or more ways of expressing a thought converge on contextual effects but diverge in processing complexity. In these cases, Manner acts like a sorting hat for which option delivers optimal relevance. We'll see a special case of when things go awry in terms of Manner below.

situations to other such situations in communication is our aim, pragmatics answers the call.[13] The pragmatic demarcation problem is thus resolved by means of a cognitive division of labour. In other words, individual psychology marks the distinction.

In a slightly more recent application, Sperber (2010) sets his sights on the body of philosophical work often associated with the continental philosophical tradition. The main protagonists here are figures like Jacques Derrida, Martin Heidegger, Jean-Paul Sartre, and others. One characteristic these authors share is a penchant for linguistic obscurity, prolixity, and convolution. Sperber's argument has a few moving parts but the basic claim is quite simple: faced with an obscurely written text from a renowned author, we're likely to associate it with profundity rather than ineptitude.

The writing of many philosophers, especially but not uniquely in the so-called continental tradition, is full of hard-to-understand passages where difficulty is presented as pertaining not to expression but to content itself, as being not a rhetorical device but a direct and unavoidable aspect of sophisticated thinking. (Sperber 2010, p. 587)

According to him, relevance theory provides us with all the tools for understanding this 'guru effect' phenomenon. Remember, relevance (and the PoR) was defined in terms of two components: (1) contextual effects produced, and (2) the processing effect required for interpretation. Thus, as Sperber (with slightly updated terminology) states, 'more cognitive effects, more relevance' and 'more effort, less relevance' (2010, p. 586). Something interesting happens when people of authority, in whom we place our trust, mess with this formula. Consider the reverse case. If someone of no authority utters an obscure phrase or sentence, we're likely to dismiss it. Our expectation of its relevance is greatly reduced. It's just not worth the time or cognitive effort. However, when an authority figure (intellectual or otherwise) utters a similar expression, we're more likely to raise our expectations and plod through the effort. In fact, this trust increases on the assumption of fruits at the end of our labours with an implicature-like triggering. In other words, more effect is created with the additional cognitive burden of the obscure text, so much so that in some cases, '[i]mpenetrability indicates profundity' (Sperber 2010, p. 587).[14]

---

[13] Szabó (2009) argues that in so far as semantic processing, as S&W describe it, requires a recursive procedure for pairing expressions with meanings, it's an inferential process itself. I don't necessarily agree, from a cognitive scientific perspective. According to one popular paradigm, semantic processes could still be at the 'System 1', automatic, intuitive level while pragmatic processes are (slightly) more deliberative and considered and thus System 2 (see Kahneman 2011). Relevance theorists seem to embrace the deliberative nature of pragmatic processing, lending some credence to this possibility. Others, such as Levinson (2000), seem to associate it with more of a System 1 approach.

[14] Most social media 'influencers' ride the wave of a highly questionable notoriety–validity equivalence, similar to the guru effect.

This seems to be a plausible account of the alleged brilliance of certain highly obscure thinkers and writers. Indeed, we might have a propensity to seek sagacity in obscurity as if some violation of clarity is an indication of hidden depth. But the guru effect doesn't really arise at the individual psychological level, as Sperber himself admits:

Are individuals on their own predisposed to commit this kind of fallacy? I see no reason to believe they are, or at least, not systematically. On the other hand something of the sort happens in the collective recognition of authorities. (2010, p. 591)

Authority, like the guru effect, is a social phenomenon that emerges when epistemic resources are distributed among a community of individuals. We just can't know everything. In many cases, we're forced to assign credibility to certain individuals (by means of reputation and other markers) so that we can go about our business with less effort. It's a bit like a Hobbesian state of nature, in which you give away some of your autonomy for increased security or just the space to pursue your own goals.[15] In any case, the application of relevance theory to the guru effect shows that something in addition to individual cognition is needed to explain certain pragmatic effects. This 'something' is sociological and not psychological. With this, we're brought to our final method of demarcation, the social-inferential approach.

One thing that unites every pragmatic theory we've seen so far is the importance of conversational and/or dialogue data. Stalnaker defines his notion of common ground in terms of the material brought to the table by conversational participants. Conversations are clearly modelled as joint activities on his view, dynamically filtering possibilities as interlocutors posit, presuppose, and proffer propositions. But conversations don't happen in vacuums, as is assumed by the linguistic-philosophical pragmatics we've considered so far. Even the move to utterance interpretation we find in relevance theory doesn't quite go far enough to capture the socially embedded nature of the pragmatic process. There's an alternative that has its roots in both the realm of classical linguistic-philosophical pragmatics and sociolinguistics. In the Introduction, I teased the possibility of linguistics as a social science. Sociolinguistics adopts this perspective to great reward. In that subfield, language is considered a social phenomenon; speakers and hearers are social actors influenced by historical, systemic, and collective factors beyond linguistic interaction. If syntax and semantics can be defined cognitively and individualistically, pragmatics seems to be more amenable to a socially informed interpretation. This is the final option I plan to discuss, namely, that the semantics–pragmatics distinction is really a division between individual psychology and social cognition. The

---

[15] See Craig's (1990) genealogical approach to epistemology that makes use of a similar metaphor.

key idea is that pragmatic phenomena are *emergent* phenomena that arise in situations beyond the utterance shared by a speaker and a hearer.

Horn & Kecskes (2013) review two trends in social-inferential pragmatics (as I call it). The two trends are grouped under the terms 'socio-cultural interactional pragmatics' (SCIP) and 'intercultural pragmatics' (IP), respectively. Both approaches aim to extend the standard philosophical intention-based approaches. It's how they do this that differentiates them. SCIP makes two strides in distancing itself from the Gricean picture. First, it broadens the scope of pragmatics to include social and cultural constraints in addition to the linguistic constraints of the mainstream theories. Second, it goes beyond the utterance and immediate context level to characterise speaker meaning through the dialogue sequence (sets of utterances) or discourse segment. IP, on the other hand, incorporates intention-based classical views more centrally while refocusing the field on emergent phenomena within communication. 'In this approach interlocutors are considered as social beings searching for meaning with individual minds embedded in a socio-cultural collectivity' (Horn & Kecskes 2013, p. 365). The theory aims to place individual traits such as prior experience and salience in interaction with societal traits like cooperation, relevance, and intention.[16]

Take Stalnaker's model again. To a certain extent, it presupposes intracultural commonalities such as common norms, conventions, and shared knowledge among interlocutors. But in an intercultural situation, these features cannot be assumed. Interlocutors in this context need to co-create a common ground (perhaps a transient one) in which standard assumptions about how implicatures work might not hold. In terms of the philosophy of science, social-inferential pragmatics seems to be asking for de-idealisation. Specifically, social and cultural components of communicative practices are to be readmitted into the models. This could mean looking beyond the utterance to sets of utterances or dialogue data, or adding cultural constraints like the social roles of speakers, authority, and register to the theories under discussion. The idea is that speaker meaning and utterance interpretation should account for things like prior experience, salience, and emergent co-created intentions. As Horn & Kecskes indicate,

The proposition the speaker produces will hardly be the same as that which will be recovered by the hearer because interlocutors are individuals with different cognitive

---

[16] Just in case there isn't already too much jargon, Kecskes (2021) considers IP a brand of sociocognitive pragmatics that 'claims that while (social) cooperation is an intention-directed practice that is governed by relevance, (individual) egocentrism is an attention-oriented trait dominated by salience' (p. 593). This interplay between social cooperation and individual egocentrism explains both production and comprehension in communication, on this view.

predispositions, prior experiences, and different histories of use of the same words and expressions. (2013, p. 368)

Haugh (2013), for instance, argues that there is a neglected moral dimension to speaker meaning that can be captured by a deontic treatment of the commitments, obligations, and responsibilities of interlocutors. 'In other words, a view of speaker meaning as socially consequential in interaction' (Haugh 2013, p. 42). He doesn't consider his view to be in opposition to the standard (neo-) Gricean approaches. But the realm of pragmatic inference he focuses on goes well beyond the remit of simple utterance interpretation between an ideal speaker–hearer pair. Camp (2017) goes further to claim that Stalnaker's informational and propositional account of conversational dynamics distorts the conventional function of language that's inherently conditioned by real-world commitments, as exemplified by the consequences of phenomena like slurs and other 'expressives'.

I think that appreciating the social, cultural milieu in which pragmatic interaction takes places does offer us a genuinely unique perspective upon which to separate semantics from pragmatics. Nevertheless, despite the promise, there are issues with this approach to the distinction. Surely some sociolinguists might want to explore semantic theory under a similar sociological or socio-cognitive lens? If there's any plausibility (and I think there is) to expanding our understanding of semantics to the social dimension, then the neat dichotomy established by these processes will dry up very quickly. Perhaps the more general point is that semantics, too, can be de-idealised and *situated*. Still, one might argue that where this could be useful in the case of semantics, it's essential to the nature of pragmatics as an inherently social phenomenon.[17] I'll leave things unresolved for now but hopefully enhanced and enlightened.

In the next section, we'll explore different linguistic theories of pragmatics and ask how they might connect to or exploit the distinctions and divisions described in this section.

5.3   Practising Pragmatics

In this section, I want to investigate the ways in which these latter philosophical views on the semantics–pragmatics interface have made an impact on linguistic pragmatics. Or at the very least, how linguistic pragmatics might track some of the philosophical distinctions discussed above. The three theories I'll focus on are (1) optimality-theoretic (OT) pragmatics, (2) game-theoretic pragmatics, and (3) Bayesian approaches to pragmatics. I'll mostly focus on the elements

---

[17] I think a possible marriage between the cognitivist and social-inferential positions could be found in a distributed notion of cognition (Hutchins 2001). Of course, the same objection would arise in terms of why semantics cannot follow a similar path.

of these theories that aim to capture different essential features of pragmatics as discussed in the previous section.[18] Let's begin with OT pragmatics.

We've already met the basic architecture of OT in the first chapter. But let's consider the underlying concepts behind the formalism before revisiting it here. Zeevat (2008) describes it as rejuvenation of Jakobson's 'markedness theory':

> In the very concept of an optimalisation problem, there is a concept of blocking: some regularity is broken because in the particular case there is a better solution ... These explanations take the form of a system of constraints, a set of demands on outputs relative to a given input that are linearly ordered. (p. 87)

In a sense, this characterisation already makes the case for OT pragmatics quite clear. The 'regularity' being blocked (by the context) is the literal semantic meaning of the sentence or expression. But let's not get ahead of ourselves. Of course, it was the initial successes in phonology (Prince & Smolensky 1993) that fuelled its application to morphology, syntax, and semantics. As previously mentioned, OT specifies a relation between input and output values. It does so by means of a GENerator, which produces a set of possible output candidates linked to the features of the input, and an EVALuator, which takes the set of universal constraints, ordered by a particular ranking, to generate the best or optimal candidate from GEN. In phonology and syntax, production is key. They're 'unidirectional'. Given a set of possible forms, the speaker or producer's perspective is paramount. Semantics and pragmatics, on the other hand, privilege not just the speaker but also the interpreter (or hearer) of the utterance. This is the first way in which OT incorporates a perspective that aims to capture some of the uniqueness of pragmatics. Blutner's (2000) notion of 'bidirectional optimisation' 'integrates the speaker and the hearer perspective into a simultaneous optimization procedure' (Blutner 2011, p. 163). This method is encoded by two conditions: (1) interpretative optimisation, and (2) expressive optimisation. (1) selects the most coherent interpretation and (2) blocks all the output that admits more efficient processing from alternatives. Specific proposals will encode these conditions by means of specific rankings of constraints (see Zeevat 2007 for one such proposal).

With this basic structure in mind, it's not hard to see how the PoR can be modelled. Blutner (2011) discusses two particular constraints that can do the job: EFFECT and EFFORT. The first would map on to the number of cognitive or contextual effects produced by the utterance and the second on the processing effort required to produce those effects. With a violable ranking from 'EFFECT>>EFFORT', one could already capture the idea of the maximum effect for minimum effort that characterises the framework. Of course, much

---

[18] All of these approaches pay due homage to Grice, of course. Thus, his influence won't be directly measured here.

more would need to be done in order to represent the full theory or to deal with tricky cases.

It's important to know that OT was initially proposed as a cognitive theory, aligned with the mentalism of generative grammar. Thus, it makes for a good partner to the cognitivist position on the pragmatic demarcation problem. But as Blutner and others have shown, more normative neo-Gricean approaches are also amenable to OT treatment. Take, for instance, Horn's concept of 'division of pragmatic labour', or the idea that 'unmarked forms tend to be used for unmarked situations and marked forms for marked situations' (Horn 1984, p. 26). To model this kind of principle, something like partial blocking (McCawley 1978) seems necessary. This is when an expected form (*fishes*) is not completely blocked by the existence of another form (*fish*). For a classic case, consider the following pair:

9. Reinhard killed the typologist.
10. Reinhard caused the typologist to die.

In (9), we have the unmarked case that maps on to the standard or stereotypical meaning (implying intention or culpability). In (10), we retrieve a weaker unintentional or accidental reading from the marked sentence. Bidirectional OT predicts that the less complex or marked form f_1 in (9) (the lexical causative) will naturally correspond with the stereotypical meaning m_1 implying direct causation. Why the alternative happens is harder to predict. 'In terms of this notion of optimality, however, Blutner is not able yet to explain how the more complex form [10] can have an interpretation at all, in particular, why it will be interpreted as non-stereotypical killing' (van Rooij & Franke 2022).[19]

From this, it's clear that the fundamental tenets of the cognitivist approach, and specifically RT, can be captured by the interplay of violable constraints. Furthermore, the PoR itself is defined in terms of optimality or the expectation of at most one optimally relevant interpretation. Although OT doesn't enforce a one-optimal-candidate output structure, a given formulation could always stipulate such a condition. The bidirectionality of the theory also tracks the dynamics of speaker–hearer interaction to great extent. So far so good. What's lacking is the modelling of more complex dialogue data or social constraints. It's unclear how to incorporate social cognition or cultural constraints within OT, especially since these kinds of constraints tend to emerge at the collective level. At its base, OT is a formal decision procedure. The kinds of ingredients it allows tend to be formally characterisable variables.

Game-theoretic approaches to pragmatics offer a home both for aspects of the social-inferential demarcation and some of the indexical conception. The

---

[19] See Blutner (2000) for a bidirectional OT treatment of partial blocking and a weakened notion of optimality in order to account for this issue.

latter should be unsurprising as Lewis' (1969) signalling games account of conventional meaning served as an inspiration not only to his own pragmatic account of scorekeeping (see above) but also later seminal developments in terms of Parikh's (1988, 1992) work on strategic inference in games of partial information. We'll start with some basics of signalling games that, despite being somewhat dated, are still seen as a foundation for the field. Then, we'll look at some advancements of this picture in terms of evolutionary approaches that could possibly account for certain social dynamics.

Lewis' (1969) account was designed to show how messages without pre-existing meaning can nonetheless convey content or communicate something. In pragmatics, the game is slightly different. The messages do have content or meaning prior to communication. A signalling game is a game with an informational imbalance between a sender s and receiver r. The imbalance favours s since she sees some state t that both participants are in. The receiver has to perform the action of interpretation, conditioned by the message sent by s. The messages are in the set of forms F and the states in their own set T. Since we are modelling pragmatics, $\forall f \in F \subset T$. This just means that each message already has a meaning. Two further important concepts from game theory are *game models* and *solution concepts*, respectively.

Game models are familiar from famous cases like the prisoner's dilemma or the Monty Hall problem. They usually consist of a formal game structure and an informal narrative explaining the situation. The game structure specifies the number of players, their individual strategies, information states, and their possible payoffs in terms of a utility function. In our case, there are two important strategies: the sender's strategy and the receiver's strategy. The former is a function from T to F. The receiver's strategy goes in the opposite direction, from F to T.[20] In standard cooperative games, the sender's and receiver's expected utility is the same since they're both seeking successful communication.[21]

The solution concept specifies what players should do or how they should behave. The most well known of these is *Nash equilibrium*. 'A Nash equilibrium is a set of choices, one for each player, such that no player would be strictly better off when only she would deviate from the specified set of choices' (Franke 2013, p. 270). It's a bit like a stalemate. Now, there might not be a unique Nash equilibrium, and thus solution concept, in every game. And other solution concepts do exist. Unfortunately, we can't get into all the details here (see the *Further Reading* section at the end of the chapter). What's important

---

[20] These are 'pure' strategies defined as functions from states to messages. Mixed strategies introduce probabilities.

[21] In the prisoner's dilemma, players cannot communicate and they're not necessarily cooperating.

for us is to attempt to understand what game theory is meant to achieve in pragmatics specifically.

Let's review. A signalling game acts like a model of one utterance, made by a speaker, and its interpretation, an action taken by a receiver/listener. In the standard case, the speaker knows the state t and the listener doesn't. The speaker has a number of alternative meaningful forms f_n at her disposal as messages she can send in order to convey the state to the listener. There's a metric for weighing things, like relevance, in terms of the utility function for each player (and disutility or costs for more costly signals). Now, things get interesting when we start to think about the strategies each player can use in a given context to achieve their shared aims (successful communication). Lastly, since this isn't a purely mathematical exercise, '[g]ame-theoretic explanations of pragmatic phenomena aim to single out those sender–receiver strategy pairs that correspond to empirically attested behavior as optimal and/or rational solution of the game problem' (van Rooij & Franke 2022). Again, Horn's division of pragmatic labour illustrates the point nicely. Faced with a choice between two forms, differing in markedness, if the sender chooses the more costly (marked) signal, the receiver is likely to interpret the signal non-stereotypically, that is, contrary to its conventional meaning.

Parikh's (1988, 1992) work, which has been highly influential in the emerging field of game-theoretic pragmatics, treats all pragmatic problems as essentially disambiguation games. He models the resolution of pragmatic problems in terms of games of partial information (GPIs), which are kinds of signalling games. Take the case of scope ambiguities familiar from semantics (see Chapter 4). In sentences like *Every linguist likes a derivation*, the more contextually costly interpretation involving all the linguists of the world fawning over one particular derivation is unlikely. But in these cases, Nash equilibrium by itself won't settle the matter (as there are two corresponding to each semantic derivation). Parikh suggests that the first, the so-called Pareto equilibrium, dominates the second one in order to resolve this issue. It's like a higher-level filter on all the equilibria generated by these games. This solution concept isn't flawless and there are others on the market. The important point is that pragmatic problems are coordination problems, on this view, involving resolutions that consider both players' individual states and strategies.

At this level, Lewis' scopekeeping model seems quite fitting. Game models can be parameterised and indexicalised. For each stage of a game, strategies can be formally represented similar to the way Lewis does for baseball in terms of player turns, runs, innings, and so on. In fact, Parikh's work at a glance can look like it endorses the indexicalist demarcation of pragmatic space. Disambiguation problems start with competing conventional semantic meanings, and a rational, utility-maximising process takes over from there, that is, pragmatics as an extension of semantics. However, this way of viewing pragmatics has its limitations.

First, one is interested not only in the equilibria upon which interlocutors eventually agree but also in the reasoning process that leads there. Second, the models tend to overgenerate ambiguities, as every difference in the complexity of a message is predicted to lead to meaning differentiation . . . Finally, it has been debated whether GPIs capture the relevant features of dialogue situations and, in particular, whether pragmatic problems should really be considered disambiguation problems. (Benz & Stevens 2018, p. 179)

Some of the recent advancements in game-theoretic pragmatics aim to capture more diachronic and social evolutionary dynamics within the broader framework. Let's take the latter first. Complex interactional models like the iterated best response (IBR) model take Grice's informal theory of mind to the next level (Franke 2011; Jäger 2011). This model takes as its core the idea that rational agents reason about each other's beliefs in an iterated manner. In other words, speakers and hearers take each other's complex states into account, such as 'I believe that you believe that I believe . . .' and so on. This approach starts with some default strategy of one participant, say the hearer, then models how each other participant reasons or responds to each possible action on the assumption of their partner's strategies. The iteration stops when it converges on a stable mapping between types and messages or states and interpretations. Diving deeper are dynamic evolutionary accounts. These don't just aim at modelling behaviour (or finding static equilibria) but explaining how an outcome was arrived at by a gradual process of adaptation over generations. Using insights from both macro- or population-level dynamics (such as replicator dynamics) or micro-level dynamics (focusing on changes in individuals over time), the theory of game-theoretic pragmatics can be richly enhanced. As Franke (2013) mentions, the micro-level evolutionary dynamics opens up a wealth of interesting applications to linguistic theory and pragmatics. The sociology of friendship networks has been used to study more realistic models of interactional structures in small-world networks and social networks (Watts & Strogatz 1998), while 'conditional imitation', a pure strategy involving occasionally surveying your neighbour's strategy and updating yours based on your observations, can account for the emergence of Horn's division of labour-style equilibria (called 'Horn-languages' in the field).

Lastly, one ubiquitous property underlying much of communicative practice in the real world is uncertainty. In our case, unknown contextual variables inevitably affect pragmatic phenomena and analysis. The standard, and in general most successful, way of modelling uncertainty in any domain is by means of probability distributions. We'll investigate probabilistic linguistics in more detail in Chapter 7. My method here will be a little more circumscribed.

First, I'll introduce Bayes' theorem and what it means. Then, I'll discuss the ways in which linguistic pragmatics can adhere to it, before connecting these issues to our general demarcation problem.

Bayes' famous theorem is a metric to calculate the probability, or rather conditional probability, of an event occurring based on a previous outcome that occurred in similar circumstances. Or in slightly more technical terminology, 'the theorem analyses the posterior probability of hypothesis H given a signal S, $p(H|S)$ as the product of the prior probability of the hypothesis $p(H)$ and the likelihood $p(S|H)$ divided by the probability of the signal $p(S)$' (Zeevat 2015, p. 2).[22] The 'prior probability', or simply the 'prior', is the probability of an event or hypothesis before the signal occurred (the hypothesis in our case can be seen as an interpretation). The 'posterior probability' is the revised probability of an event, or H, occurring after the signal or the probability of event A occurring given that event B has occurred. When you cannot compute the posterior probability by direct means, due to massive uncertainty or ambiguity, Bayes' theorem is unavoidable. In pragmatics, where conventional meaning is underdetermined by linguistic form, uncertainty abounds. Context introduces the need for probability since compositional meaning won't be sufficient for interpretation in context. As Zeevat notes, '[i]t is also easy to see that very often disambiguation cannot be explained by an appeal to hard facts and logic, but needs to appeal to what is probable in the world' (2015, p. 3). Time and time again, in this chapter, we've encountered the idea of pragmatic resolution or interpretation as a rational inference to the best explanation. Such inferences cannot ignore probabilities and might be argued to essentially depend on them.

There are different ways in which linguistic pragmatics can depend on Bayesian probability. Zeevat (2015) outlines six of them:

a. the proposal to compute the most probable NL interpretations by taking the product of prior and likelihood
b. the hypothesis that the human brain has implemented the proposal in a.
c. the Bayesian logic of interpretation: analysing rational interpretation as finding the maximum product of prior and likelihood
d. coordination on meaning using Bayesian interpretation
e. analysing intention recognition by Bayesian interpretation
f. switching to causal models for determining prior and likelihood. (p. 2)

He admits that (a) and (b) are to be settled by future science. It's (c) and (d) that most concern us here since they advocate for a Bayesian approach to the interpretation of natural language in context. For instance, according to this

[22] The standard notion for Bayes' theorem looks as follows, for two events A and B:

$$P(A|B) = \frac{P(A)P(B|A)}{P(B)}$$

approach, good interpretations require priors and likelihoods (or conditional probabilities) to be higher than zero. Interpretations with the same likelihoods need to be settled by lower priors and vice versa. With this, we can attempt to reinterpret Gricean implicatures in terms of probabilities. Again, Zeevat is optimistic that we can do this without the explicit need for the cooperative principle:

> For example, anything that increases the relevance of the utterance interpretation is automatically something that increases the likelihood of the interpretation. If manner is defined as choosing the most probable way of expressing whatever the speaker wants to express, it is also directly related to likelihood: the speaker then boosts the likelihood of the interpretation. Transgressions of manner reduce likelihood and may be the trigger of additional inferences to bring it up again. Quality is related to prior maximization: overt falsehoods do not qualify for literal interpretation. Underinformative contributions are misleading since they will lead – by the increase in likelihood due to extra relevance– to unwarranted exhaustivity effects. Overinformative contributions will merely force accommodation of extra issues and are not harmful. (2015, p. 7)

In other words, we get the logic of pragmatics without normative directives or maxims. Each instance of a maxim flouting or an implicature trigger can be explained with only reference to Bayesian statistics. The kind of reduction or parsimony the neo-Griceans and relevance theorists were after seems to be within our grasp. In addition, if other aspects of our cognition and our belief formation behaviour can be similarly explained by a generally Bayesian framework, we have a much more naturalistic approach to pragmatics. This approach dovetails with the cognitivist solution to the demarcation problem, but it would most likely embrace a more domain-general approach than relevance theory does, for example.

Zeevat's analysis indicates that pragmatics can be Bayesian in what Franke & Jäger (2016) call 'the strong sense'. The weak sense in which pragmatics can be Bayesian is if we simply represent the subjective uncertainty of language users by means of probability distributions. Some versions of the game-theoretic and even OT approaches do this to a large extent. For the strong sense, we need the weak sense and 'we also use Bayes' rule to describe how, in particular, listeners' interpretations are a form of abductive reasoning, inferring the most likely (epistemic or intentional) state that would have triggered the speaker (under a reasonable model of utterance production) to say what he actually said (and not something else)' (Franke & Jäger 2016, p. 13). In fact, they subsume game theory and Bayesian approaches under the overarching rubric of probabilistic pragmatics.

In this section, we've considered three contemporary linguistic pragmatic theories. We scanned them for traces of the philosophical distinctions we established in terms of the indexical conception, the cognitivist position, and the social-inferential view. Our forensic investigation led to some clues. Of course, OT, game-theoretic, and Bayesian approaches to pragmatics are deeply interconnected in practice.[23] As a theoretical exercise, I isolated some of their respective components, and abstracted to a certain extent over the overlap, in order to position each theory in relation to a philosophical answer to the pragmatic demarcation problem. In reality, each linguistic theory incorporates various aspects of the philosophical conceptions, with a bias towards cognitivist approaches.

5.4   Summary

This chapter has delved into the vicissitudes of contextual pragmatic inference in terms of its theoretical origins, philosophical distinctions, and practical applications. Understanding how linguistic pragmatics links up with possible answers to the demarcation of semantics and pragmatics can not only serve as a useful theoretical exercise in theory comparison but also as a tool for future hypothesis formation. Pragmatics as a field seems to be a rich mixture of logical and probabilistic phenomena, an interplay between individual psychological mechanisms and social inferential patterns, collective emergence, and rational abductive reasoning practices. The field has grown perhaps faster than any other subfield of linguistics in recent decades. The philosophy is lagging somewhat behind. My hope is that we've at least covered some important, if not neglected, topics of philosophical interest within the study of natural language pragmatics. In the next chapter, we'll traverse even more uncharted philosophical terrain in the study of phonology.

Further Reading

Although there's a lot of work on philosophical pragmatics and growing literature on linguistic pragmatics, the philosophy of pragmatics is slightly less prevalent on bookshelve across the world. Nevertheless, below are a few offerings that expand on some of the topics picked up in this chapter.

- A good place to start thinking about the distinction between semantics and pragmatics is Zoltán Szabó's (2005) volume *Semantics versus Pragmatics* (Oxford University Press). The book contains chapters by seminal figures in both the philosophy of language, such as Herman Cappelen, Stephen Neale, Scott Soames, and Francois Recanati, and linguistics, such as Mandy Simons, Kent Bach, and Robert Stainton. Many authors, like the present book, live

---

[23] For the connection between OT and game-theoretic accounts, see Dekker & van Rooij (2000) and Franke & Jäger (2012).

in both worlds. It provides clear overviews of the issues and some novel proposals on issues such as presupposition (Simons) and focus (Glanzberg).

- There are classic texts on relevance theory, cited in this chapter, by Deidre Wilson and Dan Sperber. For a more contemporary and comprehensively updated book on where the theory is now and how it connects to further debates, I recommend their *Meaning and Relevance* (2012, Cambridge University Press). Many of the chapters are authored by either Wilson or Sperber (and/or Sperber and Wilson in some combination), with some additional chapters on cross-disciplinary issues such as pragmatics and evolution and experimental pragmatics including other collaborations.

- For a volume on game-theoretic approaches, Anton Benz, Gerhard Jäger, and Robert van Rooij's (2006) *Game Theory and Pragmatics* (Palgrave Macmillan) is an essential read. It features some of the influential players in the inauguration of the field including the editors Robert Stalnaker and Prashant Parikh. The book serves well as an overview of the field but also as an indication of its application to other debates such as the pragmatics of debate and evolutionary dynamics of lexical meaning associations.

- Reinhard Blutner and Henk Zeevat's (2004) *Optimality Theory and Pragmatics* (Palgrave Macmillan) contains eleven chapters on the application of OT to pragmatics. The editor's introduction is one of the most useful guides to the philosophical underpinnings of the field, and each chapter thereafter is an exercise in linguistic pragmatics, ranging from analyses of presupposition triggers, stressed pronouns, mismatches in input–output pairs, to different demonstrative choices in Swedish.

- For a thoroughly Bayesian approach to linguistics with special focus on interpretation, Henk Zeevat's (2014) *Language Production and Interpretation: Linguistics meets Cognition* (Brill) is an excellent choice. The book takes on more than just pragmatics and pushes a controversial and ambitious project arguing that interpretation is a form of perception. It's a formally rigorous but still philosophically rich text. Chapter 4 on interpretation links most closely with the themes of the present chapter.

6   Signs, Sounds, Action!

Phonology is an extremely important subdiscipline of linguistics. Historically, phonetics and phonology headlined the work of great early linguists such as Panini and Al-Khalil Abu Amr Al-Farahidi. In the twentieth century, generative phonology fuelled the larger movement and, as we'll see, arguably retained the original transformational architecture when the rest of the framework underwent theoretical turbulence.

Despite the impact of phonology on the study of human language, philosophers have paid it surprisingly little attention. I want to remedy some of these missed opportunities. I cannot, of course, discuss every possible philosophical implication or insight hidden in the depths of phonological research. Here, I plan to resurrect one feature of a reasonably well known philosophical debate on the nature of the phoneme that dates back a few decades and directly concerns the idiosyncrasy of the field and its target domain. Although I don't endorse the erstwhile line, I'll embrace its spirit. To be more specific, in Section 6.1, I'll present the claim, courtesy of Bromberger & Halle (1989), that there's something special about phonology. I'll expand on their particular suggestion and present my own formulation in its stead. In Section 6.2, I'll broaden the scope of phonology to include modalities such as sign and touch, all the while maintaining the claim of its uniqueness. Lastly, I explore the possible connection between philosophical action theory and phonology (broadly construed) in Section 6.3.

6.1   Phonetics, Phonology, and Philosophy

One of the most interesting philosophical questions to emerge from research into the phonology of natural language revolves around the most basic unit of analysis: the *phoneme*. Theoretical work on the phoneme dates back at least to the Polish phonologist Jan Baudouin de Courtenay (1845–1929). But it was Daniel Jones (1950) who perfected the modern concept that's widely assumed in linguistics today. So what is a phoneme? According to Brown (2013), who follows most standard introductions here,

The modern position is that the phoneme is an abstract unit of a language (e.g. the English phonemic /s/) that consists of sounds that (a) are phonetically similar (i.e. produced in similar ways) and (b) function in predictable, non-overlapping environments. (p. 2)

One cannot say that the sounds are phonetically identical since /s/ will be realised differently in different phonetic contexts, that is, surrounding vowels and consonants. In words like *Sapir*, *salt*, and *linguists*, the sibilant sounds different. The idea is that these slightly different manifestations of the phoneme are *allophones*, or the physical acoustic realisations of the overarching phoneme. The second element of the definition above concerns the idea of 'non-overlapping environments'. In English, the bilabial stop /b/ and labiodental fricative /v/ are two distinct phonemes represented orthographically as 'b' and 'v', respectively. This means that 'b' and 'v' distinguish the identity or meaning of words like 'bat' and 'vat' in English. In Spanish, the letters 'b' and 'v' refer to the same sound $/\beta/$, or the voiced bilabial approximant. Thus, they're represented by the same phoneme. Again, that doesn't mean that there aren't different allophones generated by the surrounding words and syllables. For example, Spanish contains the /b/ as an onset, as in *bajo* (short) or *banco* (bank). But it does ensure that 'b' and 'v' won't mark a lexical or semantic difference generally.[1] The phoneme itself is then 'a class of sounds or phonetic segments in complementary distribution' (Egré 2018, p. 676).

Two issues immediately follow from the above definition. One relates to abstract theoretical posits of the grammar and the other to a powerful methodological tool that's transcended phonology to find uses in both syntax and semantics. We'll focus on the latter here.[2] The definition above, ubiquitous in the literature, assumes that the central unit of phonology is an abstract concept known as a phoneme. Phonemes cannot be mere collections of sounds since the sounds comprising a phoneme are not identical. Nor can they be statistical averages or approximates as the average of all the allophonic variation in a given phoneme is unlikely to yield the scientifically useful abstract concept. Determining the precise nature of the phoneme has further implications, none more important than the relationship between phonetics and phonology itself.

On the standard or generative view, the phoneme belongs to phonology, which is viewed as a formal computational theory. Phonemes are composed of binary features such as [± voiced], [± nasal], and [± anterior] denoting vocal positions from which the relevant sounds are produced. Technically, consonants are specified in terms of three parameters: voicing, place of articulation, and

[1] Of course, homophones like *baca* (luggage rack) and *vaca* (cow) do exist, but they serve only to emphasise the point.
[2] The former, or methodological, issue concerns the use of so-called minimal pairs as data for theory. Minimal pairs, in phonology, are two words with identical sounds except for one. Finding such pairs indicates contrastive distribution, a key tool in identifying phonemes. Extending this methodology to phrases and sentences is more tricky as additional material (like context, semantics, etc.) can interfere with the nature of a contrastive class.

manner of articulation. For example, a consonant can either provoke vocal cord vibration or not. This determines voice or voicelessness. Places of articulation are split between active articulators and passive ones, such as the lips, upper teeth, tip of the tongue, hard palate, and so on. The articulators themselves are like gates or air filters, and the degree to which they restrict or permit airflow determines the manner of articulation (e.g. stop, fricative, approximant). Vowels tend to be voiced for the most part (although devoiced vowels do occur). Here, the relevant parameters are the height of the tongue body with relation to the hard or soft palate, the position of the tongue at the front or back of the oral cavity, and the nature of the lip rounding. The (many) details should not detain us here.

Chomsky & Halle (1968) created a highly influential model of phonology, *The Sound Pattern of English*, or the SPE model, in which phonemes like /b/ are presented as feature matrices containing the kinds of parameters discussed above, as in Figure 6.1.

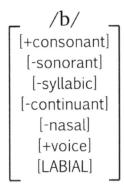

Figure 6.1 Phoneme /b/

In terms of its ontology, the phoneme is 'the basic form of a segment (consonant or vowel) that is stored in the mental grammar' (Paster 2015, p. 526). Thus, phonology is the study of a mental computational system that interfaces with physical sound systems in phonetics. A familiar story. On the SPE model, there are two levels of representation. The first is the morphophonemic level that applies to both morphological and phonology structure, and the second is the phonetic level applying to the physiological processes involved in sound production. The two levels are connected by derivation rules, similar to the syntax of the standard theory, involving transformations.[3] Like syntax, phonological structure is generally considered to be hierarchical. Consider the standard representation of syllable structure in Figure 6.2.

---

[3] In fact, the transformations of SPE were the same kind of rewrite rules used in syntax. In phonology, these kinds of rules tend to overgenerate structures.

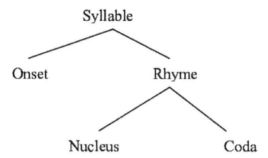

Figure 6.2 Hierarchical syllable structure

In most cases, the *onset* is usually a consonant, the *nucleus* a vowel, and the *coda* another consonant. The *rhyme* (or sometimes *rime*) contains the nucleus and the coda as daughters in the hierarchical tree.[4] In autosegmental phonology, features are represented hierarchically in a structure called a 'feature geometry' (see Figure 6.3). The initial idea was to represent universal phonological features along the lines of UG in syntax.[5]

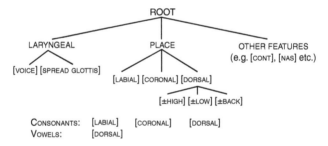

Figure 6.3 Feature geometry (from Lahiri & Reetz 2010)

Despite the possibility or prevalence of hierarchical representation, phonology differs from syntax in a number of respects. Unlike syntax, especially later generative theories, the sense in which phonetics is derived from phonology is ordered and special. Bromberger & Halle (1989) make this point forcefully. They accept that the government and binding (GB) model of generative linguistics imposes no theoretically important ordering among the principles that govern the various levels of representation. Nonetheless, they insist that phonology is different.

---

[4] Moraic phonology maintains hierarchical structure in syllables but eschews the need for a rhyme.
[5] You might be wondering where OT phonology fits into this picture. In principle, it's not incompatible with these approaches, and practitioners (including its originators) have been noncommittal about its nature as a derivational vs declarative theory (see Smolensky 2001).

Phonology, on the other hand, is primarily concerned with the connections between surface forms that can serve as input to our articulatory machinery (and to our auditory system) and the abstract underlying forms in which words are stored in memory. Whereas syntax is concerned with the relations among representations that encode different types of information requiring different types of notation, phonology is concerned with the relationship between representations that encode the same type of information–phonetic information–but do so in ways that serve distinct functions: articulation and audition, on the one hand, and memory, on the other. Since underlying phonological representations of words are stored in speakers' permanent memory, whereas phonetic surface representations are generated only when a word figures in an actual utterance, there is a clear and theoretically significant sense in which underlying representations are prior to surface representations, a sense that justifies thinking of the surface form as 'derived' from the underlying form. (Bromberger & Halle 1989, p. 53)

This, according to them, is what makes phonology special. In other words, the sequential ordering of the rules of derivation matter in phonology but not in syntax (or presumably semantics). The abstract phonological level, where the phoneme resides, is transformed into the actual phonetic surface-level pronunciation characterised by ordered rules applying to the kinds of feature matrices we mentioned before. Bromberger & Halle offer synchronic and diachronic evidence for their view. These arguments are slightly dated. I'll provide some updated evidence for their claim based on generative (or rule-based) phonology supplemented with contemporary *autosegmental representation*, which originated in Goldsmith (1976). One thing that the original SPE model struggled with was tone in tonal languages. The problem is that binary features on vowels seem to force an incompatible feature valence (both + and - for feature [H tone]) for contour tones, that is, tones that shift from one pitch to another within a single syllable or word. In autosegmental phonology, tones get their own level, or *tier*. They're linked to the vowel segments via *association lines*. This structure allows for vowels to be linked to tones in a non-one-to-one mapping, solving the issue above. Thus, the view extracts tones from standard feature matrices while retaining the ordering component.

[J]ust as feature matrices for individual segments have to be ordered from left to right in order to represent the sequential ordering of segments, the features on the tonal tier are ordered from left to right by the same convention. (Paster 2015, p. 528)

Interestingly, pace Bromberger & Halle (1989), autosegmental phonology follows a government and binding-like structure of multiple independent tiers of representation linked by association lines.[6] Phonological rules, in this theory, can modify or *transform* segments, as in SPE, but also manipulate the connections between tiers, that is, link or delink them. We'll see some further

---

[6] I'm not saying it was influenced by such a model since that would involve anachronism as GB was published after Goldstein's MIT thesis.

aspects of the theory in Section 6.3. For now, my purpose is to update Bromberger & Halle's (1989) argument as to the specialness of phonology based on its inherent sequential ordering of elements. Rules naturally impose some order of application. Paster defines the notion of 'crucial ordering' to identify those cases 'when the output of one rule affects whether (or how) another rule will apply' (2015, p. 538). She offers the case of devoicing and schwa epenthesis in English as an example. The idea is that schwa epenthesis must precede devoicing in standard examples in which the plural suffix /-z/ is realised as [ez] when the final segment is a sibilant, [s] for non-sibilants (like stops), and [z] in other cases. Triples like *garages–cats–eyes* and *horses–pilots–poems* illustrate the paradigm. The two rules that capture these data are (a) and (b) below:

a. Devoicing: z→ *s*/ [-voice]_
b. Schwa epenthesis: → *e*/ [+strident]_z

It's not hard to see that applying (a) before (b) in cases such as 'horses' will result in the wrong derivation. In order to account for the data, (b) must apply before (a). Thus, order matters to phonology. We'll return to this point below as well. Nevertheless, if we've learned anything from the pragmatic demarcation project of the previous chapter, neat dichotomies are rarely foolproof. The almost Cartesian dualistic picture of phonology as a mental rule system and phonetics as a physical acoustic one has some connections to the overarching generative programme in syntax. Phonetics is a descriptive enterprise. Given a set of sounds, the International Phonetic Alphabet (IPA), maybe a palatograph, spectograph, and/or an electroaerometer, you can determine the precise nature of the sound made by an individual on a given occasion. However, phonetics won't tell you about the distribution of these sounds, which ones are incompatible, which are absent, or which varieties map on to the same phonemes. It also won't smooth over the dialectical and idiolectical variation present in every speech event. This is the job of phonology. On this much, there seems to be agreement. Whether phonology is the study of abstract entities, mental constructs, or social norms seems to be the more prominent philosophical question.

Trubetzkoy (1958) draws the line between a speech event, accessible to our sense organs (and a fortiori our phonetic instruments), and the linguistic system as a social institution transcending individuals and space and time.

Accordingly, there are two types of the study of sounds, one that concentrates on sounds as units of speech events, and the other that concentrates on sounds as units of the linguistic system. The former, called **phonetics**, uses methodology of the natural sciences, whereas the latter, called *phonology*, uses the methodology of the human science. (Itkonen 2001, p. 4)

Phonology is, then, the study of certain kinds of social norms. Norms are not platonic objects nor individual mental entities. As previously mentioned (with the definition of phonemes), the standard position has a more mentalist ontology. But what does it mean to say that phonology studies mental computations? Again, Bromberger & Halle (1992) have a specific take on the matter. In rejecting the role of bona fide abstract types within phonology, they advocate for a thoroughly physicalist interpretation of the field. In one way, this eliminates the kind of distinction assumed by theorists like Trubetzkoy and even contemporary generative phonologists who assign phonetics and phonology different scientific statuses. For them, the central insight is that speech events are actions, and actions are brought about by intentions qua purposive mental stances. In this sense, their view is action-theoretic. I'll offer a similar view in Section 6.3. Itkonen (2001) criticises both the originality of their claims and the execution of their argument. He asks whether they 'succeed in establishing a purely physicalist phonology, and eo ipso, in obliterating the distinction between phonetics and phonology?' (p. 7). I think he misunderstands the project. Bromberger & Halle (1992) don't intend on 'obliterating' the distinction between phonetics and phonology. They distinguish between phonetic transcriptions of token utterances, 'as a record of articulator movements and positionings' (p. 24), and what they call 'phonetic intentions', which are the result of mental computations. Tools like oscillagraphs will record the sounds or speech noises produced by an individual speaker at time *t*. These noises exist in the realm of phonetics, which is a subset of acoustics or the study of all noises and sounds. They put the point somewhat jocularly as follows:

Utterances form a natural domain with other noises, the domain of acoustical theory. To deny this would be like holding that elephants, because they have a sex life, are not, like rocks, physical objects subject to the laws of mechanics! On the other hand, to deny that utterances constitute an autonomous domain, the domain of phonology, would be like holding that, because elephants are subject to the laws of mechanics, like rocks, they have no sex life! (Bromberger & Halle 1992, p. 34)

Presumably, 'sex life' here stands proxy for a domain of intentional behaviour that governs physical action. But intentions need not be occult. They too exist in the physical, causal realm. Nor are Bromberger & Halle incapable of talking about types as useful theoretical constructs (as Itkonen seems to think). They're merely denying the ontological status of types as individual nonspatiotemporal entities that somehow causally interact with the physical realm.[7] Where they do falter is in terms of the psycholinguistic proposal. If

---

[7] For a view that endorses a platonic account of phonology, see Neef (2018). See Nefdt (2018), in the same volume, for general reasons why Platonism isn't the only way to be a realist about types in linguistics. Bromberger & Halle rely quite heavily on the framework developed in Bromberger (1989) of a bottom-up scientific platonism.

phonological derivations, rules based on feature matrices, express or represent phonetic intentions to produce certain kinds of actions, then these intentions must be mental processes of some sort. Upon this much they agree. They affirm (against potential critics) that 'we view phonology as [being] about processes in real time responsible for the occurrence of tokens' (Bromberger & Halle 1992, p. 35). This is indeed a physicalist position but not clearly a generativist one. Generative linguistics, including phonology, has always pitched its mentalism at a level higher than that of real-time processing mechanisms. This is often referred to as the competence model of grammar. Bromberger & Halle seem to want to have their generativist cake and eat it. But the ideal competence model is not readily edible.[8] For an account of phonology that truly engages with real-time processes, we'll need more than just phonetic transcriptions and computational phonological rules since these latter rules can be realised in myriad *actual* ways within our cognition system. Put in stronger terms, they would need to bridge the competence–performance divide in order to make some progress on the phonetics–phonology connection. This is both a tall order and an unnecessary detour. Nevertheless, I think they were on to something with the action-theoretic part of their proposal. In the rest of the chapter, I plan to explore the deep connections between actions and phonology more closely.

For now, we can take three general properties from the above discussion: (1) phonological structure is hierarchically represented; (2) phonology is the study of ordered rules linked to fleeting or fading signals; and (3) phonology is grounded in action. In the next section, I want to follow the contemporary practice of extending phonology to sign and other modalities beyond sound and acoustics. I'll argue that these three properties are further exemplified by such a move.

6.2   Gesture and Sign

Before we set off, we should be clear about what the topic is *not* going to be. There's a sad and long history of sign languages being dismissed as mere gestural impoverished communication unequal to spoken languages. Sign languages, on these parochial, unscientific views, were not considered natural languages in the same way that English, isiXhosa, or Kiswahili are. Deaf children were often forced to lip read and sound out spoken speech. This kind of social stigma has held scientific research into the linguistic nature of sign language systems back decades. Thankfully, now, the scientific consensus as to the rich syntactic, semantic, and phonological structure of sign languages has been reached. Our focus, of course, will be on the latter. We'll proceed with a brief overview of

---

[8] For a more sophisticated generative phonological account of how phonology can be grounded in psychology, see Hale & Reiss (2000). I'll offer a different route to cognition in Section 6.3.

some of the basics of sign language phonology before highlighting some of the important properties it exemplifies of phonology in general.

The basic unit of sign language phonology is the *chereme* (from the Ancient Greek word for 'hand'). Stokoe (1960) originally analysed it in terms of three categories: handshape, location, and movement. Since then, orientation has been motivated as an additional parameter as well as nonmanual movement in the face and body (Pfau & Quer 2010). In the previous terminology, these are the articulators of sign language. Stokoe made a further claim concerning temporality. Cheremes, according to him, are organised simultaneously and not sequentially. If true, this would mark a distinction between cheremes and phonemes. Stokoe's influential insight was that sign language phonology involved signs that possess parts. He stated his position as follows:

Signs cannot be performed one aspect at a time, as speakers can utter one segment of sound at a time. Signers can of course display handshapes of manual signs ad libitum, but they cannot demonstate any significant sign action without using something to make that action somewhere. (Stokoe 1980, p. 369)

He then, somewhat cryptically, insinuates that only by 'an act of imagination', not segmentation, can we isolate aspects of the sign individually as if rotating a mental picture in one's mind. Later phonologists disagreed. There are now moraic (Perlmutter 1990) and autosegmental (Sandler 1986) models of sign language on the market. Stokoe's simultaneous bundle theory was challenged by Liddell (1984), who showed that 'the majority of signs are segmentable into sequentially-organized movements and holds' (Wilcox & Wilcox 2015, p. 844). Liddell's movement–hold model assigns identical structure to signs and spoken words. In some senses, signs are phonologically similar to spoken words, hence the need to extend phonology to cover sign languages. Sequentiality in sign languages is now well attested across grammatical models. There's some disagreement on which level of representation is the best fit for this property, but Stokoe's original claim as to simultaneity has been overturned for the most part. For example, verbal agreement, across different sign languages, tends to involve referential loci in the signing space for subject and object referents moving from the locus of the former to the latter. The most prominent model that incorporates sequentiality is the Location–Movement–Location (LML) model. Here, similar to Liddell's account, we analyse a sign as two static locations linked by a movement so that a sign is essentially assigned an LML structure. There's an inherent sequentiality to this account. As Sandler (2012) further notes, '[t]he point for phonology is that the first and last location of the sign must be independently identified by the grammar, providing good evidence for the existence of each in the phonological structure of the sign' (p. 169). Lexical compounds provide additional evidence for sequential structure in that signs can undergo a reduction or deletion of each element in

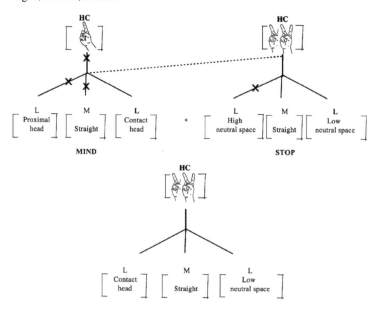

Figure 6.4 LML model for SURPRISE based on THINK + STOP compound (from Sandler 2012)

the first setting (or location), resulting in a compound of the deleted material in the second setting. Sandler (2012) provides the example of the sign word for SURPRISE in Irish Sign Language (ISL), which starts its life from the signs for THINK and STOP sequentially being deleted (see Figure 6.4). Signs, like spoken words, fade into the ether as soon as they're actioned. Thus, the sequential rules of sign language similarly apply to a set of fleeting or fading signals.

However, there are senses in which sign languages differ from spoken languages as a whole, linguistically. Wilcox & Wilcox (2015) list three syntactic differences from contemporary typological studies. Sign languages tend to be more head-marked, where spoken languages favour dependent-marking structure. Second, sign languages are more topic-prominent than subject-prominent, as we saw with SASL in Chapter 2. And lastly, crosslinguistic investigation shows surprising similarities in question formation across numerous distinct signed languages. This indicates greater crosslinguistic similarity than variation than is typically found in spoken languages, at least along one proven dimension. Nevertheless, let's return to our three properties mentioned at the end of Section 6.1, starting with hierarchy.

Hierarchical organisation is as much a part of sign language phonology as it is of spoken language. The particular organisation differs but the structure is similar. Take the hierarchical arrangement of the aforementioned parameters of signs in terms of handshape, location, and movement. In the prosodic model of sign language phonology (Anderson & Ewen 1987; van der Hulst 1993), the root node is a lexeme as opposed to a segment comprising consonants and vowels. But other than that, the model below resembles the kind of hierarchical analysis of feature geometry closely (Figure 6.5).

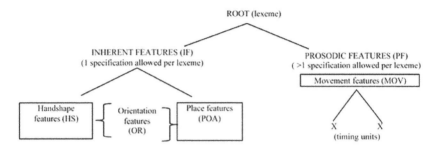

Figure 6.5 Prosodic model (from Brentari *et al.* 2018)

Hierarchical configurations of sign structure are quite common across accounts. In Sandler (1989) Hand Tier (HT) model, FINGER POSITION and PALM ORIENTATION are subordinate to SELECTED FINGERS, which is in turn beneath the overarching HAND CONFIGURATION feature class. Zooming in on the lexical level, there's a similar picture to the hierarchical syllable structure available to sign language. Take the LML structure discussed above. Recall that the syllable in spoken languages is hierarchically organised in terms of a CVC structure. Similarly, LML can be organised hierarchically as follows.

In this analysis, this two-handed, monosyllabic (if you will) sign is created from the deletion of two signs with an assimilation of the head node HAND CONFIGURATION (HC) in the final product. Both sequentiality and hierarchy seem to be abundantly apparent in sign language phonology. To see action in action, we'll need to delve into the connection between gesture and sign language more deeply.

There's a trivial sense in which sign and spoken word tokens are actions since they involve actions in their articulation, whether in terms of facial expressions, hand configurations, or puffs of air pushed through oral openings. But this isn't the sense we're after. As Bromberger & Halle (1992) argued, there's a sense in which phonology is *grounded* in actions. To get to this philosophical posit, we need to consider another essential feature of sign language phonology that links it both to actions (in the deep sense) and to gestures. In the final section, we'll put the puzzle pieces together.

One of the most fascinating properties of sign languages is its iconicity. We've already met it in our discussion of supersemantics in Chapter 4 (which itself was in part inspired by sign language). Schlenker (2019) treats an iconic sign language rule as one that incorporates the requirement that the denotation of an expression preserves properties of its form. Iconic gestures, for him, are then gestures 'which are characterized by the fact that their form resembles aspects of what they denote' (2019, p. 743). In spoken languages, iconicity expresses itself in phenomena such as onomatopoeia. Conventionalisation and grammaticalisation can affect iconicity in opposite ways. 'Emblems', like a thumbs up or the middle finger in Western culture, can have fixed meanings for certain gestures or signs (Giorgolo 2010).[9] Sign language phonologists have also noted that grammaticalisation can limit the scope of lexical iconicity. Klima & Bellugi (1979) argued that the original transparency, or roots in mimetic representation, of sign languages are gradually submerged as the language grammaticalises over time. They provide an example of the sign for SLOW in ASL (signed by first moving one's nondominant hand down – palm facing – and then sliding the other hand over the top until it reaches the bend of the arm), which is intensified by a rapid movement rather than a slower, more iconic one.

Another way of thinking about iconicity in sign language is as the reduction of Saussure's infamous 'arbitrariness of the sign' concept. In other words, iconic signs are less arbitrary. Moreover, sign languages containing such signs are less arbitrary than spoken languages. Some sign language linguists have taken inspiration from cognitive grammar to suggest that *cognitive iconicity* plays an important role in sign language phonology.

The central claim of cognitive iconicity is that phonological notions also reside in conceptual space. The phonological pole of symbolic linguistic structures reflects our conceptualization of pronunciations, which range from the specific pronunciation of actual words in all their contextual richness to more schematic conceptions, such as a common phonological shape shared by certain nouns or verbs in a particular language. (Wilcox & Wilcox 2015, p. 847)

They suggest that sign languages, like ASL, exhibit two kinds of iconicity: (1) referent iconicity (as in the cases we've mentioned) where the sign resembles its denotation's form, and (2) grammatical class iconicity. The latter is like when a noun form is expressed in the sign space usually marked for 'things' and verbal forms occupy the region assigned to 'processes'. Both of these phenomena are present in the two main routes to the codification of gesture into sign language. The first begins with a nonconventional gesture. Over time, this gesture is incorporated initially as a lexical item, after which it acquires grammatical function. Futures, evidentials, and epistemic models follow this path. The second route obviates the lexical stage and goes from gesture to prosody/intonation to grammatical marker. This latter category tends to start with a manner of movement of a manual gesture (or facial gesture). They don't

---

[9] This doesn't mean that the meaning of these gestures can't be altered by context. During a scuba dive, a thumbs up means 'end of dive' or 'take me to the surface'. Confusing it for 'everything's okay' could have dire consequences in such a setting.

lexicalise but rather enter the linguistic system as prosody or intonation for things like intensity or duration marking and stress.[10]

Again, the relationship between gesture and sign is a historically fraught one. In the backdrop of purely reductive claims about sign language, little progress could be made in this inquiry. However, enlightened research within the context of an understanding of the linguistic richness of sign languages can once again ask questions concerning the nature of this relationship and also broaden it to questions of the relationship between gesture and natural language *simpliciter*. Gesture itself is a more complex linguistic phenomenon than early theorists anticipated. Schlenker (2020) advocates for the possibility of a gestural grammar of sorts. His central thesis is that signs and nonsigners' gestures have certain properties in common. Specifically, gestural loci can be directly compared to sign language loci or positions in the signing space in terms of iconicity, pluralisation, and verbal agreement. In a way, he proposes a shadow grammar for gesture that parallels certain aspects of sign language. Of course, this shadow grammar cannot approach its counterpart in terms of complexity but its existence provides a telling glimpse into the role of action in grammar. Schlenker also focuses on the structure of 'pro-speech gestures', which replace words in spoken language, as opposed to the more studied co-speech gestures, which merely attach to them.

Returning to the foundational figure in sign language phonology, William Stokoe, we see his later view of the field transforming into an action theory linked to gesture and action:

What I propose is not complicated at all; it is dead simple to begin with. I call it semantical phonology. It invites one to look at a sign – as simply a marriage of a noun and a verb – [O]ne needs only to think of a sign as something that acts together with its action. (Stokoe 1991, p. 107)

This view again borrows from cognitive grammar in assigning inherent conceptual semantic value to the basic phonological categories (handshape, location, movement, etc.).[11] Indeed, Stokoe's work on gesture and sign language is directly informed by the possible role of gesture in natural language evolution itself. The idea that gesture is associated with the origins of language has

---

[10] There's another phonologically interesting class of languages about which little is known or studied, namely, whistling languages. These are rare languages that have developed in remote mountainous and/or tropical rainforests and savannas. Speakers of the language learn to convert or copy expressions of the spoken component of their languages into whistled signals. Meyer (2021) claims that these languages exhibit complex forms of 'sound iconicity'. Furthermore, this modality acts in tandem with spoken speech to promote carrying a signal across vast and resonant distances in which shouting is unlikely to be effective.

[11] This dovetails with Jacobson's picture, according to Egré (2018), in which phonology 'must be conceived of as a set of articulatory or motor instructions, defined on the basis of a universal set of elementary articulatory gestures' (p. 676).

occupied many theorists, from Stokoe to Armstrong *et al.* (1995) to Tomasello (2000), who argues that it's in primate social, gestural behaviour that we find the living fossils of the emergence of human language, not in their vocalisations. We'll return to issues of language evolution in Chapter 8. For now, let this discussion suffice as a case for the connection between gesture, signs, and action in natural language phonology.

So far, we've encountered a number reasons for not only extending phonology to sign language but also for appreciating the sequential, hierarchical, and action-based nature of the field. In the next section, we'll match these properties to a philosophical action theory of language.

6.3   Philosophical Action Theory of Language

What is philosophical action theory? Or, more appropriately, what is a philosophical action theory (as there are many)? The philosophy of action deals broadly with the nature and explanation of action, agency, intention, and cause. For instance, Wittgenstein (1953, §621) famously asked 'what is left over if I subtract the fact that my arm goes up from the fact that I raise my arm?' An agent's actions on views that follow him, such as Anscombe (1963), involve normative reasons not reducible to causal explanations. It's similar for the alleged incompatibility of goal-directed or teleological views of intentional action with a causal theory.

Contemporary action theories don't follow in this earlier 'anti-causalist' trajectory and fully embrace causal-rational accounts of action. This opens 'the way for a naturalistic stance in action theory and thus for an integration of philosophical and scientific enquiries' (Pacherie 2012, p. 93). Thus, on such accounts, actions are defined in terms of underlying causal psychological processes. Theories differ in terms of what they take to be relevant to these causal processes and which processes are considered action in the first place (for an overview, see Mele 1997). For example, actions can be taken as physical events with particular mental causes or causal processes themselves, as one interpretation of Bromberger & Halle (1992) would have it.

For our purposes, an important aspect of intentional action it shares with linguistic activity is its *coordinating function* that 'serve[s] to coordinate the activities of the agent over time and to coordinate them with the activities of other agents' (Pacherie 2012, p. 96).[12] One way of achieving this coordination is by means of structural connections in the face of indefinite options. This is precisely the sense of 'syntax' proposed by Horgan & Tiensen (2006):

---

[12] Millikan (1984, 2005) has developed Lewis' (1969) model of conventions to make similar points about inter-generational language production and comprehension.

Since nature did not know where in the world humans would find themselves – nor within pretty broad limits what the world would be like – nature had to provide them with a means of 'representing' a great deal of information about any of indefinitely many locations. We see no way that this could be done except by way of syntax that is, by a systematic way of producing new, appropriate representations as needed. (p. 147)

Here, syntax takes on a broader meaning involving the generation of indefinite (but not necessarily infinite) representations needed for navigating actual situations in the world. In this way, phonology could be 'syntactic'. Thus, they offer an action theory of sorts (although they never mention the term). They mount what they call the 'tracking argument' to show that syntactic structure is needed for organisms to 'survive in a complex, changing, and uncertain world', where they must 'be able to keep track of enduring individuals and of their changing properties and relations' (Horgan & Tiensen 2006, p. 148).[13] In a quasi-poverty of stimulus style, they claim that this immense ability cannot be prewired without some sort of syntactic or compositional structure.

The discussion so far has little to do with phonology explicitly. In fact, most action-based views of grammar in the literature are concerned with syntactic theory. Dynamic syntax calls itself an action-based grammatical formalism (Howes & Gibson 2021). It aims to connect syntax, semantics, and pragmatics into a model of language in terms of real-time processing and dialogue data. On the assumption of a shared neural connection between syntax and action in terms of hierarchical and compositional structure, Pastra & Aloimonos (2012) propose a Chomskyan minimalist grammar of action.

Some linguists have explicitly rejected the possible connection between syntax and action theory. Moro (2014), for example, argues against the alleged similarity between hierarchical structures in both domains, arguing that syntax, unlike action, isn't within the physical domain (despite physicalist-mentalistic interpretations of the former). He argues further for disanalogy by means of locality constraints in generative grammar and their lack of applicability to action and, similarly, a lack of an analogy with words. The former argument rests largely on the Merge operation and the view discussed in Chapter 3. While in the latter, he focuses on the lack of an analogy with function words, specifically, prepositions, determiners, and conjunctions, in actions. His discussion largely neglects the philosophical debate on basic action or 'practical atomism' that permits the possibility of word-like action units (see Lavin 2013 for a discussion), not to mention questions over how function words are represented in sign languages where some studies on lexical density – a measure of the ratio of content words to function words in corpora – suggest a high frequency of

---

[13] Bickerton (2014a), similarly suggests that syntax evolved in our early human ancestors as a means to identify and keep track of 'who did what to whom', analogous to grooming situations in other primate communities.

such linguistic items (see Johnston 2011 for an overview). Pulvermüller (2014) equally focuses his attention on relations to the minimalist syntax and action, but he's more optimistic. For instance, he claims that 'a possibly limitless human ability to embed structures into other similar structures, was first made with regard to syntax, despite the fact that the hierarchical-structural complexity of syntactic structures (defined in terms of levels of centre embedding) hardly parallels complex human action sequences' (Pulvermüller 2014, p. 219). For him, rightfully so, 'language itself is action'. I think the relationship between language and action can best be brought out by the connection between phonology and action as opposed to starting with syntax.

So far, we've shown that phonology (broadly construed) is hierarchically represented, similar to syntax. However, the hierarchical organisation in phonology is grounded in action more obviously than the formal models of syntax that are often associated with the production of infinite structural descriptions of internal thought processes. Phonology answers to phonetic possibilities, which in turn are determined by physical constraints on vocal, manual, and bodily apparatus. As we've also seen, phonological representation involves sequentiality in a way that syntax generally doesn't. In both sign and spoken language phonology, the actions derived from the ordered rules are physically fading signals. Lastly, natural language phonology seems to have deep roots in a primitive, iconic, gestural grammar. Sign languages grammaticalise over time based on this gestural underpinning that, as we saw with Schlenker's work, might have origins in a pro-speech gestural repertoire at the core of spoken language. Phonology thus offers us a sensory-motor theory of language in action.

Action theory and the field of motor cognition are intimately connected. In the contemporary setting, philosophers have generally realised the usefulness of empirical data and computational modelling, and cognitive scientists have in turn often taken and tested philosophical theories 'straight off the shelf'. One reason for the further relevance of formal phonology is brought out by the kinds of models used in motor cognition now as compared to a century ago. In the nineteenth century, motor physiology, under the auspices of figures like Charles Scott Sherrington, focused on accounts of complex actions as reactions or associative chains of behavioural sequences. Such views leave precious little for planning and programming accounts, which dominate the current theoretical landscape. But what's fascinating from our perspective is that a similar move away from natural language as associative chains or Markov processes, and behaviourist psychology, took place in linguistics around the mid-twentieth century. Chomsky & Halle's (1968) SPE model of phonology exemplifies this move. Similarly, in motor cognition, a view called 'centralism' emerged as a strong alternative.

Centralism, the idea that voluntary actions are largely driven by central internal representations rather than by external events, is one of the main tenets of contemporary theories of action generation. (Pacherie 2012, p. 98)

This view involves the idea of internal models representing the world as well as how actions of the organism might affect change in the environment.

More complex features of such models include *efference copies*, which are basically copies of the motor signals sent from the central processor to other centres for the registration of the effect, for example, a fish's central nervous system sending a copy of a tail movement to acknowledge that it's the fish's own tail and not that of another animal such as a predator, *comparators*, which compare two signals for correction and regulation, inverse models (as Figure 6.6 is a forward model), and a number of other technicalities not directly relevant to our goals here. Importantly, such systems clearly adhere to versions of sequentiality of physically fleeting signals. Even more interesting is that in many motor architectures, hierarchy is explicitly represented. 'A third key tenet of current theorizing on motor cognition … is the idea that action is hierarchically organized' (Pacherie 2012, p. 100).

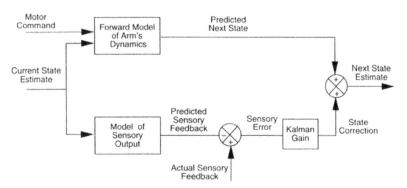

Figure 6.6 System of motor control based on internal models (from Miall & Wolpert 1996)

To see that phonology is a viable action theory, one need only appreciate that the dynamics of such systems can be modelled independently of their context and causal semantic interpretations. We can model the movement of an arm in vacuo, independently of what that movement meant for the user or the context in which it was generated. This is to suggest that autonomy is a feature of action theory and thus phonology described in terms of it. If we can describe the well-formedness of an action independently of its particular use or meaning, then systems like phonology are reasonably considered action-theoretic.

An interesting new avenue of research that could open up on this basis would be in the comparative study of impairments such as phonemic paraphasias and apraxia. Traditionally, the former are considered symptoms of aphasia in which selecting an incorrect phonemic segment involves substitution of one phonemic segment for another (e.g. 'dat' substituted for 'hat'). But there are cases in which speech is syntactically fluent yet contains numerous phonemic paraphasias (especially among posterior aphasics; see Kurowski & Blumstein 2017). Some researchers have suggested that speech impairment or error data points to a deeper inextricable bond between the phonological linguistic system and the articulatory actions associated with it (Buckingham 1986). For instance, phonomotor treatment is a powerful tool for the treatment of aphasia that's embedded in an action-theoretic approach to phonology.

The theoretical motivation behind phonomotor treatment, a connectionist, parallel distributed processing (PDP) model of phonology, has been discussed in-depth elsewhere and will only be briefly reiterated here. This PDP model proposes that phonological representations (e.g., phoneme /p/), are represented by distributed neural connections between auditory (e.g., auditory percept /p/), articulatory-motor (e.g., verbal production /p/), orthographic (e.g., letter p), and semantic/conceptual (e.g., knowledge that phoneme /p/ exists) domains that can be modified via experience and learning. Given the connectivity within and between domains, input into any domain of this phonological network will produce simultaneous activation in other domains. For example, input to the acoustic domain (e.g.,hear /p/) will automatically engage the motor domain (e.g., say p). (Madden *et al.* 2017, p. 66)

On the more theoretical side, Schwartz *et al.* (2007) propose what they call *Perception-for-Action-Control Theory* (PACT) to predict the features of vowel and consonant systems in human languages. The overarching goal is to show how the phonetic, physical, action-based substance of sound systems can be integrated with formal properties of phonological rules and theories. For some context, motor theories of speech perception take the gestural analogy literally in that they tend to consider the objects of speech perception to be gestures and not sounds. This view dovetails with some of the claims about the origins of sign language we've encountered. While auditory theories take action out of the picture, PACT puts both views together.

Our view is that speech perception is shaped both by auditory processing and motor knowledge. ... PACT assumes that speech perception not only allows listeners to follow the vocalizations of their conversation partner in order to understand them, but also to imitate and learn. In other words, perception allows listeners to specify the control of their future actions as a speaker. There is in this view an integrated process, combining perceptual shaping together with an inversion mechanism, allowing the listener to recover articulatory control in relation to his or her understanding of the perceptual goal. This process is different from both a pure 'auditory' and a pure 'motor' theory of speech perception. It integrates perceptual processing and articulatory knowledge. (Swartz *et al.* 2007, p. 114)

There are too many theories and models to consider here. What I'm offering is only a sketch of an action-theoretic account of phonology (and language) that takes both internal models and motor systems into consideration.

The last element of the sketch concerns the promise I made in Section 6.1 about cognition. Bromberger & Halle were firmly rooted in the internalist computational approach of generative phonology. Most major theories seem to assume some kind of mentalism when it comes to phonology. This is, of course, a possible avenue for the present suggestion, but I think there's a more natural setting for an action-theoretic account of the field within the burgeoning 4E approaches to cognition.

4E approaches basically take environmental factors to be constitutive of cognition in addition to incracranial properties. The first E refers to *embodied* cognition. This is the view that cognitive processes are reliant in part on factors outside of the brain of the cogniser, such as the kind of body she occupies. *Embedded* cognition goes a step further by incorporating the natural and social environment in the understanding of human cognitive processes. Thus, concepts are 'situated' in that they cannot be separated artificially from the environments in which they're found. Cognition is embedded when this 'situatedness' is internalised. The *extended* claim allows for the inclusion or extension of cognitive processes into external objects or artificial devices used to perform cognitive tasks. Standard examples are eye glasses for the visually impaired, or more, starkly, a blind person's cane used to 'extend' the perceptual domain in the absence of sight. Lastly, *enactive* cognition entails that cognition emerges by dynamic interaction between agent and environment. This latter E is probably the most incompatible with classical computationalism. Cognition, on this approach, emanates from bodily action and serves to cocreate or enact structures in the environment. It's both action-related and action-oriented.

It's not hard to see how the present view is fully *embodied* as it produces a strong analogy with the motor-sensory system. It also works well with an enactive model of cognition given its grounding in action theory.

6.4 Summary

This chapter, like its subject matter, has had a different flavour to the others so far. In it, I endeavoured to trace some of the philosophically insightful (and sadly neglected) possibilities of phonological theory to more contemporary views. I connected the phonetics and phonology of spoken languages to that of sign languages while attempting a deeper connection of this broader notion of the field to philosophical action theory. What I offer is a sketch and not a fully worked out account. However, I maintain that this sketch, based as it is in phonology rather than syntax, offers a more promising start to thinking about the intimate homologies between linguistic structure and motor action.

Further Reading

If books on the philosophy of linguistics are few and far between, then the situation is only compounded in the philosophy of phonology. Despite the dearth, there are some useful guides and studies to the more philosophical questions at the heart of this subdiscipline.

- Mark Hale and Charles Reiss' (2008) *The Phonological Enterprise* (Oxford University Press) is one of the most informed theoretical journeys into generative phonology, OT phonology, and the cognitive basis of the field in general. The authors discuss the competence–performance distinction, functionalist architectures, and how evidence is best integrated into the field among many other important topics.
- For an advanced introduction to the theory of sign language phonology, I recommend Diane Brentari's (2019) *Sign Language Phonology* (Cambridge University Press). The book goes much further than anything attempted in this chapter in terms of iconicity, processing, acquisition, and variation discussions. For a thorough grounding in this fascinating field, this is an excellent place to start but also probably sufficient if your aim is merely illumination and not continued scholarship in this direction.
- There are many works in the field of language evolution, as we'll see in Chapter 8. However, for a book on the origins of language based on social cooperative and gestural analysis of our primate relatives written by a renowned scholar of language and cognition, Michael Tomasello's (2000) *Origins of Human Communication* (MIT Press) is a solid read.
- For an edited volume on all aspects of action theory, from philosophy to cognitive science, Jesús Aguilar & Andrei Buckareff's (2010) *Causing Human Actions: New Perspectives on the Causal Theory of Action* (MIT Press) is excellent in its depth and breadth. The chapter by Fred Adams (Chapter 15) discusses the intersection between action theory and embodied cognition mentioned at the end of this chapter.

7   Computational Approaches to Language

In this chapter, I plan to make a case for the inclusion of computational approaches to linguistics within the theoretical fold. My argument is simple. Computational models aimed at application are a special case of predictive models. The status quo in the philosophy of linguistics (borrowed from the larger philosophy of science) is that explanation is scientifically prior to prediction. This is a mistake. Once corrected, the theoretical place of prediction is restored and with it computational models of language.

In Section 7.1, I'll describe the history behind the emergence of explanation over prediction views in the philosophy of science. I'll also suggest that this post-positivist intellectual milieu influenced the rejection of computational linguistics in the philosophy of theoretical linguistics. Section 7.2 is a case study of the predictive power already embedded in contemporary linguistic theory through the work on negative polarity items. In Section 7.3, I discuss the guard at the gate of theoretical linguistics, the ever steadfast competence–performance divide informed by the so-called Galilean style in linguistics. I suggest some serious drawbacks of this line of reasoning. In Section 7.4, I describe continuous methods, such as probabilistic linguistics, that showcase the explanatory and predictive possibilities of nondiscrete approaches. Section 7.5 moves to the contemporary field of deep learning in natural language Processing (NLP), where predictive possibilities are amplified. I conclude with some lessons that can be learned with the incorporation of language technology into theoretical linguistics.

7.1   Explanation over Prediction

I want to start this chapter by diagnosing the almost exclusive focus on explanation in the philosophy of theoretical linguistics. Interestingly, my initial diagnosis doesn't start with linguistics at all. In fact, it dates back to the rejection of a very different conception of science and scientific explanation in the early twentieth century. The much-maligned logical positivists had many infamous injunctions on scientific (and philosophical) practice during their heyday. Their verifiability principle insisted that meaningful statements are only those that are empirically verifiable or otherwise tautologous, that is, directly observable or based on logical proof. The focus on empirical verifiability had a number of interesting consequences. Besides the wholesale rejection of traditional metaphysics, testable scientific claims took centre stage since predicting consequences is one reliable way of testing theories. In this way, prediction was a strong indicator of empirical verifiability. Explanation, on the other hand, served the goals of positivism less so. Traditional metaphysics or theology were rich in explanation, but they failed to predict future events as they weren't based on steadfast laws of nature or precise empirical hypotheses. The balance was thus squarely in favour of theories with predictive success over explanation (where the latter also permitted 'occult' theoretical entities into the ontology).

With the weakening of positivism that came with the later logical empiricist framework, the pendulum shifted again, this time to the middle. Hempel & Oppenheim (1948) put forward 'the symmetry thesis'. As the name suggests, on this view, prediction and explanation are two sides of the same logical coin. To see how this is the case, we need to briefly discuss the covering law model of explanation. In this well-known model, scientific explanations come in packages of deductively valid arguments with sound premises in which at least one natural or general law is included. Omitting any one of these elements results in an unscientific explanation. In other words, a scientific explanation is *logically* deducible from a set of statements containing at least one reference to a general law. Under this model, prediction is just explanation at another time slice of the scientific process.

However, as Heather Douglas (2009) convincingly argues, the rejection of positivism overcorrected in many instances. In this case, the symmetry thesis was jettisoned along with the scientific interest in the role of prediction and its relationship to explanation. In the aftermath, theories of explanation flourished, with little reflection on theories of prediction. Without endorsing the symmetry thesis, Douglas emphasises the need to return to prediction as a necessary tool for understanding explanation. Moreover, she goes further to claim that without an adequate account of prediction, theories of scientific explanation face serious challenges such as overconfidence or dubious links to an even murkier concept of understanding.

[T]he relationship between explanation and prediction is a tight, functional one: explanations provide the cognitive path to predictions, which then serve to test and refine the explanations. (Douglas 2009, p. 454)

What's especially important about Douglas' characterisation is her focus. She's not interested in explanation *simpliciter* but specifically *scientific* explanation. Linguistics has taken pains to describe itself as the scientific study of language and yet it inherited the anti-positivist stance on explanation to the neglect of prediction, risking its own scientific explanatory project. Additionally, Douglas considers prediction (and the testability it brings) to be the factor that separates general explanation from scientific explanation.

In Chapter 1 (Section 1.3), I cited Chomsky's pronouncement on the positive role precise models can play in linguistics. This statement, and the early proliferation of formal models, was seen as a call to arms for computational approaches. However, the tide quickly turned when Chomsky later renounced work on so-called weak generative capacity associated with these models. Chomsky (1965, p. 61) claimed that 'discussion of weak generative capacity marks only a very early and primitive stage of the study of generative grammar' and '[q]uestions of real linguistic interest arise only when strong generative capacity (descriptive adequacy) and, more important, explanatory adequacy become the focus of discussion'. It's often assumed that this perspective was informed by his earlier work on the limitations of finite-state grammars and Markov chains, which aim to predict the next in a linear sequence of words. Let's pause on Markov processes for a moment to appreciate their apparent connection to prediction. A Markov process (or chain) is a stochastic model that encodes the relationship between a sequence of possible events in which the probability of each event depends only on the state attained in the previous event. So the idea is that predictions of future states are based solely on previous ones. In contemporary sequence-to-sequence processing, this means that the model predicts the most likely word to follow a particular word or category, for example, that the copula *is* is most likely to follow the noun phrase *the cat* in a corpus. Chomsky (1956) states unequivocally that '[w]hatever the other interest of statistical approximation in this sense may be, it is clear that it can shed no light on the problem of grammar', going on to conclude that 'there is no general relation between the frequency of a string (and its component parts) and its grammaticalness' (p. 116). These models were already quite nifty for accounting for grammatical behaviour in the mid-twentieth century, and they have only increased in power today (more below). Nevertheless, I think there are deeper philosophical reasons for the rejection of computational models within theoretical linguistics dating back to Chomsky's (1959a) famous critique of (radical Skinnerian) Behaviourism.

Pre-Chomskyan Behaviourism in psychology shared many features with logical positivism. It focused the science of mind on the observable relations between sets of stimuli and response. It eschewed theoretical constructs that weren't visible to testing directly or 'unobservable' in some sense. Chomsky (1959a) was considered a deathblow for this approach to language and mind. It ushered in a cognitive revolution in which the mind and mental phenomena could be approached with the tools and perspective of science. In particular, language acquisition was considered to be well beyond the bounds of stimulus response. The infamous poverty of stimulus argument, which claims that young children learning their first languages achieve rich mastery despite impoverished input, could allegedly not be explained on the behaviourist model. Linguistics was moved from the game of predicting behaviour to *explaining* it. Again, as in the case with the abundance of explanatory models in the philosophy of science at the time, this was an overcorrection. Linguistics at the time was a pioneer in the space of the new 'cognitive scientific revolution' (Miller 2003), so it's natural that it drew strength from the intellectual milieu in the philosophy of science that itself was a (over)reaction to positivist scientific strictures. The predicto-phobia of the larger atmosphere was thus inherited in the philosophy of this new special science.

This brings us to the present quandary: is there a role for prediction in contemporary theoretical linguistics? I've already indicated that my answer is going to be in the affirmative. Egré (2015) similarly argues that the notion of prediction is equally applicable in linguistic explanations as it is in other empirical scientific contexts. He argues, using an example of Halle's analysis of plural formation, that 'any nontrivial descriptive generalization will be predictive, provided it is testable on cases not initially considered in the inductive basis used to make the generalization' (Egré 2015, p. 455). At a basic level, this is clear across syntax and semantics as well. If you state a grammatical rule, then it should predict the form of sentences that the rules cover. If your grammar contains the rules $S \rightarrow NP\ VP$ and $VP \rightarrow V\ PP$, then the combination of these rules *predicts* that sentences that follow the pattern will be grammatical (like *Paul works on the paper*). It's already an inductive claim, as Egré notes. More complex explanatory frameworks such as Optimality Theory (OT) (see Chapter 1 for a short description) exemplify this property even more so. Using existing data (or intuitions), a ranked list of universal constraints are developed to adjudicate between rival inputs. The optimal candidate is then selected based on an algorithmic procedure that explains via prediction.[1]

In the next section, I'll provide a case study in theoretical linguistics where predictive power is in the driver's seat, in my view. After that, in Section 7.3, we'll delve a little deeper into the reasoning behind the explanation first (or only) approach in theoretical linguistics. I'll show that it has roots not only in the philosophy of science (as I've suggested above) but also in a particular interpretation of Galileo's scientific method commonly touted in favour of the competence model in generative grammar.

---

[1] OT has two kinds of constraints: *markedness* and *faithfulness*. The former concerns violations on the output (or surface representation) while the latter ensures that the input and output share some aspects, that is, that the output is 'faithful' to the input.

7.2   A Case Study in Prediction: NPI Licensing

For a clear example of the predictive power of linguistic theory, let's briefly consider some of the work on negative polarity items (NPIs) and their licensing environments. There's been a wealth of linguistic literature on the topic of NPIs in the past few decades. Part of the reason that these particles have been so widely studied is that they exhibit strange hybrid characteristics. When they are unlicensed in a particular context (cannot be appropriately used or generally not found) we're left with an infelicity akin to violations of syntactic rules. However, the linguistic situations in which these items are licensed are generally explained purely in terms of semantics (Rothschild 2009). This is interesting from our perspective because semantic considerations or entailment relations seem to be predicting where NPIs are likely to show up. This in turn informs the explanation or theory of what they are.

A precise definition of NPIs is hard to find since these particles are usually found in various contexts and don't always contribute to the meaning of those contexts. However, according to Hoeksema (1997), '[p]olarity items are words or idioms which appear in negative sentences, but not in their affirmative counterparts, or in questions, but not assertions, or in the protasis of a conditional, but not in the apodasis'.[2] Common NPIs are words such as 'ever', 'any' (ignoring the free choice 'any'[3]), and 'at all', which appear felicitously in sentences such as (1), (2), and (3) below (but not in their pairs):

1. Daniel didn't *ever* see soccer balls.
   *Daniel ever saw soccer balls.
2. Bill doesn't want *any* birds.
   *Bill wants any birds.
3. The witness never told them what they asked *at all*.
   *The witness told them what they asked at all.

The first sentences in these pairs all have something in common, namely, they all contain negations. Linguists have followed an aphorism attributed to William Ladusaw that 'NPIs live under the shade of negation'. However, the matter isn't this simple. As indicated by Hoeksema's quote above, there are many other instances of NPI licensing that don't seem to involve negation. Consider (4) below:

4. Every person who *ever* visited South Africa loved it.

The above example involves the quantifier 'every' and seems to license the NPI 'ever' without issue. What's needed is a model that not only predicts what negation and quantifiers such as 'every' have in common but also can explain

---

[2] Latin grammar school terms for antecedent and consequent of conditionals.
[3] Free choice items expand the range of possibilities.

and predict when NPIs are licensed elsewhere. Standard accounts proceed via a notion of downward entailment, or DE, on predicative contexts. A DE context is one in which you can replace a predicate with a stronger predicate (or more exclusive) without altering the truth of the sentence. All sentences involving negation and universal quantification are DE contexts. Consider the pairs in (5) and (6) below:

5. Gilles didn't *ever* see soccer balls.
   Gilles didn't *ever* see blue soccer balls.
6. Every person who *ever* visited South Africa loved it.
   Every American who *ever* visited South Africa loved it.

Thus, we can affirm the principle 'a predicative context is NPI licensing iff it's DE' in our model (or the Fauconnier–Ladusaw hypothesis). Sadly, this too fails to predict the felicity of NPIs in nonmonotonic contexts (neither upward nor downward entailing). Once again, consider the following examples:

7. Most workers enjoyed *any* job that they were offered.
8. Most people who have *ever* been to South Africa loved it.

These contexts are not downward entailing nor upward entailing since if we substitute a stronger or weaker predicate into (7), we're no longer guaranteed of the truth of the sentences:

 9. Most workers enjoyed any harmful job that they were offered.
10. Most workers enjoyed any activity that they were offered.

Similarly, adverbs, 'only' constructions, and the antecedents of conditionals seem to offer counterexamples to previous logical constraint on our models. A more successful approach makes use of tools from model theory to better predict NPI licensing and capture the data so far described. Rothschild (2009) introduces a notion of domain sensitivity (DS) to model the phenomenon of NPIs. The logical arsenal necessary is that of a model that's classically defined as containing a set of individuals (and individual events) and an interpretation function that maps predicates and names in the object language to those individuals and sets, $M = < D, I >$. Following Rothschild (2009, p. 14), '[w]e'll idealize and suppose that a given sentence S is either true or false relative to any model M'. The informal definition of domain sensitivity applies to predicates if a sentence is true in a model, then adding more objects from the domain that satisfy the predicate can make it false in that model.

Formally, DS is defined in terms of conservative extensions of the domain:

Conservative Extension – A model M' is a conservative extension of a model M if M' contains all the individuals and events in M, and at least one more individual or event not in M, and the predicate-extensions in M' are the same as in M in so far as they apply to entities of M alone.

Domain sensitivity itself is then defined like this:

Domain-Sensitivity – Given a predicative context c, with a 1-place predicate P in it, a sentence S is a domain-sensitive context if and only if for every model M such that S is true in M there exists a conservative extension of M, M', s.t.
1. S is false in M'.
2. For each $i \in [M' - M]$, Pi. (Rothschild 2009: 15).

This analysis is intended to account for and predict all of the above occurrences of NPIs (and more). Thus, by applying model-theoretic techniques to the syntactic phenomenon of NPI licensing, our semantic models are able to predict a range of data previously unaccounted for. Nothing I've claimed so far rests on the fecundity of Rothschild's analysis. The point remains the same, even if another model does a better job at the end of the day. The point is that theories of NPIs stand and fall based on their ability to predict the environments in which these little particles will show up. Every time a theory or hypothesis is put forward, it's tested against new environments in which NPIs are found. If its explanation doesn't account for the new data, the theory needs to be amended or abandoned.

I hope this brief detour already helps us to see that essential connection between explanation and prediction in linguistic theory. Before we move on to computational approaches directly, a discussion of some of the underlying assumptions of the competence model is in order.

7.3   On 'Galilean' Explanation

Linguistic theory, like any scientific endeavour, requires idealisations and abstractions in order to do its day-to-day business.[4] Chomsky introduced one famous example of such an idealisation with the competence model of grammar, setting the stage for theoretical linguistics for decades to come.

Linguistic theory is concerned primarily with an ideal speaker-listener, in a completely homogeneous speech-community, who knows its (the speech community's) language perfectly and is unaffected by such grammatically irrelevant conditions as memory limitations, distractions, shifts of attention and interest, and errors (random or characteristic) in applying his knowledge of this language in actual performance. (1965, p. 4)

This particular idealisation produced the infamous competence–performance divide. Linguistics was to be the study of ideal competence, and performance factors were to be abstracted away. The move has since become a point of massive contention recently, on a number of fronts (Kempson *et al.* 2001;

---

[4] The differences between idealisations and abstractions are a matter of debate in the philosophy of science. These differences are unlikely to detain or derail us here. See Nefdt (2016, 2019) for some discussion with relation to the case of linguistics.

Jackendoff 2002; Christiansen & Chater 2015). Although, to be honest, it's never been fully divorced from controversy. What's different about the contemporary wave of dissent is that it's largely informed by power of performance or usage-based theories, some of which stem from computational approaches. Some of the main charges involve the fact that performance data often contradict the competence model. In other words, the rules posited by the competence model are either not corroborated by corpora of actual language use or the theoretical claims, such as the poverty of stimulus, are questionable when put to the test computationally. Usage-based theories insist on the systematic nature of such data and motivate their inclusion in theoretical linguistic models. Many, if not most, computational approaches fall under usage-based theories.

Nonetheless, generative linguistics has had a tool, drawn from its philosophy of science, to stem the tide and maintain the competence model. The question that will allow us access into the nature of this tool is this: what do generative linguists say one ought to do when confronted with countervailing or contradictory evidence? On this topic, Chomsky outlines what he calls 'the Galilean style in science'. I'll include a protracted quote for full perspicacity:

> What was striking about Galileo, and what was considered very offensive at that time, was that he dismissed a lot of data; he was willing to say 'Look, if the data refute the theory, the data are probably wrong.' And the data that he threw out were not minor. ... Euler, Gauss, and so on ... just said: 'We'll live with the problems and do the mathematics and some day it will be figured out', which is essentially Galileo's attitude towards things flying off the earth. That's pretty much what happened. During the first half of the nineteenth century Gauss, for example, was creating a good part of modern mathematics, but kind of intuitively, without a formalized theory, in fact with approaches that had internal contradictions. ... now we understand it, but for a long period, in fact right through the classical period, the systems were informal and even contradictory. ... And what's true of mathematics is going to be true of everything. ... The recognition that that's the way science ought to go if we want understanding, or the way that any kind of rational inquiry ought to go – that was quite a big step and it had many parts, like the Galilean move towards discarding recalcitrant phenomena ... That's all part of the methodology of science. (Chomsky 2002, p. 98)

We won't enter into Galilean exegesis here (or Eulerian or Gaussian for that matter). These informal comments have been part of a longer adherence to this 'Galilean method' (or 'style') in which empirical inadequacies are to be discarded in favour of explanatory depth (see Chomsky 1980; Botha 1983). Note that, in terms of our dialectic, this effectively draws a sharp line on the explanation vs prediction issue. Empirical inadequacies will, no doubt, hamper predictive success. Ignoring them then results in a clear preference for explanation and, in some sense, a forced position on the usefulness of stochastic approaches.

Take the competence–performance distinction again. No matter how much performance data is amassed to contradict certain rules or principles posited by the theory, a linguist can merely evoke the distinction and relegate the recalcitrant data to performance theory (presumably beyond the remit of a tractable linguistic science). And, furthermore, how exactly the theory of competence connects to the theory of performance is a matter that can be pushed down the road with the hope that 'some day, it'll be figured out'. On the contrary, Jackendoff (2002) has suggested that the idealisation has 'hardened' so much over the years that the two are, in effect, irreconcilable.

Of course, generativists can defend the Galilean style by insisting that only unimportant 'interaction effects' are abstracted away. Allott *et al.* (2021) make precisely this case and further argue that Chomsky's philosophy of science dovetails with contemporary methodology in the natural sciences in which 'any serious science must study each system largely in highly idealized isolation from the others' (p. 519). They compare the competence and performance distinction to the elimination of friction and wind speed from Newton's laws. The idea they push is that models can isolate aspects of systems that are extraneous to those systems. This seems benign by itself. But what these authors miss in their review of critiques of the Galilean style is that critics specifically claim that relevant, nonextraneous linguistic factors are routinely ignored. And what's more is that those factors would make a difference when it comes to theory choice or acceptance.[5]

The Galilean method informs the competence model in at least two significant ways. In the first place, it cements the general naturalistic picture promoted in the field. This is known as 'methodological naturalism', or the view that linguistics ought to be continuous with the natural sciences in methodology (Chomsky 2000). This means that if science in general is Galilean in the ways described by Chomsky, then a science of language should adopt a similar strategy. The problem with this is that it's far from clear that the natural sciences, historical or contemporary, can be characterised as such. Strevens (2020) mounts a strong case for what he calls 'the Iron Rule', which places empirical considerations above all else in science. He attributes this rule to Newton and the birth of the scientific method itself. He contrasts the position with philosophical and theological theories, which he argues exhibit more natural rational human tendencies than the ultra-empirical scientific method demands of us. Thus, he classes the birth of science as an anomaly and the product of a very particular socio-political period in Europe. There's much to critique about Strevens' recent account (such as his failure to appreciate scientific endeavours in the non-Western world), but what it offers is a completely different take on scientific methodology to Chomsky's. And although the former's view on the

---

[5] Nefdt (2016) makes the link between linguistic methodology and what's known as 'Galilean idealisation' in the philosophy of science (Weisberg 2007). There, I also discuss the role of other forms of model idealisation in generative grammar.

genesis of science might be controversial, the idea that the scientific method is characterised and distinguishable by its fastidious attention to empirical details seems less so. Even if we don't follow Strevens here, the unassailable priority of explanation and theory above data (or application) seems dubious as a characterisation of scientific practice tout court. One of the most successful scientific theories of all time, quantum mechanics, lived by the mantra 'shut up and calculate', until very recently when the scientific community finally appreciated the many (and 'many worlds') interpretations of the theory.[6]

Another effect of the Galilean approach can be witnessed from the particular 'biological' constraints imposed on linguistic theory by Minimalism. Chomsky (1995b) admits that natural language is a complex biological system that emerged from messy evolutionary processes and accidental environmental conditions but nonetheless maintains that a more 'fruitful working hypothesis' is that the basic structure of language results from simplicity and elegance not common to complex organic systems (we'll evaluate other aspects of this view in Chapter 8). This is one of the ontological imports of the method that Allott *et al.* identify as 'nature is mathematically organized, and that the underlying principles of nature are in some sense elegant or simple' (2021, p. 522). Thus, the data associated with language might be messy and complex but the Galilean method allows us to abstract away from those details to home in on the true nature of language given to us by Merge and other conceptual necessities. Boeckx states of the connection between the Galilean style and Minimalism that '[s]ometimes, the mathematical results are too beautiful to be untrue, so that it seems justifiable to stick to the theory, while setting aside problematic or even conflicting data' (2006, p. 124).

Certainly, the 'Newtonian' method, described by Strevens, would require idealisation (and even *some* adherence to mathematical beauty) but presumably not in the face of relevant, strong, conflicting empirical data. The same worry applies to computational approaches to linguistics (and physics!) that privilege the data. Initially, it might have been difficult to see the theoretical consequences of corpus studies and distributional approaches. A caricature of American structuralism is that it eschewed any generalisations from individual language data to properties of languages *simpliciter*: taxonomy over theory. But times have changed. The tools and resources at the disposal of computational linguistics are vast and powerful. It would be surprising if they offered us no insights into our theoretical questions of acquisition, evolution, and communication. We might be inclined to grant a historical benefit of the doubt to Galilean methods or style, but we have never been in a better position to bridge the competence–performance divide than we are now.

---

[6] See Becker (2018) for an accessible guide to the controversies surrounding the philosophy, science, and sociology of quantum mechanics.

In the rest of the chapter, we look directly at the relevance of computational approaches. In the next section, we discuss the move from discrete (rule-based) mathematical approaches to continuous, statistical accounts. The section after that deals with the very recent introduction of deep learning techniques to natural language processing (NLP).

7.4   Discrete vs Continuous Methods

Where to begin? In the book so far, we've seen vast mathematical resources being directed at the study of the structure of natural language. We've seen formal language theory, dynamic semantics, a plethora of formal approaches to syntax, and generative phonology. What these tools share is a commitment to analysing natural language discretely. In fact, as we've seen, some linguists, from Chomsky to Moro, consider discreteness (in terms of its associated infinity) to be the sine qua non of natural language itself.

Going forward, let's be a bit more perspicacious. The central idea that has driven most linguistic theory (in various subdisciplines of theoretical linguistics) is that natural language is particularly susceptible to a particular type of grammar qua scientific theory. Pullum says it best:

As Seuren (2004) has stressed, the relevant vision of what a grammar is like, built into most linguistic theorization today at a level so deep that most linguists are incapable of seeing past it or out of it, is not just that it is explicit, but that a grammar is and must be a syntax-centered random generator. I will therefore refer to **language specification by random generation (LSRG)**. (2009, p. 12)

Randomly 'generating' sets of natural language sentences by means of recursive grammar formalisms has defined the field. In linguistics, a random generator basically describes a procedure for generating or producing an infinite set of strings (a proper subset of all the recursively enumerable sets) in accordance with the rules of the grammar. Besides Chomsky (1959b), the core texts on the general subject are due to the work of Emil Post (see Pullum 2011). One central mission of this kind of work, which has characterised much of linguistics, is the idea that the grammar needs to specify *all* and *only* the strings with the appropriate properties (grammaticality, semantic value, phonological well-formedness, etc.). We can see this with the kinds of binary structures embedded in the theory. In syntax, a string is either grammatical or not. In formal semantics, a syntactically well-formed expression either has a truth value of T(rue) or F(alse), or in the canonical textbook literally 0 or 1 (Heim & Kratzer 1998). The concept stems from the idea that a random generator is discretely decidable. If you ask it whether an object is in the set, it should give you a clear 'yes' or 'no'. I say 'should' because in most cases, in fact in the relevant ones, we're dealing with, it doesn't. Nevertheless, we don't have to decide on decidability right now.[7]

All this talk of random generation, recursively enumerable sets, and generative grammars presupposes a discrete methodology for a discrete target. Continuous methods, probabilities, and corpus studies, with their noisy, messy data, don't seem to fit well within this picture. According to Pullum (2009), mainstream theoretical linguistics had hostile reactions to four particular aspects of computational linguistics: (1) the idea of machine checking of posits of grammatical theory, (2) corpus-based studies, (3) a general aversion to statistical analysis, and (4) a rejection of the theoretical relevance of application.

Following the logic of Douglas (2009) above, application (which essentially involves prediction) and machine-based or formal checking are part and parcel of good explanation in science. Testing theories by means of predictions and applications makes for better scientific explanations. Furthermore, they might constitute the dividing line between general explanation and *scientific* explanation itself.

Instead of going through Pullum's whole list of grievances, I want to explore what it means to include stochastic methods into linguistic theory. Specifically, I'll discuss how formal grammars can be enriched with probabilities. This is the first level of computational involvement, in a sense. It aims to retain much of the structure and analysis of discrete approaches (or, as they say in probabilistic linguistics, 'categorical approaches') but with added flavour.

Before we look at one particular way of including continuous methods in linguistics, we might want to ask why we'd do such a thing in the first place. There are a number of reasons. In the previous section, we discussed the role of idealisations in scientific (and linguistic) theory. Their main purpose is functional. In other words, they are designed to make models simpler, or more tractable, testable, comparable, or bring out causal consequences. If the world is messy, sometimes sciences need to sift through the mess and find the relevant stable bits for analysis. To the point at hand, many (if not most) linguists (and philosophers of language) admit that linguistic phenomena, as they are found in nature, show a certain level of gradience. We've been adopting the simple grammatical/ungrammatical convention marked by the corner star ('*') in the book. But in reality, linguistic books and articles use a range of symbols to mark sentences of uncertain grammaticality ('?'), expressions that aren't stably grammatical across dialects, semantically anomalous sentences, and so on. In fact, it's very rare to find simple binary categories in phenomena as diverse as linguistic expressions and forms. Thus, to wrestle these objects into a discrete mathematical format requires idealisation on the part of the theorist. But what if our idealisations could accommodate some of this gradience in the grammar?

---

[7] See Pullum & Gazdar (1982) for more on that issue.

Bod (2015) argues that such admittance shouldn't be piecemeal but thorough and systematic across subdisciplines. Specifically, he states:

There is a growing realization that linguistic phenomena at all levels of representations, from phonological and morphological alternations to syntactic well-formedness judgments, display properties of continua and show markedly gradient behavior. (p. 664)

He opts for probabilities (over some of the other options we'll see below) due mainly to the pervasive appearance of 'frequency effects' across languages. These are things like the fact that we learn more frequent words and constructions faster than less frequent ones. Perceptions of grammaticality and acceptability also seem to track frequency in experience. The more you've seen or heard something, the more likely you are to recognise and interpret it. This seems to be a general cognitive phenomenon. Again, like in the Markov chains, it's previous experience that dictates future form (a theme picked up again in deep learning below). 'Whenever an expression is processed, it is seen as a piece of evidence that affects the probability distribution of language experiences' (Bod 2015, p. 666).

There are different ways to add probabilistic elements to grammatical formalisms. We could literally just mix formal grammar with probability theory. In Markov processes or finite-state machines, you could assign probabilities to the transitions between states. More complex rule-based grammars are also amenable to such treatment. In probabilistic context-free grammar, each rule is assigned a probability of application successively, which results in the probability of a particular sentence being derived from the probabilities of the rules involved in its production. It's a sort of probabilistic principle of compositionality.

'Stochasticising the grammar' by adding probabilities to the existing categorical structure is only one way of including continuous methods into linguistic theory. It also has its limitations in terms of cognitive plausibility (Fong & Berwick 2008) and, a problem inherited from finite-state and Markov processes, dealing with long-distance dependencies (Joshi 2004). A more thorough procedure is witnessable in data-oriented parsing, or DOP, advocated by Bod and others (especially Scha 1990). I'll give a brief intuitive overview of how the process works and some benefits (and limitations) it might have for theoretical linguistics here. According to Bod (2015), the general procedure involves a reinterpretation of what a corpus is.

By having defined a method for combining subtrees from a corpus of previous trees into new trees, we effectively established a way to view a corpus as a tree generation process. (p. 668)

So the idea is to associate every subtree in the corpus with a frequency distribution. Since new sentences can be constructed by joining together subtrees in

Figure 7.1 Simple combination of subtrees

different ways, they can receive analyses (parse trees) based on the probabilities of the subtrees from which they are derived. In fact, the probability of a parse tree T (like the ones below) is the sum of the probabilities of its distinct derivations (subtrees). Different derivations can produce the same parse tree. So, in effect, the grammar is analysing the most probable analysis of a sentence based on breaking down its parts and recombining them in a probability calculus. Another way of putting this is that DOP analyses new data (sentences) by probabilistically combining fragments from a corpus containing previously analysed data.

Technically, there are two separate processes in DOP. First, you define a 'bag' of subtrees in corpus C as the bag in which every subtree occurs exactly as often as it can be witnessed in a tree in C.[8] Next, you need to define the operations that combine (or concatenate) trees. In this framework, the only such operation is 'leftmost substitution' (shown in Figure 7.1), in which '[t]he composition of tree t and tree u, written as $t \cdot u$, is defined iff the label on the root node of u is identical to the label on the leftmost nonterminal leaf node of t' (Bod & Scha 1996, p. 8). With this process in place, the stochasticising can begin. First, you choose a subtree at random from the bag with a root label like S, then you combine this subtree with a subtree that's randomly chosen among the ones that it can be combined with. You repeat this process until you get a tree with only terminal leaves. So if your corpus has two trees for *Rens likes Remko* and *Henk dislikes Reinhard*, you can derive *Rens dislikes Reinhard* from the huge bag of subtrees and calculate the probabilities of different parse trees based on different combinations of subtrees.

How plausible is this model of grammar in terms of theoretical linguistics? There are two possible answers here. Since DOP can be (and has been) amalgamated with LFG, HPSG, TAG, dependency grammar, and other formalisms, it could inherit its plausibility from them. But that's the less interesting option of the two. What's more interesting about DOP (and 'Unsupervised DOP', or

---

[8] A subtree is defined precisely such that it contains more than one node, is connected, and each node in it has the same daughter nodes corresponding to nodes in the supertree (except for leaf nodes).

UDOP, Bod 2009) is that it hasn't been pitched at the level of engineering or application but rather linguistic theory. The idea of a language learner assigning parse trees based on previous experience and probabilities has been offered as a plausible model of acquisition and cognition. Bod (2009) has also merged the framework with constructional approaches (see Chapter 3) and analogy-based learning. I'm not endorsing DOP or similar accounts here; I'm merely arguing that they're clearly theoretical linguistic frameworks in their aims. Their methodology is computational, stochastic, and probabilistic. But this just shows that there's room for these approaches within theoretical linguistics. Furthermore, probabilistic, stochastic approaches can offer explanations of gradient linguistic phenomena, grammaticality judgements, and psycholinguistic effects such as syntactic priming by means of formalisms receptive to prediction as a tool for scientific insight.

One area in which this style of theorising is particularly challenging is in the resources required for its execution. Corpus-based linguistics in general requires large corpora to establish connections, patterns, and models of the data. But probabilistic approaches like DOP also require annotated corpora such as the Penn Treebank (annotated on an extract of the *Wall Street Journal*) to do much of the exciting work presented here.

The next section offers an alternative computational approach to linguistics based on an upgraded version of connectionist models of cognition of the mid-twentieth century. These models differ from the probabilistic work we've looked at here in being clearly engineering and application-oriented. Despite this, I believe they can and do hold many insights for the theoretical linguist unencumbered by the Galilean approach or a strict competence–performance divide.

7.5 Deep Learning and Theoretical Linguistics

In this final section, I'll describe what deep learning (DL) is and how it's been incorporated into NLP research. The topic is much too broad and expansive for me to comprehensively cover it here. DL is also much more developed than just its relevance to NLP evinces. For a general introduction, see Goodfellow *et al.* (2016), and for linguistic applications, see the *Further Reading* section at the end of the chapter. Image recognition, social applications, and even self-driving cars are among its recent achievements. However, our focus is on NLP, and interestingly, artificial neural networks have been frighteningly successful at language tasks. So this brings us to the central question of this section (and chapter): what does DL have to offer theoretical linguistics?

My short answer is 'a lot'. The more qualified response involves some nuance. Specifically, I think there are two main avenues of insight. The first is related to the engineering goals of computational linguistics and the space of possibilities with which it comes. In other words, language models often provide us with 'proof of concept' for learning structures. This is extremely important for the language sciences. It offers us an additional tool in our arsenal for understanding natural language and testing hypotheses, and a powerful one at that! But I think there's a *deeper* role that DL can play. This role is essentially a comparative one. Animal communication has offered us many insights into language evolution, social communicative structure, and even vocalisation possibilities. However, nonhuman animals stop short of being able to learn or produce human language in its complexity. Artificial agents, on the other hand, embodied with sophisticated artificial neural networks, might actually succeed where our linguistically impoverished earth-mates have failed. How they manage to do this, trained on what kind of data, with which inbuilt biases, can shed essential light on some of theoretical linguistics' most pressing questions related to language acquisition and even cognition. So what is DL?

DL is the most widely used and powerful computational tool in artificial intelligence (AI) currently. Applications range from natural language tasks such as machine translation (for example, Google Translate) and speech recognition (Amazon's Alexa) to image recognition, beating the world's best Go players, and medical analysis. DL itself is based on neural network architectures similar to earlier connectionist models and that of parallel distributed processing (PDP). Basically, a neural network is made up of nodes and links 'intended to model the behavior of neurons and synapses at some level of abstraction' (Buckner 2019, p. 2). However, unlike the older aspirations to cognitive neuroscience, the rebranded DL doesn't see itself as a part of neurobiology but rather machine learning, which is in turn part of AI.

The early forms of neural networks, such as McCulloch & Pitts' (1943) model, were based on threshold logic, propositional logic, and even Turing computation. There, the plan was to show that any function could be modelled through a set of idealised neurons that a network could learn. This brings us to the essence of neural network architectures and what separates them from symbolic, rule-based AI: their ability to learn from data in a particular way. Unlike these latter systems in which rules need to be explicitly encoded, DL 'relates the data to the results and comes up with rules that become part of the system. When new data is introduced, it can come up with new results that were not part of the training set' (Paluszek & Thomas 2020, p. 1). This is an important aspect of the research programme: its ability to learn from previous examples and predict or generalise to new cases. In addition, as Linzen & Baroni note in a recent review, how it does this is also of particular interest in the linguistic case:

DNN's [deep neural networks'] input data and architectures are not based on the symbolic representations familiar from linguistics, such as parse trees or logical formulas. Instead, DNNs learn to encode words and sentences as vectors (sequences of real numbers); these vectors, which do not bear a transparent relationship to classic linguistic structures, are then transformed through a series of simple arithmetic operations to produce the network's output. (2021, p. 196)

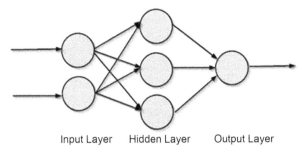

Input Layer   Hidden Layer   Output Layer

Figure 7.2 Simple feedforward neural network

This doesn't mean that DNNs can't involve parse trees or traditional linguistic structures, as we'll see. The general process uses large numbers of computational units called neural networks that take an input signal and feed it into a set of input nodes (or neurons) represented as numerical values, specifically, vectors. This information is then passed to other nodes as if they're synaptic connections or links. The links are weighted, which either inhibits or activates a node. 'Each of these units [neurons] calculates a weighted average of its inputs; this weighted average is then passed as an input to a simple nonlinear function, such as the sigmoid: $\sigma(a) = 1/(1 + e^{-a})$' (Linzen & Baroni 2021, p. 196). When the sum of incoming weights exceeds some designated threshold (depending on the function used), then the given node becomes active. This is the case with a simple feedforward network, as shown in Figure 7.2.

This isn't a very deep network. In fact, depth is determined by the number of hidden layers in a network (more than two). Essentially, DNNs are models of the data that can, in principle, approximate any function. They represent certain patterns or relationships within the datasets that in themselves are often so large that it would be impossible for us to perceive these connections. This is what makes DNNs phenomenally good at predicting things. The deeper the network, the more layers that act as input for further layers. This architecture, as well as the possibility of running it over extremely large datasets, makes DL so powerful. Of course, different network architectures perform this task in different ways, and even respond to data differently (see below). Importantly, the real game changer comes in after the network assigns initial weights to individual connections. It literally corrects itself based on the expected value of the output. This is what's known as backpropagation.

Given an input, the network is used to predict an output. If the network's output fails to match the correct output, yielding an error, the weights are changed slightly in the direction of generating the correct activation pattern. (Pater 2019, p. e51)

This all happens during the training phase. It happens over multiple epochs or cycles and not all at once. The process involves 'computing the gradient of a loss (error) function and proceeding down the slope, by specified increments, to an estimated optimal level' (Lappin 2021, p. 8). Basically, the network assigns weights, then checks these against expected output and adjusts them piecemeal until the distance between the network's values and that of expected output is reduced to a minimum. There are many details being left out of this sketch. For instance, in *supervised learning*, the network is trained on annotated data. *Unsupervised learning* removes the labels and expects the network to find connections and patterns in the raw data through probability distributions or other means.[9]

Once backpropagation does its thing, the training phase is over. All the relevant patterns have been identified in the data or at least a local maximum of correct prediction has been reached. Next comes the all-important testing phase. Learning technically occurs in the first phase. The DNN is usually trained using historical data (or text from Wikipedia and so forth), and testing is done using a new set of data to check the ability of the trained network to generalise beyond instances it's already observed. In NLP, there are three main areas in which DNNs are tested (and trained): to classify data (e.g. grammatical or ungrammatical); in language models to assign probabilities to the next words in a sequence (similar to Markov processes or DOP); and seq2seq setting, in which a network generates a sequence based on a sequence (e.g. machine translation).

Prior to the Transformer revolution (Vaswani *et al.* 2017), the most common kind of DNN in NLP was a recurrent neural network (RNN), which differed from the feedforward networks (Figure 7.2) in important respects. Let's briefly discuss RNNs and their offspring long short-term memory (LSTM) in order to understand how these networks process linguistic information (see Figure 7.3). RNNs come equipped with context layers where patterns of activation are copied from hidden layers of previous cycles. In essence, '[t]hey retain information from previous processing phases in a sequence, and so they have a memory span of the input' (Lappin 2021, p. 10). This short-term memory enables the network to use its recent context to process new input. If the text or sound can be encoded as an ordered string, the RNNs are good at processing it. You can improve the performance of RNNs in a few ways. One way to do it is by adding 'gates'. Gates add control that the basic RNN lacks since it can only process information from the previous state (or hidden layer). This kind of control is especially useful with processing long-distance dependencies between words. LSTMs have three kinds of gates: a 'forgetting' gate that discards certain information from the previous state, an input gate that adds the retained information to the new state, and an output gate that determines the vectors that get passed on.[10]

---

[9] See Clark & Lappin (2012) for a thorough comparison.

[10] As Linzen & Baroni (2021) note, if the network can be equipped with a large amount of information from all previous states, then the mechanism of recurrence (as in RNN) can be dropped. Transformers, which operate by means of *attention*, work this way.

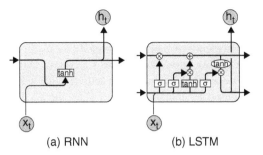

(a) RNN   (b) LSTM

Figure 7.3 (a) RNN vs (b) LSTM (from Olah 2015)

There are other kinds of gated RNNs (such as GRUs – gated recurrent units) and many other kinds of neural networks (convoluted neural networks (CNNs), transformers such as BERT or GPT-3, etc.), but these details won't detain us here. Now that we have a basic understanding of what DNNs are and how they're structured to process information, let's briefly move on to some linguistic applications. Again, there are too many to mention here. Anyone who's ever used Google Translate has witnessed first-hand the usefulness (and problems) with machine translation via DL.

One area in which DNNs have been incorporated with some success is in processing syntactic agreement phenomena. Generally, in many languages, agreement involves the correspondence of parts of sentences in terms of case, gender, number, and person. In English, subject and verb have to agree on number, as in the following sentences:

11. Marco *works* on NLP.
     *Marco *work* on NLP.

We say that there's a dependency between the subject *Marco* and the verb *works* in (11). Most computational models, even before DL, can handle these sorts of agreement phenomena. Things become more tricky, however, when more 'attractors' are added to the initial signal, as in (12):

12. The importance of the *articles* is/*are …

In (12), *articles* is an 'attractor' because it gets in between the head subject and its verb. This means that in order '[t]o correctly predict the number of the verb, the DNN must derive an implicit analysis of the structure of the sentence and resist the lure of the proximal but irrelevant attractor' (Linzen & Baroni 2021, p. 198). In this task, both LSTMs and GRUs have achieved considerable success. For the latter, Linzen *et al.* (2016) trained a network to predict the number of the verb in examples like (2), extracted from corpora in a supervised setting. In the testing phase, the network made correct predictions 99 per cent of the time. Even in the presence of up to four attractors, the DNN still achieved 82 per cent accuracy. The reduction in accuracy tracks human-level competence, which also drops with the presence of more attractors.[11]

Another area in which DNNs have found some success is with filler-gap dependencies. Filler-gap dependencies are constructions with a wh-element (filler) and a position licensed by that filler (gap). Why these constructions might matter from a theoretical point of view is that we know that DNNs are very good at finding patterns and connections between observable data, but these phenomena ask whether they can also find patterns in unobservables such as empty categories or positions. Consider the following examples from Wilcox *et al.* (2018):

13. (a) I know what the lion _ devoured at sunrise.
     (b) *I know that the lion devoured _ at sunrise.

They tested (with unsupervised feedback) whether the DNNs would pick up on the pattern by extracting direct objects in licensing environments (and nonlicensing ones) and measuring the *surprise* factor experienced by the network, where *surprise* is measured in terms of assigning lower probabilities. Their findings showed that DNNs were indeed sensitive to the filler-gap patternings in natural language data. What's more fascinating, again from a theoretical linguistic perspective, is that the models also showed some sensitivity to island constraints (Ross 1967/1983) that block certain filler-gap dependencies, although some others were inaccessible to the DNN.

Nested agreement phenomena such as centre-embedding have proven more difficult for DNNs to process (Marvin & Linzen 2018). This could be the case for a number of reasons. For one thing, they're not attested very much in corpora, so it's hard to train the network. Another more interesting concern is that they might require structural syntactic appreciation beyond the heuristics that these systems use in general. If Chomskyans are corrected about the importance of hierarchical nested structure for language, then the failure of these systems to capture this property would be detrimental to their use in theoretical linguistics.

So what's the proof of concept here? Well, it seems to be that DNNs can learn a reasonable amount of syntactic structure purely based on data and statistical processes. This would militate against the purely structural symbolic accounts of linguistic science. In addition, they can also learn theoretical posits like gaps not present in the input data ostensibly. As Penn (2012) notes, Chomsky's earliest objection to computational linguistics was that statistical models 'could not distinguish between a low/high assigned probability on

---

[11] Bernardy & Lappin (2017) generalised these results by means of GRUs and CNNs, which lack the memory-based mechanisms of RNNs. Their results were also largely successful.

account of grammaticality or other formal aspects of a candidate sentence's syntax' (p. 149). The DNNs we've looked at already falsify this claim.

On another level, DNNs also go some way in defeating the Galilean ideology of generative linguistics. DL and DNNs are data-hungry. The more data they can access, the more connections they can establish, discard, or retain. DL proves that minimalist tendencies are not the only game in town when explaining linguistic data. But we still haven't shown that they tell us anything about how human beings access that data and use it to go on to produce (and understand) natural language. Proofs of concept are good for business but I promised a deeper relevance to theoretical linguistics. So here goes.

In the previous section, I briefly mentioned that DOP was added to a number of formal (symbolic) syntactic frameworks such as HPSG and LFG. Is a similar procedure possible for DL? The answer is yes. RNNs generally process left-to-right sequences of information, but they can be designed to take a tree as input (Pollack 1990; Dyer *et al.* 2016). Linzen (2019) describes the process in the following way:

To create a representation of the sentence *the man eats pizza*, for example, a tree-shaped neural network would first create vector representations for *the man* and *eats pizza*, and then combine the two.

It's a bit like teaching Merge to a network. McCoy *et al.* (2018) report findings that this methodology allowed the DNN to learn English question formation with an error rate similar to that of children. This would indicate a strong bias for hierarchical structure, a claim Lappin & Shieber (2007) dispute. In fact, they argue that computational learning theory can directly inform language acquisition debates in theoretical linguistics. Specifically, they claim that machine learning offers an alternative to the principles and parameters (P&P) paradigm of generative linguistics. This model assumes strict fixed and universal principles of the language faculty shared by all humans. External linguistic stimuli not only activate this inbuilt faculty but also set certain parameters that are language-specific like a switchboard: '[w]hen switches are set one way, we have Swahili; when they are set another way, we have Japanese' (Chomsky 2000, p. 3). From an engineering perspective, this indicates strong learning biases innately programmed into young children before they acquire their first languages.

Before we delve into their argument, we need to add one extra element to our description of DNNs. They're often faced with a dearth of data and the functions they extract can be ambiguous. For instance, given an endless series of input and output pairs such as $f(2, 1) = 2, f(3, 1) = 3, f(4, 1) = 4$, and so on, it's indeterminate whether or not the function is division or multiplication. In practice, this situation is addressed by either adding more data or by encoding inductive biases where 'machine learning algorithms that have a strong inductive bias pay less attention to the dataset when selecting a function' (Kelleher 2019, p. 19). In other words, a DNN can be equipped with inductive biases that allows it to sift through the data in particular ways.

Theoretical linguists have been largely persuaded by poverty of stimulus (POS)-style arguments that the data young children experience is hopelessly too impoverished to account for the grammars they develop within a short period of time.[12] What Lappin & Shieber argue is twofold. In the first place, experiments based on machine learning show that the inductive biases are distributional and not categorical (which is a special case of the former). Next, they claim that, based on work in unsupervised grammar induction, successful learning requires even weaker biases. Let's review in sequence.

A distributional bias is a linguistically motivated bias that 'words form distributional patterns by virtue of falling into classes' (Lappin & Shieber 2007, p. 10). If one incorporates such a 'weak bias' into old arguments about the alleged identical probabilities of the following two sentences (from Chomsky 1957), then the first, contra Chomsky, becomes considerably more likely to be grammatical than the second. A result proven by Pereira (2000) for simple 'maximum likelihood estimator' n-grams (similar to those used in Markov processes) with the addition of a 'smoothing mechanism'.

14. (a) Colorless green ideas sleep furiously.
    (b) Furiously sleep ideas green colorless.

The idea, which we saw in Chapter 3, was that statistical analysis alone cannot distinguish a grammatical string from a nonsensical one if they're both absent or rare in a corpus. As further evidence, Lappin & Shieber offer Collins' (1999) work, which incorporates weak structural biases such as hierarchical structure (like the tree RNNs) and headed constituency to great effect in supervised parsing. In the unsupervised case, if we're concerned that children receive less negative feedback, the biases of the models are even fewer. Here, they cite Klein & Manning's (2002) work on grammar induction, which scored high on the segment of the *Wall Street Journal* contained in the Penn Treebank for learning constituent structure from input with only a bias for sentences with binary branching trees.

Even if we don't agree with their conclusions that the strong learning bias of the P&P model is refuted by this data, we do need to accept that these models provide relevant information for the issue of language acquisition. Perhaps in their current states, they run on input quite alien to the input a young human language learner experiences. They certainly don't benefit from the social interaction of a linguistic community, for instance. Children don't learn

---

[12] There are notable non-DL arguments against POS. See Pullum & Scholz (2002) for one prominent example.

language by scanning the *Wall Street Journal*. But these additional 'real-world' features can be modelled if we acknowledge the relevance of DL experiments to questions of human language acquisition for future theoretical work.

My proposal is essentially this: viewing DNNs as nonhuman agents capable of advanced linguistic performance can provide a comparative perspective from which to judge human-level linguistic performance. Over and over in this book, and countless others, have we encountered the claim that human beings are uniquely linguistic. No other animal on the planet can process and produce the complex linguistic structures we do on a daily basis. This is no longer true if we admit DNNs into our class of fellow fauna. They might not process language in the exact same ways that we do, but understanding how they achieve the levels of performance they do can assist in understanding our own linguistic abilities, either by debunking myths about learning or by providing us with resources for genuinely novel insights. Before concluding, I want to address two possible objections that might militate against including DL into theoretical linguistics.

The first is familiar from the general philosophical (and policy) work on DL AI: the issue of epistemic opacity. Unlike traditional symbolic AI systems that are designed to follow rules and operate transparently, given the architecture of DNNs, with hundreds of thousands of hidden layers making millions of weighted connections, accessing their inner workings is sometimes impossible. They've been called 'black boxes' for this reason. In response, there's been an explosion of work on explainable AI (XAI) in recent years. I myself have argued that this issue produces problems for determining whether the principle of compositionality is involved in DL within NLP (Nefdt 2020a, 2022). There are two immediate responses to this kind of concern. The first passes the buck to the emerging work on XAI and draws from its initial successes here. The second pushes the buck back a bit. Human linguistic neurobiology is in its infancy. Our inner workings are far from transparent. Expecting DNNs to offer transparency where we don't, in terms of linguistic processing, seems unfair at best.

There's a more serious interpretation of the previous worry, captured in a recent article by Dupre (2021), that might question the narrative of the chapter so far. The issue brings us back to the competence–performance distinction. Dupre asks whether DL can contribute to theoretical linguistics in any meaningful way. Unlike myself, and the authors cited in this chapter, he takes a negative approach. There are a few components to his argument, summed up below:

i. DL systems are performance-based.
ii. Theoretical linguistics is about linguistic competence.
iii. Competence and performance can differ arbitrarily.
iv. Therefore, DL offers little in the way of insight for theoretical linguistics.

It should come as no surprise that the only premise with which I agree is (i). For (ii) to work, we'd need to reduce all of theoretical linguistics to a specific form of generative grammar. Dupre makes this assumption. He also accepts the conceptual divergence between competence and performance that I take to be seriously problematic, as is clear from Section 7.3. Nevertheless, his argument for (iii) is strong and needs addressing.

He argues that the negation of (iii) involves the idea that performance is competence with noise. DNNs are very good at noise reduction. Thus, their performance on linguistic data can reflect competence by some sort of backward engineering of the output of competence. Scientifically, this means that we could abstract away from some performance data to get to the heart of competence. Dupre rejects this picture based on the fact that not only are there multiple paths back from performance to underlying structures but 'performance deviates from competence in substantial ways' (2021, p. 629). He cites ordinary utterances such as nonconstituent conjunction and subject dropping as possible expressions of language not derived from the language faculty at all but common in corpora.[13] The second divergence concerns theoretical posits of generative theory that include invisible copies left behind by movement. However, he doesn't consider the work on filler-gap dependencies or the possibilities of including parse trees with hierarchical structure into the RNN input.

Boiled down, Dupre's argument is that we shouldn't expect DL to pick out human-level, linguistically relevant structures. It's entirely an empirical matter as to whether they do this or not. This makes sense, of course. But it ignores much of the literature on how DNNs have been and can be designed to test linguistic hypotheses. This is my main point of contention and also the primary reason that I believe DL has a lot to offer theoretical linguistics. In keeping with the dialectic of this chapter, testing hypotheses by predicting future forms, answering questions, or transforming input is an important aspect of scientific explanation. In other words, DL in NLP is based on prediction, and prediction is essential for explanation. Hunkering down on the strict competence–performance distinction won't change this reality.

7.6   Summary

In this chapter, I've made a case for an increased appreciation for the role that prediction can play in linguistic explanation. I've suggested that neglecting this element is in part based on historical reactions to logical positivism in the general philosophy of science and also partly based on the specific manifestation of the 'explanation only' manifesto of the Galilean style in generative linguistics, that is, the strict competence–performance distinction.

---

[13] Veres (2022) goes further to advocate for a change in terminology such that the term 'language model' in DL is replaced with 'corpus model' to reflect that language models are not models of language itself.

This brought us to the realm of computational linguistics, where prediction figures significantly in theory. I first evaluated what it would mean to move from the categorical, discrete mathematics-based approaches of formal linguistics to continuous methods in probabilistic linguistics. After this, I took it a step further to consider what contemporary DL technology could contribute to theoretical linguistics.

In the book so far, we've seen a number of different methodologies all geared at tackling the hard problems in language science such as acquisition, action, meaning, and form. I've presented a picture of theoretical linguistics as a broad and methodologically pluralist science. However, one remnant of the narrow conception of linguistics still dominates an important scientific question: how did language evolve? In the final chapter, I'll argue against a minimal answer to this question and present a framework that can, in principle, take many of the theories and perspectives discussed in the book so far into account.

Further Reading

This chapter has covered a lot of ground from logical positivism and explanation to computational linguistics and DL. Thankfully, all of these topics are well represented in the literature. Here, I'll suggest some volumes and books that provide either more context or more depth to the discussion of the chapter.

- For a comprehensive treatment of all aspects of logical positivism/empiricism, Alan Richardson & Thomas Uebel's (2007) *Cambridge Companion to Logical Empiricism* (Cambridge University Press) is a good place to start. In fact, if you don't go much further, then you'll probably be fine. It provides useful historical background as well as chapters on the nature of scientific theory under the view. In Part 3, it contains chapters that explore the effects of logical positivism in fields such as psychology and the social sciences.
- For a book that both explains and criticises the competence–performance divide in theoretical linguistics, Peter Matthews' (2014) *Generative Grammar and Linguistic Competence* (Routledge) is a strong option. Matthews links the distinction to a traditional view in the philosophy of mind and finds no support within linguistics. He covers topics such as variation in speech communities and lexical meaning to make his case.
- For a defence of the Galilean view, Noam Chomsky's (2012) *The Science of Language* (Cambridge University Press) contains a series of interviews with James McGilvray and Chomsky on various issues in the language sciences. The topic of Galilean science comes up often in discussions ranging from the biology of language evolution to reflections on simplicity in theory.
- Moving to the computational linguistics content of the chapter, an excellent general introduction to probability theory and linguistics is Rens Bod,

Jennifer Hay, & Stefanie Jannedy's (2003) edited volume *Probabilistic Linguistics* (MIT Press). It covers much more than I was able to here. Probabilistic approaches to morphology, phonology, semantics, and sociolinguistics all find a home in the expansive volume. The explanations are generally accessible and present a clear picture of the field and its potential for theoretical linguistic significance.

- For a careful, thorough and radical approach to converting generative grammar structures, formal features, and insights into a novel probabilistic approach, I highly recommend Chater *et al.* (2015) *Empiricism and Language Learnability* (Oxford University Press). It delves into Bayesian probabilistic methods for theoretical linguistics and provides a fascinating application of the notion of minimal description length to formal language theory.
- Lastly, as referenced in the chapter, Shalom Lappin's (2021) *Deep Learning and Linguistic Representation* (CRC Press) is a recent book-length discussion of the content of Section 7.5 by an expert in both computational and theoretical linguistics. Lappin covers the structure and nature of DL in NLP in some detail and specifically focuses on what relevance contemporary research in DL has for theoretical debates in linguistics.

8   Language and Evolution

In this final chapter, we take on an issue that perhaps precedes all the others: how and why did language evolve? Linguistic theory has recently pivoted to amass considerable research on these questions. As we've seen over and over in the book, simpler structures have been posited across frameworks to account for the need to explain how language evolved. However, in this book, we've seen many distinct approaches to understanding human language. A view of language evolution that permits the pluralism of the book would be consistent with the broad approach of this work. Therefore, in this chapter, I want to turn the minimalist research agenda on its head with an alternative thesis: *natural language is a complex system and its emergence is likely to have been prompted by multiple interacting factors.*

In Section 8.1, we'll assess the current state of the art in biolinguistics and the strong saltation claim that goes with it. Section 8.2 will challenge the assumptions that have resulted in the saltation picture of language evolution. Section 8.3 argues for a radical approach to language evolution in terms of complexity science, while Section 8.4 puts forward my own unique view on how this general approach can be instantiated.

8.1   Chomsky's Controversial Gambits

As we've seen over and over again in this book, one of the most profound claims of modern linguistic theory has its roots in the early recursion and proof-theoretic leanings of the Standard Theory (Chomsky 1956, 1957; Lobina 2017). The idea is that natural language is in some important sense infinite. Where recursion theory comes in is as a means of capturing how a finite system such as the human brain can generate an infinite output – what generative linguists call 'Humboldt's problem', in honour of the linguist Wilhelm von Humboldt (Boeckx 2015). Formal 'generative' grammars are devices for capturing this essential property of natural language. Recursive rules are incorporated into the grammars that allow for discretely infinite output. The infinitude claim takes on many forms. As we've seen in Chapter 3, in some cases, the essential property is described as 'discrete infinity'; in others, it's 'recursion'. In the language evolution literature, this property gets a further name: 'the Basic Property', or 'each language provides an unbounded array of hierarchically structured expressions that receive interpretations at two interfaces, sensorimotor for externalization and conceptual-intentional for mental processes' (Chomsky 2013, p. 647). Again, in Chapters 2 and 3, we've seen that these properties come apart. As Pullum & Scholz (2010) show, recursive structures don't entail infinite output. In other words, not all grammars with recursive rules allow for infinite output. And when discrete infinity is a feature of a formal grammar's output, this doesn't mean that the languages the latter models inherit this property. It could merely be a feature of the formal model and not the target system (Tiede & Stout 2010; Nefdt 2019). What's more important for our purposes is that this family of properties, whatever label it takes, limits the application of analogies from biology, even according to biolinguists themselves.

> Some basic properties of language are unusual among biological systems, notably the property of discrete infinity. A working hypothesis in generative grammar has been that languages are based on simple principles that interact to form often intricate structures, and that the language faculty is nonredundant, in that particular phenomena are not 'overdetermined' by principles of language. These too are unexpected features of complex biological systems, more like what one expects to find (for unexplained reasons) in the study of the inorganic world. (Chomsky 1995b, p. 154)

Thus, biolinguistics starts with a very controversial assumption, namely, that its actual target is biologically anomalous. This might indeed be the case, but I don't believe that the biological resources were exhausted prior to this determination. In fact, as I'll show, the allegedly biological anomaly of natural language draws from a controversial claim about its emergence or evolution. It's important to note that I'm not saying that human language (or competence) isn't biologically unique. It might very well be the case that it is. Nor am I claiming that biological uniqueness is out of step with biology *simpliciter*. My argument is that biological uniqueness is a stronger claim that requires stronger evidence to prove. Unfortunately, the counterevidence is compelling, as we'll see.

To see how this is the case, let's consider the evolutionary claim of Hauser *et al.* (2002), developed further in Berwick & Chomsky (2016). The central Merge operation, which produces a single object from two separate syntactic objects and projects the head of one of them to the overarching structure, is said to be an evolutionary mutation responsible for the alleged rapid emergence of human language.

> At some time in the very recent past, apparently sometime before 80,000 years ago, if we can judge from associated symbolic proxies, individuals in a small group of hominids in East Africa underwent a minor biological change that provided the operation Merge – an operation that takes human concepts as computational atoms and yields structured

expressions that, systematically interpreted by the conceptual system, provide a rich language of thought. These processes might be computationally perfect, or close to it, hence the result of physical laws independent of humans. (Berwick & Chomsky 2016, p. 87)

There are a few components to this evolutionary thesis. The first is that Merge is supposed to be a single genetic mutation that emerged in an individual or a few individual hominid ancestors of ours. It was a *macro mutation*, or a mutation that had a massive effect on the organism going forward, one that essentially rewired the human brain and gave rise to language. The reason for the need for a single macro mutation, according Berwick & Chomsky, is temporal. Language emerged around 100,000 years ago in our species.[1] Thus, the usual resources of natural selection are unavailable to us since their processes tend to take much longer to effect change.

Another limiting assumption of this proposal is the claim that language evolved exclusively for the purpose of internal thought and not communication. Any evidence from the neurobiology of speech production, animal vocalisations, or symbolic processing in bees or other species is rendered 'peripheral' at best by this assumption. The internal computational system at the heart of this view is central, and 'there is no empirical evidence that any non-human species has such a system, suggesting that language is human-specific' (Friederici *et al.* 2017, p. 717), while they also claim that 'communication is merely a possible function of the language faculty, and cannot be equated with it' (p. 713). Of course, for Chomskyans, the evolutionary biology has limited analogies, but it isn't out of step entirely with a Darwinian picture since the mutation was selected for its benefits to thinking, which is meant to also explain the rapidity of its spread.

Furthermore, there are no half measures when it comes to the emergence of Merge. The emergence was purchased wholesale not piecemeal from nature. This, again, is in part motivated on the basis of the timeline assumption and in part on the nature of discrete infinity. However, Martins & Boeckx (2019) use the theory-internal claims about Merge, that is, that it's separated into 'internal Merge', applying to its own products, and 'external Merge', applying to two distinct objects, to argue that Merge could have emerged in more than one step. They therefore separate the emergence of the process of Merge from the property of recursion.

Thus, the biological anomaly that is language emerged from a single mutation, in one instantaneous step, around 100,000 years ago in our recent ancestors, and led to the property of recursion, or the production of 'an infinite array of hierarchical structured expressions' (Berwick & Chomsky 2016, p. 107).

---

[1] The number in the above quote is 80,000, but it tends to vary between this number and 120,000 years.

Essentially, minimalism reduces language evolution to the evolution of the computational system via its proxy Merge. Each assumption of this picture is prompted by the minimalist aims of economy, simplicity, and computational efficiency.

As an explanation of what's innate about language, it returns the answer of Merge, or the computational system. In terms of explaining the diversity of the world's languages, it opts for an alternative route. In fact, the answers are related. The innate initial state of the language faculty is remarkably simple and similar across languages and persons. What differs are peripheral externalisation characteristics. These give the impression, or rather 'illusion', that language itself is diverse. But language in a minimalist sense, recall, is just Merge. Perhaps a more charitable interpretation would have Berwick & Chomsky making use of the 'scientific vs manifest image' distinction in the philosophy of science. Prima facie, it certainly seems that the emergence of a vast array of different languages is an evolutionary explanandum. But what the science tells us, in this case, evolutionary biology, is that for language to have evolved so rapidly, it needed to be an extremely simple macro mutation. '[T]he appearance of complexity and diversity in a scientific field quite often simply reflects a lack of deeper understanding, a very familiar phenomenon' (Berwick & Chomsky 2016, p. 93).

As a theory of language evolution, Berwick & Chomsky's saltation account might be plausible given their assumptions. Of course, it really depends on what we mean by 'plausible'. One popular take on language evolution is that 'there is no end to plausible storytelling' (Lewontin 1998, p. 129). Nevertheless, even if this controversial claim is true, some accounts are more plausible than others. The minimalist account of Berwick & Chomsky eschews complexity in favour of a particular brand of simplicity; in the next section, we'll challenge this assumption and its resulting vision of language evolution.

8.2   The Complexity of Language Evolution

There are many points of contention in the above account. In this section, I want to highlight two recent objections, both of which are related to the failure of minimalist accounts of language evolution to appreciate the complexity of language.[2] The first concerns the issue of the timeline, which plays a central role

---

[2] There are more objections to more specific elements of linguistic theory from a biological perspective. Bickerton (2014a), for instance, mounts an argument against the use of theory-internal covert movement in the minimalist program (MP). He suggests that it amounts to what Poeppel & Embick (2005) call a 'granularity mismatch' in that there's a mismatch between the levels and/or processes involved in syntactic analysis and those of neurobiology. Unlike overt movement in which the same syntactic object lives at two locations but is pronounced at only one of them, Bickerton claims that covert movement is unlikely to find equal or any empirical footing.

in saltation accounts such as Berwick & Chomsky's. The second challenges the evolutionary logic of their response to their own assumptions. In both cases, the issues point to a more complex target.

Let's begin with the first claim, namely, that the paleontological record strongly suggests that human language evolved between 80,000 and 120,000 years ago within our hominid lineage. Dediu & Levinson (2013), Everett (2017a), and Steedman (2017) all dispute this projection. For Dediu & Levinson, evidence from various sources – including genetics, brain size, cultural artifacts, and skeletal morphology – indicate that early Homo sapiens, Denisovans, and Neanderthals had some form of language. This pushes the timeline back at least 400–500,000 years; 'language as we know it must then have originated within the 1 million years between *H. erectus* and the common ancestor of Neandertals and us' (Dediu & Levinson 2013, p. 10). They don't, however, suggest that 'full language' was present prior to modern humans and allow for the possibility that syntax, speech, and vocabulary size were significantly impoverished in this common ancestor. The cross-species prevalence of the FOXP2 gene as well as evidence that suggests its (or a variant's) possible presence in Neandertals (Krause *et al.* 2007) also serve to challenge the uniqueness and rapidity claims of saltation views (which assumed the gene was unique to humans). Everett (2017a), on the other hand, goes further to suggest that the epoch that produced full language was that of Homo Erectus. He rejects the notion of protolanguage on the basis of claims about the culture, cranial capacity, and vocal capabilities of this early hominid. Everett's account stretches the timeline for the emergence of language back to around 1.9 million years ago. Both the tools of natural selection and sexual selection are thus fully available to us.[3] Steedman (2017) homes in on a piece of evidence that he considers more suggestive of the presence of language, namely, the lengthening of the vocal tract with the Homo genus, which created a much wider array of possible sounds than any other primate vocalisations. He suggests that '[t]his evolutionary adaptation has been so rapid and extreme as to leave adult humans alone among animals in not being able to swallow and breathe at the same time, a change that would otherwise seem to be maladaptive as it can cause them to die prematurely by choking on food' (p. 581). Taking fossil evidence into consideration, this vocal tract lengthening (and larynx lowering) started at least two million years ago.

The important point, for our purposes, is that rejecting the strictures of the timeline assumed by Berwick & Chomsky opens us up to the standard resources of evolutionary biology. Specifically, it was the strict timeline, or

---

[3] However, the 'stretch' is often based on controversial assumptions about the culture and vocal capabilities of Erectus. His view also delves into the internecine debates on recursion, Pirahã, and UG.

what Martins & Boeckx (2019) call the 'Great Leap Forward', that was supposed to force us towards the biological uniqueness of the emergence (and subsequent nature) of natural languages. Without this assumption, language can be treated like any other biological phenomenon in need of evolutionary explanation. Progovac (2015), for instance, proposes a gradualist, incremental approach to the evolution of syntax and language, more generally.[4] Her account starts with MP but then quickly moves beyond it. She, unlike Everett, embraces the possibility of proto-grammar by identifying ('fossilised') flat paratactic binary compounds found across languages (like *rattle-snake*, *cry-baby*) as the foundation for later hierarchical, more complex syntax. Her account fits the adjusted timeline and, more importantly, unlike Berwick & Chomsky, relies on language variation as a source of evolutionary insight. Furthermore, she envisages testable neuroimaging hypotheses:

When linguistic reconstructions can identify ancestral proto-structures, and distinguish them from more recent structures, neuroscience can test if these distinctions are correlated with a different degree and distribution of brain activation, and genetics can shed light on the role of some specific genes in making necessary connections in the brain possible. (Progovac 2016, p. 10)

On a gradualist, incrementalist approach, we're not compelled towards the reduction of language to syntax, and syntax to Merge, on simplicity grounds. Language (and syntax) is thus more complex than the minimalist assumptions would have it. Moreover, Progovac suggests that postulates of syntactic theory, such as subjacency, are explained by this approach.[5]

The second objection I want to briefly consider derives complexity from Berwick & Chomsky's own assumptions. De Boer *et al.* (2020) take on board, for the sake of argument, all of the assumptions of their particular minimalist saltation theory and show that it's incorrect from a probabilistic perspective. 'Specifically, we formalize the hypothesis that fixation of multiple interacting mutations is less probable than fixation of a macro mutation in this time window, and show that this hypothesis is wrong' (p. 452). They use extreme value theory to determine the a priori probability of a mutation occurring and diffusion analysis to plot the probability of it leading to fixation in a population (modelled on the evidence of likely human population sizes around 140,000 years ago). The result of their study is that it's more likely, even within the limited

---

[4] See Pinker & Bloom (1990) and Pinker & Jackendoff (2005) for earlier arguments for this kind of picture as opposed to the saltation account.

[5] The literature on subjacency is vast, and the idea has been refined and updated a number of times. But basically, the 'subjacency condition' was proposed in Chomsky (1973) to account for multiple island effects, where an 'island' is a constituent that blocks items from moving outside of it (like a relative clause) within one structural principle. More specifically, it's a condition on movement to ensure that all movement is local such that an element cannot move over more than one cyclic node, like a noun phrase.

time period, that smaller biological changes contributed to the emergence of language gradually rather than the rapid saltation scenario involving a single macro mutant. Furthermore, their view doesn't rule out communication as a selective advantage, nor the possible 'smaller biological changes' involving phonology, gestures, or pragmatic elements (or a combination of all of these).

The precise details are beyond the present scope, but in the next sections, we'll embrace both the methodological pluralism and the possibility of multiple interacting elements at various levels resulting in the emergence of language. It seems that even with the Chomskyan gambits in hand, complexity is a more likely outcome (and initial state) than simplicity. And what's more, 'the alternative scenario for gradual evolution of linguistic ability proposes that the evolution of language happened in a way that is far less exceptional by biological standards' (De Boer *et al.* (2020), p. 453). As Martins & Boeckx note:

> The evolution of something as complex as human language deserves integration of results and insights from different corners of the research landscape, namely the fields of neurobiology, genetics, cognitive science, comparative biology, archaeology, psychology, and linguistics. (2019, p. 5)

This is all to show that the minimalist moves are not benign, biologically speaking. Accepting the timeline relegates many of the resources of comparative biology and natural selection to the periphery. Endorsing the single mutation logic of Merge, and recursion as metonymous for language, attenuates the biodiversity of languages and accepts a parochial concept partly divorced from other biological phenomena.

Berwick & Chomsky believe that unlike the laws of physics, biology is more like a case study where individual cases generate particular explanations. In what follows, I'll argue that this only seems like the case on the assumption of individual biology, but patterns and generalisations emerge when the purview is shifted from the individual to biological systems.

8.3 The Maximalist Programme and Complex Systems

Much like the MP, the maximalist programme (or MP+), I'll advocate, isn't a theory but an approach or a strategy. First, I'll outline what a complex system is with reference to the ten standard features outlined in Ladyman & Wiesner (2020). Thereafter, I'll briefly mention three prominent examples of this general approach, each of which exemplify a few of these features, before proffering my own account, which aims to incorporate additional features. Finally, I explain why my view is biolinguistic in Section 8.4.

Complex systems are studied from various angles, with a bent towards computational and probabilistic methods. Language, too, can be studied from various angles. Yet, the dominant position for generations has been that the science of language cannot be a 'science of everything', and the scientific demarcatable aspect of such a study is an *I*-language (Chomsky 1965, 2000). An I-language is an *internal, individual, intensional*[6] mental/brain state of an individual language cogniser (at the appropriate 'level of abstraction'). With this focus, social *externalia* hold little currency among scientifically minded linguists. Such pursuits are best left to philosophers of language, sociolinguistics, ethnographers, or abandoned entirely, it's often argued. At the heart of an I language is a grammar viewed as a scientific theory. As we saw with MP, grammars are considered to require the postulation of simple mechanisms responsible for grammatical complexity. There is, however, another way to do things.

The science of language could embrace complexity without becoming a theory of everything and without eschewing scientific idealisation. Chomsky himself hints at this option before dismissing it lines later:

[L]anguage is a biological system, and biological systems typically are 'messy', intricate, the result of evolutionary 'tinkering', and shaped by accidental circumstances and by physical conditions that hold of complex systems with varied functions and elements. (Chomsky 1995b, p. 29)

A few lines later, he reaffirms the need to be minimalist (with a nod to the competence–performance distinction) as a 'working hypothesis' of the basic structure of language based on simplicity and elegance. Language use might indeed be more complex in the above sense, he concedes.[7] Before I argue for complexity science–based linguistics more holistically, a few properties of complex systems need to be considered. I'll closely follow Ladyman & Wiesner's (2020) recent characterisation, although there are other excellent introductions, for the sake of clarity and due to their ecumenical approach (which draws from a range of other work).[8]

One way of thinking about complex systems involves emergent phenomena. Indeed, emergence is an important, perhaps inextricable, aspect of complexity science. Individual honeybees exhibit simple random behaviour in isolation, but when they act in unison, they display highly complex collective behaviour including advanced symbolic communication (the famous 'waggle dances'),

---

[6] *Internal* means internal to the language user or intracranial; *individual* pertains to the fact that the grammar doesn't consider relational facts outside of the individual speaker; and lastly, *intensional* marks the functional or generative procedure for getting at the expressions of a language as opposed to the external set containing all such expressions.

[7] It should be noted that Chomsky is assuming something like the distinction between the faculty of language broadly (FLB) and narrowly construed (FLN) (later proffered by Hauser *et al.* 2002). The former includes semantics, pragmatics, and other linguistically relevant cognitive systems while the latter only includes narrow syntax. Many linguists accept that FLB might meet the criteria of complex systems but Chomskyans insist that FLN doesn't.

[8] See Morin (2008), Mitchell (2011), and Thurner *et al.* (2018) for other prominent accounts.

the ability to deliberate on hive creation, temperature regulation, and swarming. Eusocial insects like bees and ants often display the adaptive behaviour characteristic of multicellular organisms for survival of the colony above that of any individual (see Hölldobler & Wilson 2008). This is one expression of how a complex system can emerge from simple components, or as Ladyman & Weisner put it, 'complexity can come from simplicity (2020, p. 9). In fact, they highlight a number of other 'truisms of complexity science' including that coordinated behaviour doesn't require centralised control, complex systems are often modelled as networks and information processing systems, the field is interdisciplinary, inorganic systems can produce order, and so on. More directly to the point of this section is the list they provide of the standard features of complex systems:

1. Numerosity.
2. Disorder and Diversity.
3. Feedback.
4. Non-equilibrium.
5. Order and Self-Organisation.
6. Nonlinearity.
7. Robustness.
8. Nested Structure and Modularity.
9. History and Memory.
10. Adaptive Behaviour. (Ladyman & Wiesner 2020, p. 10)

The list above doesn't constitute a set of necessary and sufficient conditions. Rather, some systems exemplify some of these features and not others. For instance, they argue that adaptive behaviour is a hallmark of living systems (although artificial neural networks do exhibit a facsimile of this capability). Different complex systems also display these features to different degrees. The universe involves more numerosity in terms of its elements and its interactions than other systems do. While many systems such as the climate and economies strive towards equilibrium (but don't necessarily achieve it), nonequilibrium physical systems such as chemical reactions can be captured by stochastic characterisation. Complex systems tend to be open, dynamic, and not at equilibrium (Kauffman 1995). Systems like the human brain also exhibit feedback (and reinforcement) via millions of neuronal and synaptic connections, and hierarchical nested structure in its functions and organisation. Evolution tends towards the establishment of robust structures for the sake of stability without which it would be nearly impossible to attempt to describe a complex organic system. However, the diversity of targets and methods is part of the reason complexity science has taken so long to establish itself as a distinct discipline. We cannot, of course, discuss every feature and its instantiation in particular complex systems, but with these features in mind, and the examples provided, we can describe what a complex system can generally be.

Complexity science studies how real systems behave. The models of the traditional sciences often treat systems as closed. Real complex systems interact with an environment and have histories. Complexity is not a single phenomenon but the features of complex systems identified [above] are common to many systems. If it is right that the hallmark of complex systems is emergence and that there are different kinds of emergent features of complex systems, then instead of defining kinds of emergent features of complex systems, it is possible to identify different varieties of complex systems according to what emergent features they exemplify. (Ladyman & Wiesner 2020, p. 126)

This is the key to understanding the maximalist approach to language sciences. We'll be guided by this latter insight going forward. By focusing on which features of complex systems are present in or give rise to linguistic phenomena and how one might measure these to produce or support theoretical claims, we can work within the overarching framework. In other words, instead of viewing language as an isolated biologically unique outlier characterised entirely by simple mechanisms, we should embrace the complexity and attempt to show how language emerges from the interaction of many parts. Thus, our working definition of language will be something of the following sort:

Language is a complex system in which robust structures emerge from the dynamic interaction of multiple interconnected parts.

The evolution of language can similarly be approached from multiple angles. There's no need for any reduction to the emergence of a single factor, as De Boer *et al.* (2020) suggest (Section 8.2). And, more importantly, there are new ways in which to connect the study of language to biology. There are many possible arguments and evidence to explore starting from different features of complex systems exhibited by language, each of which constitutes a specific hypothesis and thus is a member of the MP+ (see the *Further Reading* section for some examples). In the final section of the book, I'll offer my own sketch of a theory of language evolution that embraces complexity.[9] As Ladyman & Wiesner emphasise, not all complex systems exhibit all ten features listed above.

---

[9] What's interesting is that many of the historical developments of modern linguistics, such as the influence of cybernetics, dynamical systems theory, and so on, were pursued under the umbrella of the classical cognitive revolution of the mid-twentieth century. Linguistics was a core member of that approach to the study of mind (Miller 2003). Its early methods, such as formal language theory and automata theory, are directly related to fields such as cellular automata theory, which laid the foundations for complexity science. Yet, although Ladyman & Wiesner add the brain to their list of complex systems, they leave out the mind and language. They include them only as emergent phenomena of the brain, but this is too parochial and internalist. No other general introductions or advanced discussions include language explicitly. And yet language exhibits many of the fundamental features of complex systems. Besides multiple interacting parts, in sound, form, and meaning, feedback is characteristic of the practice of communication and information transfer as well as decentralised organisation and modularity. Nested structure is the hallmark of linguistic analysis, with hierarchical trees forming the primary methodology. More below.

8.4 Systems Biolinguistics

My aim in this final section is to offer the biolinguist a way to ground or constrain their field in terms of the biological sciences (see Nefdt 2023b). I'll outline the beginnings of such an approach here while focusing on systems biology, what I'll call *systems biolinguistics*. My strategy is to show that many of the sui generis concepts of biolinguistics (and MP) can be reinterpreted within this framework (and complexity science more generally) to yield more scientific, less isolationist, and more measurable results. In what follows, my chief goal will be to show that this novel perspective can offer three main advantages over generativist and/or individualist theories of language evolution: (1) significant theoretical incorporation/integration, (2) better naturalisation of concepts in linguistic theory as per the goal of biolinguistics, and (3) a specific route to methodological pluralism.

One criticism of MP was that it resorted to a strong uniqueness claim about language, severing it from case studies in other biological sciences. Uniqueness leads to isolation and cognitive modularity. If language is an outlier in the biological world, then it cannot be easily integrated with other systems of which we might know more. Thus, knowledge transfer is hindered. MP+ rejects this assumption in principle and views aspects of language such as phonetic distribution, symbolic signalling, and semantic significance as emergent phenomena within a complex network of interacting internal and environmental factors. The first question to confront is how to apply a complex systems analysis to language via biology. The novel answer I provide is that this possibility should be relocated within an understanding of systems biology.

Systems biology is a holistic approach to the life sciences. It's an extremely collaborative interdisciplinary field that includes biology, computer science, physics, engineering, and mathematics. Whereas the nexus of traditional biology might've been individual organisms, cells, plant life, and so on, systems biology abstracts away from these to home in on their complex interactions with the environment. There are a number of specific subdisciplines of this larger field, such as metagenomics or the study of diverse microbial communities.

Like many theoretical offshoots, systems biology started with critical reflection on the limitations of both standard microbiology, with its focus on microbes such as viruses and bacteria, and mainstream biology, with its focus on individual macroorganisms such as plants and animals. For instance, classical concepts such as multicellularity are ill defined on the entity-based accounts since they fail to capture the multicellular nature of symbiotic organisms such as lichens, which exhibit interdependent existence. Cellular cooperation, competition, communication, and certain developmental processes require a broader perspective than the object-oriented accounts can provide. Some have put forward the claim that microbial communities can be considered multicellular organisms themselves (O'Malley & Dupré 2007).

Dupré & O'Malley (2007) survey the literature on metagenomics or environmental genomics that 'consists of the genome-based analysis of entire communities of complexly interacting organisms in diverse ecological contexts' (p. 835). In this field, microorganisms aren't placed in isolated artificial settings but rather assumed to be essentially coupled with their environments and interactions with other organisms. A proper investigation of biodiversity seems to require the analysis of metagenomes or large amounts of DNA collection within the environment. One additional reason for this shift is that evolution seems to require a larger perspective of this kind. As they state:

> Conceptually, metagenomics implies that the communal gene pool is evolutionarily important and that genetic material can fruitfully be thought of as the community resources for a superorganism or metaorganism, rather than the exclusive property of individual organisms. (Dupré & O'Malley 2007, p. 838)

On this view, one might consider human bodies to be complex symbiotic systems composed partly of human cells, viruses, the bacteria hosted by prokaryotes, and so on. But this perspective is also too limited. Systems biology assumes that there's no nonarbitrary distinction to be had between an individual organism and its environmental conditions. No clear 'self' vs 'other' is discernible. The immune system is a clear case where the human host and the prokaryote communities form one complex system that benefits the organisms (Kitano & Oda 2006). Dupré & O'Malley use these considerations and more to suggest an ontological shift is necessary and/or present in biology, one that moves from entities or organisms to processes and systems as the basic ontological categories. There is no useful concept of a static genome–organism correspondence as '[g]enomes, cells, and ecosystems are in constant interactive flux: subtly different in every iteration, but similar enough to constitute a distinctive process' (2007 p. 841).

Systems biology conceives of biological entities at the systemic level not only as individual components but interacting systems, processes, and their emergent properties. Clark (1996) offers a related picture of language as a dance in which coordination between participants results in the emergence of the joint action. In this sense, language is an action or activity that requires multiple partners acting on convention, coordination, in order to establish common ground. These kinds of views have also been proffered by philosophers of language such as Davidson (1986) and, more recently, Ludlow (2014). The idea is that language exchanges create passing languages or microlanguages in which the static rules of grammar aren't generally present. Emergence plays a major role in such accounts.

In order to accommodate the analysis of big data, the complex inter-organism interactions, and their environments, statistical and network approaches have become prominent, if not dominant, in the field. Thus, biological systems are usually represented as dynamic networks that form complex sets of binary

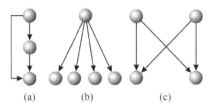

Figure 8.1 Transcriptional regulatory networks: (a) feedforward; (b) hierarchy; (c) multiple input (from Costa *et al.* 2008, p. 596)

interactions or relations between different entities and their contexts. Graph theory has proven a very useful tool in the representation of biological networks, as it has in linguistics. The vertices represent different biological entities such as proteins and genes in biological networks, and edges convey information about the links or interactions between the nodes. The links can be weighted or assigned quantitative values to encode various properties of interest, either topological or otherwise. More complex networks of networks can model the interaction between systems themselves (Gao *et al.* 2014). It's this aspect of systems biology that I think makes it especially applicable to biolinguistics as per the 'truism' that 'complex systems are often modelled as networks or information processing systems' (Ladyman & Wiesner 2020, p. 9).

Networks can take the form of *trees* or *forests*. See Figure 8.1 for some of the different kinds of networks used in molecular systems biology (for yeast and *E. coli* bacteria). (a) is a feed-forward loop (similar to a finite-state automaton), while (b) models a simple input module similar to both hierarchical constituency trees (if we add more layers) or rooted dependency graphs. Lastly, (c) involves multiple input that's useful for modelling dialogue dynamics and signalling games in linguistics. These are examples of directed acyclic graphs (DAGs).

The idea in complexity science and systems biology is that these (graph-theoretic) tools aren't merely instruments but tell us something ontologically important about organic life and reality, respectively. Silberstein, for instance, claims that 'reality is more like multiscale complex networks or structured graphs of extrinsic dispositions' (2022, p. 600). He insists that this view is commonplace in network neuroscience. Deacon (2008) argues that life itself is a third-order emergent property characterised by self-organisation and processes that involve some form of history or memory. Thus, if we apply the analogy, language would also count as a case of third-order emergence characteristic of living organisms that 'inevitably exhibits a developmental and/or evolutionary character' (p. 137). For him, the robustness of these emergent structures and patterns sustained over time involves a kind of 'self-similarity maintenance' in which '[i]n the jargon of complexity theory, such patterns are called "attractors", as though they exerted a "pull" toward this form' (p. 120). In linguistics, the attractors could be universal forms that connect the world's languages. Deacon's example of choice is snow crystal formation in which external environmental factors can shape individual snowflakes whose general form is compelled by the crystal lattice structure.

Deacon's picture of complexity and emergence involves three nested kinds of emergent phenomena arranged into a hierarchy of increasing topological complexity. Third-order emergent processes ('teleodynamics'), where he locates life and mind, require second-order emergent processes ('morphodynamics') or chemical processes as necessary conditions, while at the base are self-amplifying (nonequilibrium) first-order emergent processes ('thermodynamics') to create their necessary conditions, basically, the laws of physics. What's interesting for us is that both Deacon's and Silberstein's accounts of complex systems allow for law-like patterns emerging not just at the level of physics and chemistry but also biology and cognition. However, in both cases, a systems purview is required to appreciate these patternings.

It's well known that formal linguistics since the mid-twentieth century embraced very similar network and graph-theoretic analyses of language. Early formal language theory emphasised the importance of the nested hierarchy of formal languages that characterises the rules and complexity of human language. The type of rules a generative grammar possesses maps its output to a given class of formal languages. Regular grammars express the regular languages. Context-free grammars produce the regular languages and the context-free languages. In context-free languages, we find patterns like $a^n b^n$ (ab, aabb, aaabbb …) but not more complex (and harder to parse) patterns like $a^m b^n c^m d^n$ (aaabbcccdd). The formalisms of formal language theory (which can be represented as both graphs and automata) aren't just supposed to be tools but reflect the actual structure and complexity of language.

If the formal language hierarchy represents the relationship between different complex configurations (i.e. languages) at the systems level, the individual tree diagrams represent the individual construction level where most linguists ply their trade. Of course, graphs and networks are common mathematical tools across disciplines. As we've seen, most linguists believe that hierarchical constituent structure is the essence of language. For them, language is in a sense graph-theoretic. Whether or not we hold this strong syntactic view, network structure clearly plays an important role in every linguistic discipline from phonology to pragmatics. Moreover, the connections between different linguistic systems are often modelled as mappings or *structural morphisms*. As we've seen, Jackendoff's (2002) Parallel Architecture (PA) is one prominent example of multiple generative systems with interface principles linking them to and across one another (in opposition to the syntax-centred approaches of classical and minimalist generative grammar).

The key insight of systems biolinguistics is to ascend to the level of grammars that characterise more than just individuals by adding more systematic information from other aspects of language and the social environment. What the biological systems (and complexity science) perspective brings with it is a clear way to integrate information from different systems as networks of networks. The tendency among biolinguists under MP has been to simplify trees and isolate the syntactic information from the phonetic, semantic, and pragmatic. But there are deep, ontologically important interactions between these elements that can be modelled as networks of networks. One clear example that aims to capture the compositional connections between syntax and semantics is Shieber & Schabes' (1991) framework of synchronous grammars. If we allow ourselves for a moment to take a grammar to be a network of some sort (since it can be represented as a tree or graph structure), then formalisms that map one or more grammars on to each other are networks of networks.[10] The resulting complex analysis is rather structural, but this is in keeping with both systems biology French (2011) and complexity science.

The general idea behind synchronous grammars is to create nested information structures with syntax and semantic information encoded as couples. Specifically, take a pair of trees, one representing the syntax and other the semantics of a particular sentence. Some nodes in the trees form links. These links then conjoin the nodes such that operations on the tree pairs occur on both sides of the link.[11] So if you move one part or constituent of the syntactic tree, you move its semantic couple. The insight is that single operations (such as adjunction or substitution) can happen on pairs of trees and not just segments of individual trees. In principle, there's nothing stopping us from incorporating contextual (or environmental) parameters, phonological markers, and even neurological regions creating quadruples or further tuples of trees and tree segments. The important aspect is finding the links between systems that become the units of our analysis over and above isolated fragments such as syntactic constituents. These are the nodes of our networks of networks. For instance, what counts as grammatical or acceptable is in part based on community standards and conventions, and these can vary between dialects of the same language in distinct regions. Grammars aren't (only) inside the head!

What I'm advocating is similar to a practice in cognitive neuroscience in which researchers construct multiple distinct graphs and look for invariant structure across them. As Sporns notes, 'studies of brain networks using a

---

[10] In computational linguistics and machine translation, *transducers* compare two or more languages.

[11] This marks a departure from frameworks such as LFG that split the syntax into constituent structure (C-structure) and functional structure (F-structure), reserving semantic correspondence for the latter only. Other aspects of LFG, however, are highly conducive to a systems biolinguistic or MP+ approach more generally. See Börjars (2020).

variety of parcellations ... have converged on a set of fundamental attributes of human brain organization that are largely consistent with those found in nonhuman primates' (2014, p. 653). These studies have uncovered empirically significant features such as robust 'hubs' in particular brain regions, where a hub is a node that has the most number of edges attached to it. In our case, this would be a node in a synchronous tree that allows for the most links or connections across grammars.

In terms of theoretical integration or the first stated advantage of this approach, notice that this picture can retain the computationalism of generative grammar without endorsing its individualism. The most prominent example of a network of networks is one of Ladyman & Weisner's cases of a complex system, namely, the Internet. Consider a local area network, or LAN. These can be configured in a number of ways, but ring and mesh networks seem most appropriate as models of linguistic communities since either each computer is connected to neighbouring computers to form closed circuits (ring) or each computer is connected to every other computer in a distributed fashion (mesh). In order to communicate or exchange information, certain protocols need to be observed between senders and receivers. In evolving systems, these interactions can shape future structures and create robustness.

Hutchins (1995) applies a very similar idea to ship navigation on board a small aircraft carrier. Navigation is, in a sense, an emergent computational phenomenon that draws from the hierarchical and socially distributed connections of individual officers without a central controller. Again, one of Ladyman & Weisner's truisms of complexity science is that 'coordinated behaviour does not require an overall controller' (2020, p. 9). What Hutchins develops is a cognitive social computational model that abstracts away from individual cognisers' internal states but still incorporates environmental conditions constitutively. In language, the individual cognitive states are important (as the CPUs are in computer networks) but they don't determine the language. The language emerges when a number of these states are connected in the right kinds of ways within a particular environment towards shared and varied tasks. Evolution plays a central role in what kinds of networks evolve for which purposes and how certain structures are stabilised over time. But many distinct components could have evolved simultaneously, as De Boer *et al.* (2020) argue for language evolution above. In fact, Seyfarth & Cheney (2014) specifically integrate formal language theory, social cognition, neurobiology, and comparative evolutionary biology into a single framework. They argue that many of the discrete combinatorics characteristic of human language can be found in simpler forms within nonhuman primate social cognition. They focus on features of the complex social groupings of baboons and argue that 'human and nonhuman primates exhibit many homologous brain mechanisms that have evolved to serve similar social functions' (p. 5). Again, they show that social cognition offers a system-level purview from which to appreciate the connections of social structure and language evolution involving 'discrete, combinatorial, rule-governed, and open-end systems of communication in which a finite number of signals can yield a nearly unlimited number of meanings' (p. 7).

The idea of situated social cognition invites analogies with the 4E approaches to cognition, which have dominated the cognitive scientific landscape recently. Both systems biolinguistics and 4E approaches start with the criticism of the individualistic computationalist approach to language and cognition, respectively. Prima facie, the move to the 4E approaches to cognitive science resembles the move to systems from individual organisms in biology. Most of the 4E approaches take environmental factors to be constitutive of cognition and advocate integrating social sciences into the cognitive sciences. The idea is that cognition (and 'mind' itself) is *embodied, extended, embedded* or situated, and *enacted* in the environment and not located squarely within the skull of the cogniser (Varela *et al.* 1991). The last three components emphasise the sometimes active (in the case of *enacted*) role the environment plays in mental phenomena. Take the concept of extended cognition for a moment (Clark & Chalmers 1998). This framework allows for 'cognitive coupling' in which an external device can be connected with internal processes for the completion of a task such as a calculator making certain calculations possible. Similarly, Google Translate (or even a dictionary) can be said to operate in tandem with a language user to linguistically interact with her environment, thereby extending the language.

In terms of the second advantage over rival approaches, complexity science has the tools to *naturalise* a number of notions in MP and biolinguistics more generally. The concept of naturalisation here tracks the extent of biological involvement it contains or continuity with the biological sciences. I'll consider two such possibilities here. The first is the idea of an I-language or steady state of the language faculty. This term is meant to capture the idea of a mature state achieved by a language learner after the primary linguistic data (PLD) has set various parametric settings of the innate UG capacity (Chomsky 1986). Unlike the alleged externalised or socio-political concept of a language like English or Kiswahili spoken in a particular community, I-languages are supposed to be more scientifically tractable. However, a common criticism of this picture is that it produces a static view of language that ignores various dynamic aspects of the system. This is because the steady state or I-language is identified with a narrow concept of the syntactic or the computational component of the faculty of language (Hauser *et al.* 2002). Where complexity science can assist is by reinterpreting this steady state of a language learner as a dynamic equilibrium where 'a system is said to be in "dynamic equilibrium" or "steady state" if some aspect of its behaviour or state does not change significantly over time' (Ladyman & Wiesner 2020, p. 72). In biological systems, this state is related to the concept of *homeostasis*. Homeostasis is in turn related to feedback from the environment (e.g. linguistic interlocutors in your community) and robustness of structure (features (3) and (7) in the list above). Notice that the proposal here is not merely about nomenclature. Homeostasis is intimately linked to the environment. It's not a completely isolated internal system or UG only reflecting some sort of activation by external stimulus. Mature language is then not an internal component of a human mind or brain but a complex steady state attained by intricate calibration with the linguistic (and nonlinguistic) environment, that is, individual networks are fine-tuned or updated by connections to other networks like in the LAN case.[12] The upshot of this shift in interpretation is that, unlike the previous view, dynamic equilibrium is measurable. We have tools from biology, chemistry, and physics to use as templates. In addition, it tracks linguistic maturity better than a static view. Consider the concept in chemistry. Dynamic equilibrium happens when the rate of the forward reaction is equal to the rate of the reverse reaction. It can look like nothing is changing, but processes *are* happening continuously. It's a steady state but also a moving target. In language, our environment places learning constraints on us that require us to quickly achieve a state in which we can communicate effectively (we might also be helped by innate catalysts). There's a 'critical period' in which our internal machinery is particularly attuned to environmental stimuli. But mastery of language is an ongoing process. Static or mechanical equilibrium, by contrast, occurs when the reaction has stopped completely. Sometimes, generative linguists seem to imply this idea when they speak of a mature state of the language faculty being 'set' or 'achieved', but this is misleading.

This brings me to the second concept in need of naturalisation in terms of systems biology, namely, the infamous idea of a linguistic community. Generative linguists have long argued that the linguistic community has no significant theoretical or scientific role to play in a theory of language. It is too amorphous and thus not conducive to formal characterisation. The idea of an external environment of speakers linguistically interacting in sometimes imperfect ways was considered a 'theory of everything' and as such a scientific nonstarter (Chomsky 2000). Conventions, regularities, and patterns among speakers within such a community, although favoured by some philosophers (Lewis 1975; Millikan 1984), have thus not received due theoretical investi-

---

[12] For those worried about acquisition and poverty of stimulus issues here, I refer them to the growing literature on neural networks and pattern recognition (Youguo *et al.* 2007; Mattson 2014). These are learning models completely based on empiricist mechanisms and sometimes minimal inductive biases programmed in and represent yet another way in which complexity science can illuminate linguistic phenomena and processes such as language acquisition. See Yang & Piantadosi (2022) for a recent empiricist model of language learning that uses data from seventy-four languages.

gation within the philosophy of linguistics. With these elements, the social aspect of language has been banished to the realms of sociolinguistics and anthropology. But systems biology offers us a means of reintegrating many of these elements within theoretical biolinguistics. We can start by asking what a system is on this view.

Importantly for our purposes, there are two concepts of 'system' in systems biology. They differ in terms of ontological commitment. As O'Malley & Dupré state:

The first account is given by scientists who find it useful for various reasons (including access to funding) to refer to the interconnected phenomena that they study as 'systems'. The second definition comes from scientists who insist that systems principles are imperative to the successful development of systems biology. We could call the first group 'pragmatic systems biologists' and the second 'systems theoretic biologists'. (2005, p. 1271)

The pragmatic approach dominates in the field. However, some systems biologists insist that such an approach offers little philosophical insight. Taking systems to be some collection or conglomeration of parts misses aspects of interconnection, emergent structures, and symbiosis. The alternative, one I endorse here, is that '[s]ystems are taken to constitute a fundamental ontological category' (O'Malley & Dupré 2005, p. 1271). In our case, the linguistic community is a complex semiotic system and language is an emergent phenomenon therein. The system involves language users, learners, gestures, external linguistic resources (books, computers, etc.), nonlinguistic animals, and the external environment. If biolinguists are sceptical about the latter's inclusion, it's actually been well documented in dialectometry for years that geographical location affects language variance in systematic ways. This isn't to endorse anything as strong as the Sapir–Whorf hypothesis that states that language, cognition, and location are linked deterministically (see Reines & Prinz 2008). Omar & Alotaibi (2017) conducted a study to show that geographical distance can influence the use and frequency of intensifiers (*really*, *very*, *extremely*, etc.) across populations of the same language (Arabic) speakers based on location (in Egypt and Saudi Arabia) (see also Huisman *et al.* 2019; Reed 2020). Thus, the linguistic community is even broader than many philosophers have taken it to be. There seems to be an underexplored link between the concepts of linguistic diversity and other types of conditions that influence biodiversity in plants and animals.

Again, there are various tools, some from neglected fields, such as dialectometry and cognitive anthropology, and others from complexity science, such as network analysis and Shannon information theory, that can aid us in understanding the complex dynamics that give rise to linguistic structure. Besides Kirby's (2013) work on signalling systems, Skyrms (2010) adds elements of deception and the introduction of new symbols, thereby connecting semantics to information theory. Mapping the interconnected aspects of language, communication, and the environment offers a much more promising analogy with the emergence and structure of genes and genetics than does the claims of organ-hood along the lines of a more individualist ontology. A methodological cornucopia unfolds.

Returning to the issue of how biological constraints might play a role in biolinguistics, we can see that simplicity and optimality conditions (such as those discussed within MP) are not enough to shape the field into a more biological direction, even from an evolutionary perspective. Language evolution must take culture and general cognition into consideration. One prominent example of such an approach is Bickerton (2014b), who aims to connect MP to cultural evolution and primatology. According to him, each component only tells one part of an interconnected story of how complex language evolved in human populations. His story involves the property of discreteness (symbolic representation) witnessed in bee and ant colonies transposed to a particular primate, Homo sapiens, triggering brain reconfiguration due in part to the construction of a new niche imposed by a change in the hunting environment of our ancestors. Culture then shaped the linguistic diversity we find across the world. Bickerton's work remains highly speculative in parts, but as we've seen, in Section 8.2, many biologists and biolinguistics have objected to the single mutate theory of MP precisely on complexity grounds. For instance, the possibility of niche construction theory playing a role in language emergence and variation is empirically approached by Blasi et al. (2019), who assess the impact the transition from prehistoric forager societies to more industrialised agricultural societies had on our spoken language by means of paleodental data. Under MP, this evidence is peripheral at best; under MP+, it's much more central because it tells us how the environment might have exerted a force on our linguistic development.

The last advantage, already indicated by the myriad possible theoretical convergences of systems biolinguistics, is the methodological pluralism this perspective forces into linguistics. What were considered rival theoretical and formal frameworks, such as lexical functional grammar, head-driven phrase structure grammar, dependency grammar, construction grammar, probabilistic linguistics, and more semantic approaches such as dynamic syntax, all have a place within MP+. Synchronous grammars, sociolinguistics, pragmatics, social cognition, and neurobiology are especially important for systems biolinguistics, as I've described it, more specifically. But the possibilities extend beyond traditional avenues of connection. By adding natural language to the established list of complex systems examples such as brains, economies, climates, eusocial insects, the Internet, and the universe itself, we open ourselves up to analogies and models drawn from these well-studied phenomena, no longer relegating the study of language to the realm of the biologically unique.

In terms of the complex systems features in use in systems biolinguistics, this view would aim to incorporate (1) numerosity, (2) feedback, (7) robustness, (8) nested structure and modularity, (9) history and memory, and (10) adaptive behaviour into the study of language. We've mostly seen snapshots of (1), (7), (8), and (10) here. Of course, future work would precisify these aims but, for now, the chief goal is to present an argument for a maximalist approach to language sciences as a means of capturing the true essence of a viable biolinguistics.

Further Reading

There are a number of extant linguistic accounts that treat natural language as a complex system, either implicitly or explicitly. Each focuses on one or two different features of complex systems as the core linguistic explananda.

- A classic text on language as an emergent phenomenon is Herbert Clark's (1996) *Using Language* (Cambridge University Press). Clark argues that language is like a dance that emerges within a particular joint action setting. Coordination between participants on content and process require a rich mixture of convention and common ground to sustain the linguistic activity. Dialogue data and the appreciation of social relationships above and beyond individual communicative acts pervade the analysis.
- The next candidate more explicitly embraces the idea of language as a complex system. William Kretzschmar's recent (2015) book *Language and Complex Systems* (Cambridge University Press) homes in on the features of (1) numerosity, (3) feedback, and (6) nonlinearity, or what he calls the 'A-curve' in the corpus data he evaluates. He states that 'no linguist can afford to ignore the fact that human language is a complex system' and that, furthermore, '[a]ll approaches to human language must begin with speech, and all speech is embedded in the complex system' (Kretzschmar 2015, p. 2). One specific complex feature that Kretzschmar shows to be omnipresent in his corpus data is an emergent nonlinearity characteristic of market economies, namely, the Pareto, or 80/20, principle in which 80 per cent of wealth is concentrated within 20 per cent of the populace based on Zipf's law. He claims that the Pareto principle shows up all over the data at various levels and that 'we in language studies can and should make good practical use of the 80/20 Rule on a conceptual basis' (2015, p. 85).
- Neither Clark's nor Kretzschmar's work really engages with the biological aspects of linguistics. This is unsurprising since neither prescribe to biolinguistics explicitly. A complex systems analysis of language that does aspire to biolinguistics is the work of Simon Kirby, and his colleagues, on computational evolutionary theory. His earlier book (1999) *Function,*

Selection, and Innateness: The Emergence of Language Universals (Oxford University Press) sets up the idea of approaching language as an adaptive system. He considers the approach 'a new way of thinking about the role of cultural transmission in an explanatory biolinguistics' (Kirby 2013, p. 460). Specifically, the method of 'iterated learning models' in computational language evolution research, pioneered by this latter approach, aims to explain how complex syntactic structure, such as discrete infinity, is generated by creating highly simplistic models involving generational simulations of populations with no language to begin with (see Brighton & Kirby 2001). This work exemplifies both the truism 'complexity can come from simplicity' and the feature of the role of history and memory (9), discussed by Ladyman & Weisner.

9 Conclusion

There's not much more that I can say about the philosophy of linguistics here (see Nefdt 2023a for a different but related take). In this book, we've covered linguistic fields from generative syntax and phonology to game-theoretic pragmatics, deep learning NLP, formal semantics, language evolution, and much in between. This doesn't mean that we haven't been forced to neglect important domains such as sociolinguistics, psycholinguistics, and language acquisition, at least as independent chapters. In fact, the issue of the goals or success conditions of specific theories covered in the text haven't always been presented explicitly. In Chapter 7, we added predictive success to the goals of linguistic theory. However, what individual linguists are working towards in building their models of, say, the semantics of a particular phrase, or the role minimal pairs or counterexamples play in a given theory, has remained relatively implicit. But as I mentioned in the Preface, no one book can cover all of the topics of philosophical interest in a field as diverse and developed as linguistics. What I've attempted to do is discuss, dissect, and discover new topics that connect linguistic theory to the philosophy of mind, evolutionary theory, cognitive science, modal metaphysics, and the philosophy of science. In the process, I hope to have convinced any reader, who made it this far, that linguistic theory is indefatigably fascinating from a contemporary philosophical perspective.

Although each chapter offered up a new purview, scope, and range of data and theories for scrutiny and reflection, there were overarching themes that connected the many strands. For one thing, I think methodological pluralism within subfields (and across them) is unavoidable. Linguistic theory isn't monolithic. Many books on the subject have adopted particular theoretical persuasions and held fast to them in the face of alternative formalisms and models. I, for my part, have tried to do justice to the vast array of competing and complementary theoretical possibilities.

Natural language is perhaps the single most important human development. This book has shown, through its scientific study, just how complex it is to capture the many interconnected elements of this uniquely human cognitive and social achievement. While I highlighted the significant accomplishments that have brought us to our present level of knowledge, I also suggested places in which we can improve, integrate, and develop new models based on adjacent fields and alternative approaches. I see this as one of the primary roles of philosophy. The step back it asks us to take can often lead to the development of new tools or at least deeper appreciation of our present ones.

There are no neutral philosophers. We all come with our favoured theoretical outlooks and biases. I'm no different in that way. I've flagged places in the text where I've personally contributed to the literature in one direction or another. In some places, I've even taken up strong positions (for the sake of argument) on where I think juicier fruit might be located in a particular domain and where appreciation of historical debates in the philosophy of other sciences might resolve or dissolve current controversies. Despite this, my approach has been eclectic and, in every chapter, my primary goal was fair exposition of alternatives before offering my own views on the matters at hand.

Finally, this book was designed to start multiple conversations across sub-fields of the study of language, which often receive little to no philosophical airtime. The philosophy of theoretical linguistics isn't a novella or even a novel; it's a Proustian series of deep conversations about a theoretical project so fundamental to the way we understand ourselves, our interlocutors, and the worlds in which we converse with one another.

References

Adger, D. 2018. The autonomy of syntax. In Hornstein, N., Lasnik, H., Patel-Grosz, P., & Yang, C. (eds.), *Syntactic Structures after 60 Years*, pp. 153–75. De Gruyter.

Aguilar, J., & Buckareff, A. 2010. *Causing Human Actions: New Perspectives on the Causal Theory of Action*. MIT Press.

Allott, N., Lohndal, T., & Rey, G. 2021. Chomsky's 'Galilean' explanatory style. In Allott, N., Lohndal, T., & Rey, G. (eds.), *A Companion to Chomsky*, pp. 517–28. Wiley & Sons, Inc.

Altshuler, D. (ed.). 2022. *Linguistics Meets Philosophy*. Cambridge University Press.

Anderson, J., & Ewen, C. J. 1987. *Principles of Dependency Phonology*. Cambridge University Press.

Ankeny, R., & Leonelli, S. 2011. What's so special about model organisms? *Studies in the History and Philosophy of Science* 41: 313–23.

Anscombe, E. 1963. *Intention* (2nd ed.). Cornell University Press.

Armstrong, D.F., Stokoe, W.C., & Wilcox, S.E. 1995. *Gesture and the Nature of Language*. Cambridge University Press.

Asher, N. 2011. *Lexical Meaning in Context: A Web of Words*. Cambridge University Press.

   2012. Context in content composition. In Kempson, R., Fernando, T., & Asher, N. (eds.), *Philosophy of Linguistics*, pp. 229–69. Elsevier B.V. North Holland.

Austin, P., & Bresnan, J. 1996. Non-configurationality in Australian aboriginal languages. *Natural Language and Linguistic Theory* 14: 215–68.

Baggio, G. 2018. *Meaning in the Brain*. MIT Press.

Ball, D. 2018. Semantics as measurement. In Ball, D., & Rabern, B. (eds.), The Science of Meaning: Essays on the Metatheory of Natural Language Semantics (online ed.). Oxford Academic.

Ball, D., & Rabern, B. (eds.) 2018. *The Science of Meaning*. Oxford University Press.

Bechtel, W., & Abrahamsen, A. 2005. Explanation: a mechanist alternative. *Studies in the History and Philosophy of Biological and Biomedical Sciences* 36: 421–41.

Becker, A. 2018. *What Is Real? The Unfinished Quest for the Meaning of Quantum Physics*. Basic Books.

Benz, A., & Stevens, J. 2018. Game-theoretic approaches to pragmatics. *Annual Review of Linguistics* 4: 173–91.

Benz, A., Jäger, G., & van Rooij, R. 2006. *Game Theory and Pragmatics*. Palgave Macmillan.

Bernardy, J., & Lappin, S. 2017. Using deep neural networks to learn syntactic agreement. *Linguistic Issues in Language Technology* 15: 1–15.

Berto, F., & Jago, M. 2019. *Impossible Worlds*. Oxford University Press.

Berwick, R., & Chomsky, N. 2016. *Why Only Us? Language and Evolution*. MIT Press.

Berwick, R., Friederici, A., Chomsky, N., & Bolhuis, J. 2013. Evolution, brain, and the nature of language. *Trends in Cognitive Sciences*, 17(2): 89–98.

Bever, T. 2021. How *Cognition* came into being. *Cognition* 213: 104761.

Bickerton, D. 2014a. Some problems for biolinguistics. *Biolinguistics* 8: 73–96.

   2014b. *More than Nature Needs: Language, Mind, and Evolution*. Harvard University Press.

Blasi, D., Moran, S., Moisik, S., Widmer, P., Dediu, D., & Bickel, B. 2019. Human sound systems are shaped by post-Neolithic changes in bite configuration. *Science* 363(6432): eaav3218.

Blome-Tillmann, M. 2013. Conversational implicatures (and how to spot them). *Philosophy Compass* 8(2): 170–85.

Blutner, R. 2000. Some aspects of optimality in natural language interpretation. *Journal of Semantics* 17: 189–216.

Blutner, R. 2011. Some experimental aspects of optimality theoretic pragmatics. In Nemeth, E., & Bibok, K. (eds.), *The Role of Data at the Semantics–Pragmatics Interface*. pp. 161–204. De Gruyter Mouton.

Blutner, R., & Zeevat, H. (eds.) 2004. *Optimality Theory and Pragmatics*. Palgrave Macmillan.

Boas, H., & Sag, I. (eds.) 2012. *Sign-Based Construction Grammar*. CSLI Publications.

Bod, R. 2009. From exemplar to grammar: a probabilistic analogy-based model of language learning. *Cognitive Science* 33: 752–93.

   2015. Probabilistic linguistics. In Heine, B., & Narrog, H. (eds.), *The Oxford Handbook of Linguistic Analysis*, pp. 663–92. Oxford University Press.

Bod, R., & Scha, R. 1996. Data-oriented language processing: an overview. *ILLC Technical Report LP-96-13*.

Bod, R., Hay, J., & Jannedy, S. 2003. *Probabilistic Linguistics*. MIT Press.

Boeckx, C. 2006. *Linguistic Minimalism: Origins, Concepts, Methods, and Aims*. Oxford University Press.

   2015. Beyond Humboldt's problem: reflections on biolinguistics and its relation to generative grammar. *Language Sciences* 50: 127–32.

Boleda, G. 2020. Distributional semantics and linguistic theory. *Annual Review of Linguistics* 6: 213–34.

Borg, E. 2004. *Minimal Semantics*. Clarendon Press.

Börjars, K. 2020. Lexical-functional grammar: an overview. *Annual Review of Linguistics* 6(1): 155–72.

Borsley, R. 1991. *Syntactic Theory: A Unified Approach*. Edward Arnold.

Botha, R. 1983. On the 'Galilean style' of linguistic inquiry. *Lingua* 58: 1–50.

Brandom, R. 1994. *Making It Explicit*. Harvard University Press.

Brentari, D. 2019. *Sign Language Phonology*. Cambridge University Press.

Brentari, D., Fenlon, J., & Cormier, K. 2018. Sign language phonology. In Aronoff, M. (ed.), *The Oxford Research Encyclopedia of Linguistics*, pp. 1–23. Oxford University Press.

Bresnan, J. (ed.) 1982. *The Mental Representation of Grammatical Relations*. MIT Press.

Bresnan, J., Asudeh, A., Toivonen, I. & Wechsler, S. 2016. *Lexical-Functional Syntax*. Wiley, Blackwell.

Brighton, H., & Kirby, S. 2001. The survival of the smallest: stability conditions for the cultural evolution of compositional language. In Kelemen, J., & Sosik, P. (eds.), *Advances in Artificial Life*. Springer.

Bromberger, S. 1989. Types and tokens in linguistics. In George, A. (ed.), *Reflections on Chomsky*, pp. 58–90. Basil Blackwell.

Bromberger, S., & Halle, M. 1989. Why phonology is different. *Linguistic Inquiry* 20(1): 51–70.

    1992. The ontology of phonology. In Bromberger, S. (ed.), *On What We Know We Don't Know*, pp. 206–30. University of Chicago Press.

Brown,   A.   2013.   Phonetics   and   phonology: historical   overview.   In Chapelle,   C.   A.   (ed.),   *The   Encyclopedia   of   Applied   Linguistics*. https://doi.org/10.1002/9781405198431.wbeal0910

Buckingham, H. W. (1986). The scan-copier mechanism and the positional level of language production: evidence from phonemic paraphasia. Cognitive Science 10(2): 195–217.

Buckner, C. 2019. Deep learning: a philosophical introduction. *Philosophy Compass* 14(10): e12625.

Bunt, H. 2007. The semantics of semantic annotation. In Chae, H.-R., Choe, J.-W., Jun, J. S., Jun, Y., & Yoo, E.-J. (eds.), *Proceedings of the 21st Pacific Asia Conference on Language, Information and Computation* (PACLIC21, pp. 13–28). The Korean Society for Language and Information (KSLI).

Burgess, A., & Sherman, B. (eds.) 2014. *Metasemantics: New Essays on the Foundations of Meaning*. Oxford University Press.

Burgess, A., Cappelen, H., & Plunkett, D. (eds.) 2020. *Conceptual Engineering and Conceptual Ethics*. Oxford University Press.

Camp, E. 2017. Pragmatic force in semantic context. *Philosophical Studies: An International Journal for Philosophy in the Analytic Tradition* 174(6): pp. 1617–27.

Cann, R. 1993. *Formal Semantics: An Introduction*. Cambridge University Press.

Cann, R., Kempson, R., & Wedgwood, D. 2012. Representationalism and linguistic knowledge. In Kempson, R., Fernando, T., & Asher N. (eds.), *Philosophy of Linguistics*, pp. 356–401. Elsevier B.V. North Holland.

Cappelen, H., & Lepore, E. 2005. *Insensitive Semantics: A Defense of Semantic Minimalism and Speech Act Pluralism*. Blackwell.

Cartwright, N. 1983. *How the Laws of Physics Lie*. Clarendon Press.

Chater, N., Clark, A., Goldsmith, J. & Perfors, A. 2015. *Empiricism and Language Learnability*. Oxford University Press UK.

Chomsky, N. 1956. Three models for the description of language. *IRE Transactions on Information Theory* IT-2: 113–23.

    1957. *Syntactic Structures*. Mouton Press.

    1959a. Review of Skinner's *Verbal Behavior*. *Language* 35: 26–58.

    1959b. On certain formal properties of grammars. *Information and Control* 2(2): 137–67.

    1965. *Aspects of a Theory of Syntax*. MIT Press.

    1966. *Cartesian Linguistics: A Chapter in the History of Rationalist Thought* (3rd ed., 2009). Harper & Row.

1973. Conditions on transformations. In Anderson, S., & Kiparsky, P (eds.), *A Festschrift for Morris Halle*, pp. 232–86. Holt, Rinehart & Winston.

1980. *Rules and Representations*. Blackwell.

1981. *Lectures on Government and Binding*. De Gruyter Mouton.

1986. *Knowledge of Language: Its Nature, Origin, and Use*. Praeger.

1995a. Bare phrase structure. In Campos, H., & Kempchinsky, P. (eds.), *Evolution and Revolution in Linguistic Theory: Essays in Honor of Carlos Otero (Georgetown Studies in Romance Linguistics none)*, pp. 51–109. Georgetown University Press.

1995b. *The Minimalist Program*. MIT Press.

1995c. Language and nature. *Mind* 104: 1–61.

2000. *New Horizons for the Study of Mind and Language*. Cambridge University Press.

2001. Derivation by phase. In Kenstowicz, M. (ed.), *Ken Hale: A Life in Language*. MIT Press.

2002. *On Nature and Language*. Cambridge University Press.

2012. *The Science of Language*. Cambridge University Press.

2013. Lecture I: what is language? The Journal of Philosophy 110(12): 645–62.

2021. Simplicity and the form of grammars. *Journal of Language Modelling* 9(1): 5–15.

Chomsky, N., & Halle, M. 1968. *The Sound Pattern of English*. Harper & Row.

Christiansen, M., & Chater, N. 2015. The language faculty that wasn't: a usage-based account of natural language recursion. *Frontiers in Psychology* 6. doi.org/10.3389/fpsyg.2015.01182

Clark, H. 1996. *Using Language*. Cambridge University Press.

Clark, A., & Chalmers, D. 1998. The extended mind. *Analysis* 58(1): 7–19.

Clark, H., & Fox Tree, J. 2002. Using *uh* and *um* in spontaneous speaking. *Cognition* 84: 73–111.

Clark, A., & Lappin, S. 2012. Computational learning theory and language acquisition. In Kempson, R., Fernando, T., & Asher, N. (eds.), *Philosophy of Linguistics*, pp. 445–75. Elsevier B.V. North Holland.

Collins, M. 1999. Head-Driven Statistical Models for Natural Language Parsing. Ph.D thesis, University of Pennsylvania.

Cooper, R. 1983. *Quantification and Syntactic Theory*. D. Reidel.

Costa, L., Rodrigues, F., & Cristino, A. 2008. Complex networks: the key to systems biology. *Genetics and Molecular Biology* 31(3): 591–601.

Cowie, F. 1999. *What's Within? Nativism Reconsidered*. Oxford University Press.

Craig, E. 1990. *Knowledge and the State of Nature: An Essay in Conceptual Synthesis*. Clarendon Press.

Croft, W. 2001. *Radical Construction Grammar: Syntactic Theory in Typological Perspective*. Oxford University Press.

2005. Logical and typological arguments for radical construction grammar. In Östman, J.-O., & Fried, M. (eds.), *Construction Grammars: Cognitive Grounding and Theoretical Extensions [Constructional Approaches to Language 3]*, pp. 273–314. John Benjamins.

2013. Radical construction grammar. In Hoffmann, T., & Trousdale, G., (eds.), *The Oxford Handbook of Construction Grammar*. Oxford University Press.

Culicover, P., & Jackendoff, R. 2005. *Simpler Syntax*. Oxford University Press.

Curtiss, S., Fromkin, V., Krashen, S., Rigler, D., & Rigler, M. 1974. The linguistic development of Genie. *Language* 50(3):528–54.

Dabrowska, E. 2015. What exactly is Universal Grammar, and has anyone seen it? *Frontiers in Psychology* 6: Article 852.

Davidson, D. 1965. Theories of meaning and learnable languages. Reprinted in *Inquiries into Truth and Interpretation*, 2001, pp. 3–16. Clarendon Press.

Davidson, D. 1967. Truth and meaning. *Synthese* 17(1): 304–23.

Davidson, D. 1986. A nice derangement of epitaphs. In Lepore, E. (ed.), *Truth and Interpretation: Perspectives on the Philosophy of Donald Davidson*, pp. 433–46. Blackwell.

Deacon, T. 2008. Emergence: the hole at the wheel's hub 1. In Clayton, P., & Davies, P. (eds.), *The Re-Emergence of Emergence: The Emergentist Hypothesis from Science to Religion*, pp. 111–50. Oxford University Press.

De Boer, B., Thompson, B., Ravignani, A., & Boeckx, C. 2020. Evolutionary dynamics do not motivate a single-mutant theory of human language. *Scientific Reports* 10(1): 1–9.

Debusmann, R. 2000. An introduction to dependency grammar. *Hausarbeit fur das Hauptseminar Dependenzgrammatik SoSe* 99, pp. 1–16. Universitat des Saarlandes.

Debusmann, R., & Kuhlmann, M. 2010. Dependency grammar: classification and exploration. In Crocker, M., & Siekmann, J. (eds.), *Resource-Adaptive Cognitive Processes*, pp. 365–88. Springer Verlag.

Dediu, D., & Levinson, S. 2013. On the antiquity of language: the reinterpretation of Neandertal linguistic capacities and its consequences. *Frontiers in Psychology* 4: 397.

Dekker, P. 2012. *Dynamic Smenatics*. Springer Verlag.

Dekker, P., & van Rooij, R. 2000. Bi-directional optimality theory: an application of game theory. *Journal of Semantics* 17: 217–42.

de Marneffe, M. C., & Nivre, J. 2019. Dependency grammar. *Annual Review of Linguistics* 5: 197–218.

Derbyshire, D., & Pullum, G. 1981. Object initial languages. *International Journal of American Linguistics* 47(3): 192–214.

Dever, J. 2012. Formal semantics. In García-Carpintero, M., & Kölbel, M. (eds.), *The Continuum Companion to the Philosophy of Language*, pp. 47–83. Continuum International.

Devitt, M. 2006. *Ignorance of Language*. Oxford University Press.

2013a. The 'linguistic conception' of grammars. *Filozofia Nauki* Rok XXI: 2(82).

2013b. What makes a property 'semantic'? In Capone, A., Lo Piparo, F., & Carapezza, M. (eds.), *Perspectives on Pragmatics and Philosophy. Perspectives in Pragmatics, Philosophy & Psychology*, Volume 1, pp. 87–111. Springer.

Ding, N., Melloni, L., Zhang, H., Tian, X., & Poeppel, D. 2015. Cortical tracking of hierarchical linguistic structures in connected speech. *Nature Neuroscience* 19: 158–64.

Dorr, C. 2010. Review of James Ladyman and Don Ross. *Every Thing Must Go: Metaphysics Naturalized. Notre Dame Philosophical Reviews* 6.

Douglas, H. 2009. Reintroducing prediction to explanation. *Philosophy of Science* 76(4): 444–63.

Dowty, D. 2007. Compositionality as an empirical problem. In Barker, C., & Jacobson, P. (eds.), *Direct Compositionality*, pp. 14–23. Oxford University Press.

Dupre, G. 2021. (What) can deep learning contribute toÂtheoretical linguistics? *Minds & Machines* 31: 617–35.

Dupre, G. 2023. Idealisation in semantics: truth-conditional semantics for radical contextualists. *Inquiry: An Interdisciplinary Journal of Philosophy* 66(5): 917–46.

Dupré, J., & O'Malley, M. 2007. Metagenomics and biological ontology. *Studies in History and Philosophy of Biological and Biomedical Sciences* 38(4): 834–46.

  2009. Varieties of living things: life at the intersection of lineage and metabolism. *Philosophy and Theory in Biology* 1(3): 1–25.

Dummett, M. 1993. What do I know when I know a language? In Dummett, M. (ed.), *The Seas of Language*, pp. 94–105. Clarendon Press.

Dyer, C., Kuncoro, A., Ballesteros, M., & Smith, N. 2016. Recurrent neural network grammars. In *Proceedings of the 2016 Conference of the North American Chapter of the Association for Computational Linguistics: Human Language Technologies*, pp. 199–209. Association for Computational Linguistics.

Egré, P. 2015. Explanation in linguistics. *Philosophy Compass* 10(7): 451–62.

Egré, P. 2018. Philosophy of linguistics. In Baberousse, A., Bonnay, D., & Cozic, M. (eds.), *The Philosophy of Science: A Companion*, pp. 654–728. Oxford University Press.

Elffers, E. 2020. Linguistics and brain science: (dis-)connections in nineteenth century aphasiology. In Nefdt, R. M., Klippi, C., & Karstens, B. (eds.), *The Philosophy and Science of Language*, pp. 239–74. Palgrave Macmillan.

Erk, K. 2020. Variations on abstract semantic spaces. In Nefdt, R. M., Klippi, C., & Karstens, B. (eds.), *The Philosophy and Science of Language*, pp. 71–99. Palgrave Macmillan.

Eshghi, A., Hough, J., Purver, M., Kempson, R., & Gregoromichelaki, E. 2012. Conversational interactions: capturing dialogue dynamics. In Larsson, S., & Borin, L. (eds.), *From Quantification to Conversation: Festschrift for Robin Cooper on the Occasion of His 65th Birthday*, pp. 1–27. College Publications.

Evans, N., & Levinson, S. 2009. The myth of language universals: language diversity and its importance for cognitive science. *Behavioral and Brain Sciences* 32(5): 429–48.

Everett, D. 2005. Cultural constraints on grammar and cognition in Pirahã: another look at the design features of human language. *Current Anthropology* 46: 621–46.

  2007. Cultural constraints on grammar in Piraha: a reply to Nevins, Pesetsky, and Rodrigues. http://ling.auf.net/lingBuzz/000427

  2017a. *How Language Began: The Story of Humanity's Greatest Invention*. W. W. Norton.

  2017b. A dozen years of misunderstanding. *Letters* 3(2).

Field, H. 1980. *Science without Numbers: A Defense of Nominalism*. Princeton University Press.

Fillmore, C., Kay, P., & O'Connor, M. 1988. Regularity and idiomaticity in grammatical constructions: the case of *let alone*. *Language* 64: 501–38.

Firth, J. 1957. *Papers in Linguistics*. Oxford University Press.

Fong, S., & Berwick, R. 2008. Treebank parsing and knowledge of language: a cognitive perspective. *Proceedings CogSci 2008*, Washington, DC.

Forst, M. 2011. Computational aspects of lexical functional grammar. *Language and Linguistics Compass* 5(1): 1–18.

Francez, N., & Dyckhoff, R. 2010. Proof-theoretic semantics for a natural language fragment. *Linguistics & Philosophy* 33(6): 447–77.

Frank, S., Bod, R., & Christiansen, M. 2012. How hierarchical is language use? *Proceedings of the Royal Society B: Biological Sciences* 279: 4522–31.

Franke, M. 2011. Quantity implicatures, exhaustive interpretation, and rational conversation. *Semantics & Pragmatics* 4(1): 1–82.

2013. Game theoretic pragmatics. *Philosophy Compass* 8(3): 269–84.

Franke, M., & Jäger, G. 2012. Bidirectional optimization from reasoning and learning in games. *Journal of Logic, Language and Information*, 21(1): 117–39.

2016. Probabilistic pragmatics, or why Bayes' rule is probably important for pragmatics. *Zeitschrift für Sprachwissenschaft* 35(1): 3–44.

Frege, G. 1892 [1948]. On sense and reference. *The Philosophical Review* 57(3): 209–30.

Freidin, R. 2012. A brief history of generative grammar. In Russell, G., & Fara, D., (eds.), *The Routledge Companion to Philosophy of Language*, pp. 895–916. Routledge.

French, S. 2011. Shifting the structures in physics and biology: a prophylactic promiscuous realism. *Studies in History and Philosophy of Biological and Biomedical Sciences* 42: 164–73.

Friederici, A., Chomsky, N., Berwick, R., Moro, A., & Bolhuis, J. 2017. Language, mind and brain. *Nature Human Behaviour* 1(10): 713–22.

Futrell, R., Mahowald, K., & Gibson, E. 2015. Large-scale evidence of dependency length minimization in 37 languages. *Proceedings of the National Academy of the Sciences USA* 112(33): 10336–41.

Futrell, R., Stearns, L., Everett, D., Piantadosi, S., & Gibson, E. 2016. A corpus investigation of syntactic embedding in Pirahã. *PLoS ONE* 11(3): e0145289.

GAMUT. 1991. *Logic, Language and Meaning, Volume II: Intensional Logic and Logical Grammar*. Translation and revision of *Logica, taal en betekenis II*. University of Chicago Press.

Gao, J., Li, D., & Havlin, S. (2014). From a single network to a network of networks. *National Science Review* 1(3): 346–56.

Garde, P. 1977. Ordre linéaire et dépendance syntaxique: contribution á une typologie. *Bulletin de la Societe de Linguistique de Paris*. Paris, 72(1): 1–26.

Gazdar, G., Klein, E., Pullum, G., & Sag, I. 1985. *Generalized Phrase Structure Grammar*. Blackwell and Harvard University Press.

Gil, D. 1999. Riau Indonesian as a pivotless language. In Raxilina, E., & Testelec, Y. (eds.), *Tipologija i Teorija Jazyka, Ot Opisanija k Objasneniju, K 60-Letiju Aleksandra Evgen'evicha Kibrika (Typology and Linguistic Theory, from Description to Explanation, for the 60th Birthday of Aleksandr E. Kibrik)*, pp. 187–211. Jazyki Russkoj Kul'tury.

Gil, D. 2005. Word order without syntactic categories: how Riau Indonesian does it. In Carnie, A., Harley, H., & Dooley, S. A. (eds.), *Verb First: On the Syntax of Verb-Initial Languages*, pp. 243–63. John Benjamins.

Giorgolo, G. 2010. Space and Time in our Hands. Ph.D Thesis, Uil-OTS, Universiteit Utrecht.

Goldberg, A. 2013. Constructionist approaches. In Hoffmann, T., & Trousdale, G. (eds.), *The Oxford Handbook of Construction Grammar*, pp. 15–31. Oxford University Press.

Goldberg, A. 2015. Compositionality. In Reimer, N. (ed.), *Routledge Semantics Handbook*, pp. 419–33. Routledge Press.

Goldsmith, J. 1976. Autosegmental Phonology. MIT Ph.D Thesis.

Goodfellow, I., Bengio, Y., & Courville, A. 2016. *Deep Learning*. MIT Press.

Greenberg, J. 1963. Some universals of grammar with particular reference to the order of meaningful elements. In Greenberg, J. (ed.), *Universals of Language*, pp. 73–113. MIT Press.

Grice, H. P. 1967. Logic and conversation. In Grice, H. P. (ed.), *Studies in the Way of Words*, pp. 41–58. Harvard University Press.

Grice. H. P. 1975. Logic and Conversation. In Cole, P., & Morgan, J. (eds.), *Syntax and Semantics*, Volume 3, pp. 41–58. Academic Press.

Grice, H. P. 1989. *Studies in the Way of Words*. Harvard University Press.

Groenendijk, J., & Stokhof, M. 1982. Semantic analysis of wh-complements. *Linguistics & Philosophy* 5: 175–233.

Groenendijk, J. & Stokhof, M. 1991. Dynamic predicate logic. *Linguistics and Philosophy* 14: 39–100.

Hale, K. 1983. Warlpiri and the grammar of non-configurational languages. *Natural Language and Linguistic Theory* 1: 5–47.

Hale, M., & Reiss, C. 2000. Phonology as cognition. In Burton-Roberts, N., Carr, P., & Docherty, G. (eds.), *Phonological Knowledge*, pp. 161–84. Oxford University Press.

2008. *The Phonological Enterprise*. Oxford University Press.

Haspelmath, M. 2021. General linguistics must be based on universals (or non-conventional aspects of language). *Theoretical Linguistics* 47(1–2): pp. 1–31.

Haugh, M. 2013. Speaker meaning and accountability in interaction. *Journal of Pragmatics* 48(1): 41–56.

Hauser, M., Chomsky, N., & Fitch, W. 2002. The faculty of language: what is it, who has it, and how did it evolve? *Science* 298: 1569–79.

Hawthorne, J., & Magidor, O. 2009. Assertion, context, and epistemic accessibility. *Mind* 118(470): pp. 377–97.

Hays, D. 1961. Grouping and dependency theories. *Research Memorandum RM-2538*, The RAND Corporation.

1964. Dependency theory: a formalism and some observations. *Language* 40: 511–25.

Heim, I. 1982. The Semantics of Definite and Indefinite Noun Phrases. Ph.D Dissertation, University of Massachusetts.

Heim, I., & Kratzer, A. 1998. *Semantics in Generative Grammar*. Blackwell.

Hempel, C., & Oppenheim, P. 1948. Studies in the logic of explanation. *Philosophy of Science* 15: 135–75.

Hockett, C. 1960. The origin of speech. In Wang, W. (ed.), *Human Communication: Language and its Psychobiological Bases*, pp. 4–12. Scientific American, 1982.

1968. *The State of the Art*. Mouton.

Hoeksema, J. 1997. *Corpus Study of Negative Polarity Items*. University of Groningen. IV–V Jornades de corpus linguistics 1996–97, Universitat Pompeu Fabre, Barcelona.

Hoffmann, T. 2022. *Construction Grammar: The Structure of English*. Cambridge University Press.

Hoffmann, T., & Trousdale, G. 2013. Construction grammar: introduction. In Hoffmann, T., & Trousdale, G. (eds.), *The Oxford Handbook of Construction Grammar*, pp. 1–12. Oxford University Press.

Hölldobler, B., & Wilson, E. (2008). *The Superorganism*. W. W. Norton.

Horgan, T., & Tiensen, J. 2006. Cognition needs syntax but not rules. In Stainton, R. (ed.), *Contemporary Debates in Cognitive Science*, pp. 149–58. Blackwell.

Horn, L. 1984. Towards a new Taxonomy of pragmatic inference: Q-based and R-based implicature. In Schiffrin, D. (ed.), *Meaning, Form, and Use in Context: Linguistic Applications*, pp. 11–42. Georgetown University Press.

   2004. Implicature. In Horn, L., & Ward, G. (eds.), *Handbook of Pragmatics*, pp. 3–28. Blackwell.

Horn, L., & Kecskes, I. 2013. Pragmatics, discourse, and cognition. In Anderson, S., Moeschler, J., & Reboul, F. (eds.), *The Language–Cognition Interface*, pp. 353–75. Librairie Droz.

Hornstein, N. 2009. *A Theory of Syntax: Minimal Operations and Universal Grammar*. Cambridge University Press.

Howes, C., & Gibson, H. 2021. Dynamic syntax. *Journal of Logic, Language, and Information* 30: 263–76.

Hudson, R. 1990. *English Word Grammar*. Basil Blackwell.

Huisman, J., Majid, A., & van Hout, R. 2019. The geographical configuration of a language area influences linguistic diversity. *PLOS ONE* 14(6): e0217363.

Hutchins, E. 1995. *Cognition in the Wild*. MIT Press.

Hutchins, E. 2001. Distributed cognition. *International Encyclopedia of the Social & Behavioral Sciences*: 2068–72.

Isaac, M., Koch, S., & Nefdt, R. 2022. Conceptual engineering: a road map to practice. *Philosophy Compass* 17(10): e12879.

Itkonen, E. 1978. *Grammatical Theory and Metascience*. John Benjamins.

   1997. The social ontology of linguistic meaning. *SKY Journal of Linguistics*: 49–80.

   2001. Concerning the philosophy of phonology. *Puhe ja kieli* 21: 3–11.

   2006. Three fallacies that recur in linguistic argumentation. *Puhe ja kieli* 26(4): 221–6.

   2019. Concerning the scope of normativity. In Mäkilähde, A., Leppänen, V., & Itkonen, E. (eds.), *Normativity in Language and Linguistics*, pp. 29–68. John Benjamins.

Jackendoff, R. S. 1977. *X Syntax: A Study of Phrase Structure*. MIT Press.

Jackendoff, R. 1990. *Semantic Structures*. MIT Press.

   2002. *Foundations of Language: Brain, Meaning, Grammar, Evolution*. Oxford University Press.

   2007. Linguistics in cognitive science: the state of the art. *The Linguistic Review* 24: 347–401.

   2017. In defense of theory. *Cognitive Science* 41: 185–212.

   2019. Conceptual semantics. In Maienborn, C., Heusinger, K., & Portner, P. (eds.), *Semantics – Theories*, pp. 86–113. De Gruyter Mouton.

Jackendoff, R., & Wittenberg, E. 2014. What you can say without syntax: a hierarchy of grammatical complexity. In Newmeyer, F., & Preston, L. (eds.), *Measuring Linguistic Complexity*, pp. 65–82. Oxford University Press.

Jacobson, P. 2012. Direct compositionality and 'uninterpretability': the case of (sometimes) 'uninterpretable' features on pronouns. *Journal of Semantics* 29(3): 305–43.

Jäger, G. 1997. Game-theoretical pragmatics. In van Benthem, J., and ter Meulen, A. (eds.), *Handbook of Logic and Language*, pp. 467–91. Elsevier.

Jäger, G., & Rogers, J. 2012. Formal language theory: refining the Chomsky hierarchy. *Philosophical Transactions of the Royal Society B: Biological Sciences* 367(1598): 1956–70.

Janssen, T. 2012. Compositionality: its historic context. In Hinzen, W., Machery, E., & Werning, M. (eds.), *The Oxford Handbook of Compositionality*, pp. 19–46. Oxford University Press.

Johnson, M., & Lakoff, G. 2002. Why cognitive linguistics requires embodied realism. *Cognitive Linguistics* 13(3): 245–63.

Johnson-Laird, P., & Byrne, R. 1991. *Deduction*. Lawrence Erlbaum Associates.

Johnston, T. 2011. Lexical frequency in sign languages. *The Journal of Deaf Studies and Deaf Education* 17(2): 163–93.

Jones, D. 1950. *The Phoneme: Its Nature and Use*. Heffer.

Joshi, A. 1987. An introduction to tree adjoining grammars. In Manaster-Ramer, A. (ed.), *Mathematics of Language*, pp. 87–114. John Benjamins.

Joshi, A. 2004. Starting with complex primitives pays off: complicate locally, simplify globally. *Cognitive Science* 28: 637–68.

Joshi, A. & Schabes, Y. 1997. Tree-adjoining grammars. In Rozenberg, G. & Salomaa, A. (eds.), *Handbook of Formal Languages*, pp. 69–123. Springer.

Kac, M. 1994. A nonpsychological realist conception of linguistic rules. In Lima, S., Corrigan, R., & Iverson, G. (eds.), *The Reality of Linguistic Rules*, pp. 43–50. John Benjamins.

Kahane, S. 1997. Bubble trees and syntactic representations. In Becker, H., & Krieger, U. (eds.), *Proceedings of the 5th Meeting of Mathematics of Language*, pp. 70–76. Deutsches Forschungszentrum für Künstliche Intelligenz.

Kahneman, D. 2011. *Thinking, Fast and Slow*. Macmillan.

Kamp, H. 1981. A theory of truth and semantic representation. In Groenendijk, J., Janssen, T., & Stokhof, M. (eds.), *Formal Methods in the Study of Language, Mathematical Centre Tracts* 135, pp. 277–322. Mathematisch Centrum.

Kamp, H., Van Genabith, J., & Reyle, U. 2011. Discourse representation theory. In Gabbay, D., & Guenthner, F. (eds.), *Handbook of Philosophical Logic*, Volume 15, pp. 125–394. Springer.

Kaplan, D. 1989. Afterthoughts. In Almog, J., Perry, J., & Wettstein, H. (eds.), *Themes from Kaplan*, pp. 565–614. Oxford University Press.

Karlsson, F. 2007. Constraints on multiple center-embedding of clauses. *Journal of Linguistics* 43(2): 365–92.

Karttunen, L. 1977. The syntax and semantics of questions. *Linguistics and Philosophy* 1: 3–44.

Katz, J. 1981. *Language and Other Abstract Objects*. Rowman and Littlefield.

1996. The unfinished Chomskyan revolution. *Mind & Language* 11(3): 270–94.

Kauffman, S. 1995. *At Home in the Universe: The Search for the Laws of Self-Organization and Complexity*. Oxford University Press.

Kay, P., & Michaelis, L. (2012). Constructional meaning and compositionality. In Maienborn, C., von Heusinger, K., & Portner, P. (eds.), *Semantics: An International Handbook of Natural Language Meaning*, pp. 2271–96. Mouton de Gruyter.

Kecskes, I. 2021. Sociocognitive pragmatics. In Haugh, M., Kádár, D., & Terkourafi, M. (eds.), *The Cambridge Handbook of Sociopragmatics*, pp. 592–615. Cambridge University Press.

Keenan, E., & Moss, L. 2016. *Mathematical Structures in Language*. CSLI Publications.

Kelleher, J. 2019. *Deep Learning*. MIT Press.

Kempson, R., Viol, W., & Gabbay, D. 2001. *Dynamic Syntax: The Flow of Language Understanding*. Blackwell.

Kempson, R., Fernando, T., & Asher, N. (eds.) 2012. *Philosophy of Linguistics*. Elsevier.

Kennedy, C., & McNally, L. 2005. Scale structure, degree modification, and the semantics of gradable predicates. *Language* 81(2): 345–81.

Kepa, K., & Perry, J. 2020. Pragmatics. In Zalta, E. N. (ed.), *The Stanford Encyclopedia of Philosophy*. Metaphysics Research Lab, Stanford University. https://plato.stanford.edu/archives/spr2020/entries/pragmatics/

Kirby, S. 1999. *Function, Selection, and Innateness: The Emergence of Language Universals*. Oxford University Press.

  2013. Language, culture and computation: an adaptive systems approach to biolinguistics. In Boeckx, C., & Grohmann, K. (eds.), *Cambridge Handbook of Biolinguistics*. Cambridge University Press.

Kitano, H., & Oda, K. (2006). Self-extending symbiosis: a mechanism for increasing robustness through evolution. *Biological Theory* 1: 61–6.

Kitcher, P. 1989. Explanatory unification and the causal structure of the world. In Kitcher, P., & Salmon, W. (eds.), *Minnesota Studies in the Philosophy of Science, Volume XIII: Scientific Explanation*, pp. 410–505. University of Minnesota Press.

Klein, D., & Manning, C. 2002. Corpus-based induction of syntactic structure: models of dependency and constituency. In Scott, D. (ed.), *Proceedings of the 42th Annual Meeting of the Association for Computational Linguistics*, pp. 478–85. Association for Computational Linguistics.

Klima, E., & Bellugi, U. 1979. *The Signs of Language*. Harvard University Press.

Kratzer, A. 1977. What must and can must and can mean. *Linguistics & Philosophy* 1: 337–55.

  1981. Notional category of modality. In Einkmeyer, H., & Rieser, H. (eds.), *Words, Worlds, and Contexts: New Approaches in Word Semantics*, pp. 38–74. De Gruyter.

Krause, J., Lalueza-Fox, C., Orlando, L., Enard, W., Green, R., Burbano, H., Hublin, J., Hänni, J., Fortea, J., Rasilla, M., Bertranpetit, J., Rosas, A., & Pääbo, S. (2007). The derived FOXP2 variant of modern humans was shared with Neanderthals. *Current Biology* 17: 53–60.

Kretzschmar, W. 2015. *Language and Complex Systems*. Cambridge University Press.

Kubota, Y., & Levine, R. 2020. *Type-Logical Syntax*. MIT Press.

Kukla, A. 1996. The theory–observation distinction. *The Philosophical Review*, 105(2): 173–230.

Kurowski, K., & Blumstein, S. 2017. Phonetic basis of phonemic paraphasias in aphasia: evidence for cascading activation. *Cortex* 75: 193–203.

Labov, W. 1969. Contraction, deletion, and inherent variability of the English Copula. *Language* 45: 715–62.

Labov, W. 2010. Unendangered dialect, endangered people: the case of African American Vernacular English. *Transforming Anthropology* 18(1): 15–28.

Ladyman, J., & Ross, D. 2007. *Everything Must Go: Naturalized Metaphysics*. Oxford University Press.

Ladyman, J., & Wiesner, K. 2020. *What Is a Complex System?* Yale University Press.

Lahiri, A., & Reetz, H. 2010. Distinctive features: phonological underspecification in representation and processing. *Journal of Phonetics* 38(1): 44–59.

Lakoff, G. 1973. Fuzzy grammar and the performance/competence terminology game. In *Cognitive Linguistics Bibliography*. Chicago Linguistic Society.

   1991. Cognitive versus generative linguistics: how commitments influence results. *Language & Communication* 11(1/2): 53–62.

Langacker, R. 1991. *Concept, Image, and Symbol*. De Gruyter.

Langendoen, T. 2003. Merge. In Carnie, A., Hayley, H., & Willie, M. (eds.), *Formal Approaches to Function in Grammar: In Honor of Eloise Jelinek*, pp. 307–18. John Benjamins.

   2008. Coordinate grammar. *Language* 84: 691–709.

   2022. *The Vastness of Natural Languages Revisited*. Unpublished manuscript.

Langendoen, T., & Postal, P. 1984. *The Vastness of Natural Languages*. Blackwell.

Lappin, S. 2021. *Deep Learning and Linguistic Representation*. Chapman & Hall/Crc.

Lappin, S., & Shieber, S. 2007. Machine learning theory and practice as a source of insight into univeral grammar. *Journal of Linguistics* 43: 393–427.

Larson, R., & Segal, G. 1995. *Knowledge of Meaning*. MIT Press.

Lavin, D. 2013. Must there be basic actions? *Nous* 47(2): 273–301.

Lenci, A. 2008. Distributional semantics in linguistic and cognitive research. *Rivista di Linguistica* 20(1): 1–31.

Leng, M. 2021. Models, structures, and the explanatory role of mathematics in empirical science. *Synthese*, 199: 10415–40.

Lesmo, L., & Robaldo, L. 2006. Dependency tree semantics. In *Foundations of Intelligent Systems*, pp. 550–9. Springer.

Levinson, S. 2000. *Presumptive Meanings: The Theory of Generalized Conversational Implicature*. MIT Press.

Lewis, D. 1969. *Convention*. Harvard University Press.

   1970. General semantics. *Synthese* 22: 18–67.

   1975. Languages and language. In Gunderson, K. (ed.), *Minnesota Studies in the Philosophy of Science*, pp. 3–35. University of Minnesota Press.

   1979. Scorekeeping in a language game. In *Philosophical Papers*, Volume I, pp. 233–49. Oxford University Press.

   1980. Index, context and content. In Kanger, S., & Ohman, S. (eds.), *Philosophy and Grammar*, pp. 79–100. Reidel.

   1983. New work for a theory of universals. *Australasian Journal of Philosophy* 61: 343–77.

Lewis, K. 2014. Do we need dynamic semantics? In Burgess, A., & Sherman, B. (eds.), *Metasemantics: Essays on the Foundations of Meaning*, pp. 231–58. Oxford University Press.

Lichte, T. & Kallmeyer, L. 2017. Tree-adjoining grammar: a tree-based constructionist grammar framework for natural language understanding. In Steels, L., & Feldman, J. (eds.), *Proceedings of the AAAI 2017 Spring Symposium on Computational Construction Grammar and Natural Language Understanding* (Technical Report SS-17–02), pp. 205–12. Association for the Advancement of Artificial Intelligence.

Liddell, S. 1984. THINK and BELIEVE: sequentiality in American Sign Language. *Language* 60: 372–99.

Lipton, P. 2004. *Inference to the Best Explanation*. Routledge.

Linnebo, O. 2008. *Compositionality and Frege's Context Principle*. Unpublished manuscript.

Linzen, T. 2019. What can linguistics and deep learning contribute to each other? Response to Pater. *Language* 95(1): e99–e108.

Linzen, T., & Baroni, M. 2021. Syntactic structure from deep learning. *Annual Review of Linguistics* 7: 195–212.

Linzen, T., Dupoux, E., & Goldberg, Y. 2016. Assessing the ability of LSTMs to learn syntax-sensitive dependencies. *Transactions of the Association for Computational Linguistics* 4: 521–35.

Lobina, D. 2017. *Recursion: A Computational Investigation into the Representation and Processing of Language*. Oxford University Press.

Lewontin, R. 1998. The evolution of cognition: questions we will never answer. In Gleitman, L., Liberman, M., & Osherson, D. N. (eds.), *An Invitation to Cognitive Science*, Volume 4, pp. 107–32). MIT Press.

Ludlow, P. 2011. *Philosophy of Generative Grammar*. Oxford University Press.

    2014. *Living Words: Meaning Underdetermination and the Dynamic Lexicon*. Oxford University Press.

Madden, E., Robinson, R., & Kendall D. 2017. Phonological treatment approaches for spoken word production in aphasia. *Seminars in Speech and Language* 38(1): 62–74.

Mallory, F. 2023. Why is generative grammar recursive? *Erkenntnis* 88: 3097–111.

Manaster-Ramer, A., & Kac, M. 1990. The concept of phrase structure. *Linguistics & Philosophy* 13(3): 325–62.

Manning, C. 2003. Probabilistic syntax. In Bod, R., Hay, J., & Jannedy, S. (eds.), *Probabilistic Linguistics*, pp. 289–342. MIT Press.

Marantz, A. 2007. Generative linguistics within the cognitive neuroscience of language. *The Linguistic Review* 22: 429–46.

Marr, D. 1982. *Vision*. W.H. Freeman and Company.

Martins, P., & Boeckx, C. 2016. What we talk about when we talk about biolinguistics. *Linguistics Vanguard* 2(1): 1–15.

    2019. Language evolution and complexity considerations: the no half-Merge fallacy. *PLoS Biology* 17(11): e3000389.

Marvin, R., & Linzen, T. 2018. Targeted syntactic evaluation of language models. In Riloff, E., Chiang, D., Hockenmaier, J., & Tsujii, J. (eds.), *Proceedings of the 2018 Conference on Empirical Methods in Natural Language Processing*, pp. 1192–202. Association of Computational Linguistics.

Matthews, P. 2014. *Generative Grammar and Linguistic Competence*. Routledge.

Mattson, M. 2014. Superior pattern processing is the essence of the evolved brain. *Frontiers in Neuroscience* 8(265): 1–17.

McCawley, J. 1978. Conversational implicature and the lexicon. In Cole, P. (ed.), *Syntax and Semantics 9: Pragmatics*, pp 245–59. Academic Press.

McCoy, T., Frank, R., & Linzen, T. 2018. Revisiting the poverty of the stimulus: hierarchical generalization without a hierarchical bias in recurrent neural networks. In Kalish, C., Rau, M. A., Zhu, X., & Rogers, T. T. (eds.), *Proceedings of the 40th Annual Conference of the Cognitive Science Society*, pp. 2093–8. Cognitive Science Society.

McCulloch, W., & Pitts, W. 1943. A logical calculus of the ideas immanent in nervous activity. *The Bulletin of Mathematical Biophysics* 5(4): 115–33.

McNally, L. 2013. Semantics and pragmatics. *WIREs Cognitive Science* 4: 285–97.

McNally, L., & Szabó, Z. 2022. *A Reader's Guide to Classic Papers in Formal Semantics*. Springer Verlag.

Mel'cuk, I. 1988. *Dependency Syntax: Theory and Practice*. State University Press of New York.

Mele, A. (ed.) 1997. *The Philosophy of Action*. Oxford University Press.

Meyer, J. 2021. Environmental and linguistic typology of whistled languages. *Annual Review of Linguistics* 7: 493–510.

Miall, C., & Wolpert, D. 1996. Forward models for physiological motor control. *Neural Networks* 9(8): 1265–79.

Miller, G. 2003. The cognitive revolution: a historical perspective. *TRENDS in Cognitive Science* 7(3): 141–4.

Miller, G., & Chomsky, N. 1963. Introduction to the formal analysis of natural languages. In Duncan Luce, R., Bush, R., & Galanter, E. (eds.), *The Handbook of Mathematical Psychology* (Volume II), pp. 269–321. Wiley.

Millikan, R. G. 1984. *Language, Thought, and Other Biological Categories: New Foundations for Realism*. MIT Press.

　　2005. *Language: A Biological Model*. Clarendon Press.

Mitchell, M. 2011. *Complexity: A Guided Tour*. Oxford University Press.

Montague, R. 1968. Pragmatics. In Thomason, R. (ed.), *Formal Philosophy*, pp. 95–118. Yale University Press, 1974.

Montague, R. 1970. Universal Grammar. *Theoria* 36: 373–98. Reprinted in Montague, R. 1974. *Formal Philosophy*. (ed.) R. Thomason (ed.), pp. 222–46. Yale University Press.

Morin, E. 2008. *On Complexity*. Hampton Press.

Moro, A. 2014. On the similarity between syntax and actions. *Trends in Cognitive Sciences* 18: 109–10.

Moro, A. 2016. *Impossible Languages*. The MIT Press.

Müller, S. 2018. *Grammatical Theory: From Transformational Grammar to Constraint-Based Approaches*. Language Science Press.

　　2020. *Grammatical Theory: From Transformational Grammar to Constraint-Based Approaches* (4th ed.) (Textbooks in Language Sciences 1). Language Science Press.

Müller, S. 2021. HPSG and construction grammar. In Müller, S., Abeillé, A., Borsley, R., & Koenig, J. (eds.), *Head-Driven Phrase Structure Grammar: The Handbook*, pp. 1497–553. Language Science Press.

Napoletano, T. 2019. How important are truth-conditions for truth-conditional semantics? *Linguistics and Philosophy* 42: 541–75.

Neef, M. 2018. Autonomous declarative phonology: a realist approach to the phonology of German. In Christina, C., & Neef, M. (eds.), *Essays on Linguistic Realism*, pp. 185–202. John Benjamins.

Nefdt, R. 2016. Scientific modelling in generative grammar and the dynamic turn in syntax. *Linguistics & Philosophy* 39(5): 357–94.

2018a. Languages and other abstract structures. In Behme, C., & Neef, M. (eds.), *Essays on Linguistic Realism*, pp. 139–84. John Benjamins.

2018b. Structuralism and inferentialism: a tale of two theories. *Logique et Analyse* 61(244): 489–512.

2019. Infinity and the foundations of linguistics. *Synthese* 196(5): 1671–711.

2020a. A puzzle about compositionality in machines. *Minds & Machines* 30: 47–75.

2020b. Formal semantics and applied mathematics: an inferential account. *Journal of Logic, Language & Information* 29(2): 221–53.

2021. Structural realism and generative linguistics. *Synthese* 199: 3711–37.

2022. Are machines radically contextualist? *Mind & Language* 38(3): 750–71.

2023a. *Language, Science, and Structure: A Journey into the Philosophy of Linguistics*. Oxford University Press.

2023b. Biolinguistics and biological systems: a complex systems analysis of language. *Biology & Philosophy* 38(12).

Nefdt, R., & Baggio, G. 2023. Notational variants and cognition: the case of dependency grammar. Erkenntnis.

Newmeyer, F. 1991. Functional explanation in linguistics and the origins of language. *Language and Communication* 11(1–2): 3–28.

1996. *Generative Linguistics: A Historical Perspective*. Routledge.

Nevins, A., Pesetsky, D., & Rodrigues, C. 2009. Pirahã exceptionality: a reassessment. *Language* 85: 355–404.

Nowak, E., & Michaelson, E. 2022. Meta-metasemantics, or the quest for the one true metasemantics. *The Philosophical Quarterly* 72(1): 135–54.

O'Grady, W. 1998. The syntax of idioms. *Natural Language & Linguistic Theory* 16: 279–312.

Olah, C. 2015. https://colah.github.io/posts/2015–08-Understanding-LSTMs/

Omar, A., & Alotaibi, M. 2017. Geographic location and linguistic diversity: the use of intensifiers in Egyptian and Saudi Arabic. *International Journal of English Linguistics* 7(4): 220–9.

O'Malley, M., & Dupré, J. 2005. Fundamental issues in systems biology. *BioEssays* 27: 1270–76.

2007. Size doesn't matter: towards an inclusive philosophy of biology. *Biology and Philosophy* 22: 155–91.

Osborne, T. 2005. Beyond the constituent: a dependency grammar analysis of chains. *Folia Linguistica* 39(3–4): 251–97.

2014. Dependency grammar. In Carnie, A., Sato, Y., & Siddiqi, D. (eds.), *The Routledge Handbook of Syntax*, pp. 604–27. Routledge.

Osborne, T., Putnam, M., & Gross, T. (2012). Catenae: introducing a novel unit of syntactic analysis. *Syntax* 15(4): 354–96.

Pacherie, E. 2012. Actions. In Frankish, K., & Ramsey, W. (eds.), *The Cambridge Handbook of Cognitive Science*, pp. 92–111. Cambridge University.

Paluszek, M., & Thomas, S. 2020. *Practical MATLAB Deep Learning: A Project-Based Approach*. Springer.

Parikh, P. 1988. Language and Strategic Inference. Ph.D Thesis, Stanford University.

Parikh, P. 1992, A game-theoretic account of implicature. In *Proceedings of the 4th TARK Conference*, pp. 85–94. Morgan Kaufmann.

Partee, B. 1996. The development of formal semantics in linguistic theory. In Lappin, S. (ed.), *The Handbook of Contemporary Semantic Theory*, pp 11–38. Blackwell Reference.

  2009. Perspectives on semantics: how philosophy and syntax have shaped the development of formal semantics, and vice versa. Conference 'Russian in Contrast', special guest lecture. University of Oslo. https://udrive.oit.umass.edu/partee/Partee2009Oslo.ppt.pdf

  2014. A brief history of the syntax–semantics interface in Western formal linguistics. *Semantics–Syntax Interface* 1(1): 1–21.

Partee, B., Meulen, A., & Wall, R. 1993. *Mathematical Methods in Linguistics*. Kluwer Academic Publishers.

Paster, M. 2015. Phonological analysis. In Heine, B., & Narrog, H. (eds.), *The Oxford Handbook of Linguistic Analysis*, pp. 525–44. Oxford University Press.

Pastra, K., & Aloimonos, Y. 2012. The minimalist grammar of action. *Philosophical Transactions of the Royal Society B* 367: 103–17.

Patel, P., Mascarenhas, S., Chemla, E., & Schlenker, P. 2023. Super linguistics: an introduction. *Linguistics and Philosophy* 46: 627–92.

Pater, J. 2019. Generative linguistics and neural networks at 60: foundation, friction, and fusion. *Language* 95(1): e41–e74.

Penn, G. 2012. Computational linguistics. In Kempson, R., Fernando, T., and Asher, N. (eds.), *Philosophy of Linguistics*, pp. 143–73. Elsevier B.V. North Holland.

Peregin, J. 2015. *Inferentialism: Why Rules Matter*. Palgrave Macmillan.

Pereira, F. 2000. Formal grammar and information theory: together again? In Philosophical Transactions of the Royal Society, pp 1239–53. Royal Society.

Perlmutter, D. 1990. On the segmental representation of transitional and bidirectional movements in ASL phonology. In Fischer, S., & Siple, P. (eds.), *Theoretical Issues in Sign Language Research. Volume 1: Linguistics*, pp. 67–80. University of Chicago Press.

Pfau, R., & Quer, J. 2010. Nonmanuals: their prosodic and grammatical roles. Sign Languages: 381–402.

Pietroski, P. 2018. *Conjoining Meanings: Semantics without Truth Values*. Oxford University Press.

Pinker, S., & Bloom, P. 1990. Natural language and natural selection. *Behavioral and Brain Sciences* 13: 707–26.

Pinker, S., & Jackendoff, R. 2005. The faculty of language: what's special about it? *Cognition* 95: 201–36.

Pollack, J. 1990. Recursive distributed representations. *Artificial Intelligence* 46: 77–105.

Pollard, C., & Sag, I. 1994. *Head-Driven Phrase Structure Grammar*. University of Chicago Press.

Poole, G. 2002. *Syntactic theory*. Palgrave.

Postal, P. 2003. Remarks on the foundations of linguistics. *The Philosophical Forum* XXXIV(3–4): 233–52.

Postal, P. 2003. *Skeptical Linguistic Essays*. Oxford University Press.

Postal, P. 2009. The incoherence of Chomsky's 'biolinguistic' ontology. *Biolinguistics* 3(1): 104–23.

Prince, A., & Smolensky, P. 1993. *Optimality Theory: Constraint Interaction in Generative Grammar*. Blackwell.

Progovac, L. 2015. *Evolutionary Syntax*. Oxford University Press.

Progovac, L. 2016. A gradualist scenario for language evolution: precise linguistic reconstruction of early human (and Neanderthal) grammars. *Frontiers in Psychology* 7(1714): 1–14.

Pullum, G. 1983. How many possible human languages are there? *Linguistic Inquiry* 14(3): 447–67.

2007. Ungrammaticality, rarity, and corpus use. *Corpus Linguistics and Linguistic Theory* 3: 33–47.

2009. Computational linguistics and generative linguistics: the triumph of hope over experience. In Baldwin, T., & Kordoni, V. (eds.), *ILCL '09: Proceedings of the EACL 2009 Workshop on the Interaction between Linguistics and Computational Linguistics: Virtuous, Vicious or Vacuous?*, pp. 12–21. Association for Computational Linguistics.

2011. The mathematical foundations of *Syntactic Structures*. *Journal of Logic, Language & Information* 20(3): 277–96.

2013. The central question in comparative syntactic metatheory. *Mind & Language* 28(4): 492–521.

2014. Fear and loathing of the English passive. *Language & Communication* 37: 60–74.

2018. *Why Linguistics Matters*. Polity Press.

2019. Formalism, grammatical rules, and normativity. In McElvenny, J. (ed.), *Form and Formalism in Linguistics*, pp. 197–224. Language Science Press.

Pullum, G., & Gazdar, G. 1982. Natural languages and context-free languages. *Linguistics and Philosophy* 4(4): 471–504.

Pullum, G., & Scholz. B. 2001. On the distinction between model-theoretic and generative-enumerative syntactic frameworks. In de Groote, P., Morrill, G., & Retore, C. (eds.), *Logical Aspects of Computational Linguistics*, pp. 17–43. Springer.

2002. Empirical assessment of stimulus poverty arguments. *The Linguistic Review* 19: 9–50.

Pullum, G. & Scholz, B. 2010. Recursion and the infinitude claim. In van der Hulst, H. (ed.), *Recursion in Human Language (Studies in Generative Grammar 104)*, pp. 113–38. Mouton de Gruyter.

Pulvermüller, F. 2014. The syntax of action. *Trends in Cognitive Sciences* 18: 219–20.

Pustejovsky, J. 1991. The generative lexicon. *Computational Linguistics* 17: 409–41.

1995. *The Generative Lexicon*. MIT Press.

Pustejovsky, J., & Jezek, E. 2008. Semantic coercion in language: beyond distributional analysis. *Italian Journal of Linguistics* 20(1): 181–214.

Pustejovsky, J., Rumshisky, A., Batiukova, O., & Moszkowicz, J. L. 2014. Annotation of compositional operations with GLML. In Bunt, H., Bos, J., Pulman, S. (eds.), *Computing Meaning: Text, Speech and Language Technology*, Volume 47, pp. 217–34. Springer.

Putnam, H. 1973. Meaning and reference. *Journal of Philosophy* 70: 699–711.

1981. *Reason, Truth and History*. Cambridge University Press.

Rambow, O., & Joshi, A. 1997. A formal look at dependency grammars and phrase-structure grammars, with special consideration of word-order phenomena. In Wanner, L. (ed.), *Recent Trends in Meaning-Text Theory* 39, pp. 167–90. John Benjamins.

Reali, F., & Christiansen, M. 2005. Uncovering the richness of the stimulus: structure dependence and indirect statistical evidence. *Cognitive Science* 29(6): 1007–28.

Recanati, F. 2004. *Literal Meaning*. Cambridge University Press.

Reed, P. 2020. Place and language: links between speech, region, and connection to place. *Wiley Interdisciplinary Review of Cognitive Science* 11(3): e1524.

Reines, M., & Prinz, J. 2009. Reviving Whorf: the return of linguistic relativity. *Philosophy Compass* 4(6): 1022–32.

Rey, G. 2020. *Representation in Language*. Oxford University Press.

Richardson, A., & Uebel, T. 2007. *Cambridge Companion to Logical Empiricism*. Cambridge University Press.

Roberts, C. 2015. Accommodation in a language game. In Loewer, B., & Schaffer, J. (eds.), *A Companion to David Lewis*, pp. 345–66. Wiley-Blackwell.

Ross, J. 1967/1983. Constraints on Variables in Syntax. Ph.D dissertation. MIT.

Ross, J. 1973. A fake NP squish. In Bailey, C., & Shuy, R. (eds.), *New Ways of Analyzing Variation in English*, pp. 96–140. Georgetown University Press.

Rothschild, D. 2009. *Definite Descriptions and Negative Polarity*. Unpublished manuscript.

Sag, I. 2012. Sign-based construction grammar: an informal synopsis. In Boas, H. C., & Sag, I. A. (eds.), *Sign-Based Construction Grammar* (CSLI Lecture Notes 193), pp. 69–202. CSLI Publications.

Sag, I., Wasow, T., & Bender, E. 2003. *Syntactic Theory: A Formal Introduction* (2nd ed.). CSLI Publications.

Sampson, G. 2007. Grammar without grammaticality. *Corpus Linguistics and Linguistic Theory* 3(1): 1–32.

Sampson, G., & Babarczy, A. 2013. *Grammar without Grammaticality: Growth and the Limits of Grammatical Precision*. De Gruyter Mouton.

Sandler, W. 1986. The spreading hand autosegment of American Sign Language. *Sign Language Studies* 50: 1–28.

Sandler, W. 1989. *Phonological Representation of the Sign: Linearity and Non-Linearity in American Sign Language*. Foris.

Sandler, W. 2012. The phonological organization of sign languages. *Language and Linguistics Compass* 6(3): 162–82.

Savitch, W. 1993. Why it might pay to assume that languages are infinite. *Annals of Mathematics and Artificial Intelligence* 8: 17–25.

Scha, R. 1990. Taaltheorie en taaltechnologie; competence en performance. In de Kort, Q., & Leerdam, G. (eds.), *Computertoepassingen in de Neerlandistiek*, pp. 7–22. Landelijke Vereniging van Neerlandici.

Schlenker, P. 2018. What is super semantics? *Philosophical Perspectives* 32(1): 365–453.

2019. Gestural semantics. *Natural Language and Linguistic Theory* 37: 735–84.

2020. Gestural grammar. *Natural Language and Linguistic Theory* 38: 887–936.

Sellars, W. 1954. Some reflections on language games. *Philosophy of Science* 21: 204–28.

Seyfarth, R., & Cheney, D. 2014. The evolution of language from social cognition. *Current Opinion in Neurobiology* 28: 5–9.

Sgall, P., Hajicova, E., & Panevova, J. 1986. *The Meaning of the Sentence in Its Semantics and Pragmatic Aspects*. D. Reidel.

Shieber, S. 1985. Evidence against the context-freeness of natural language. In *The Formal Complexity of Natural Language*, pp. 320–34. Springer Netherlands, 1987.

Shieber, S., & Schabes, Y. 1990. Synchronous tree-adjoining grammars. In Karlgren, H. (ed.), *Proceedings of the 13th International Conference on Computational Linguistics*, pp. 253–8. University of Helsinki.

1991. Synchronous tree-adjoining grammars. *Technical Reports* (CIS).

Sinha, C. 2010. Cognitive linguistics, psychology, and cognitive science. In *The Oxford Handbook of Cognitive Linguistics*, pp. 1–30. Oxford University Press.

Skyrms, B. 2010. *Signals: Evolution, Learning and Information*. Oxford University Press.

Sider, T. 2010. *Logic for Philosophy*. Oxford University Press.

Silberstein, M. 2022. Context is king: contextual emergence in network neuroscience, cognitive science, and psychology. In Wuppuluri, S., & Stewart, I. (eds.), *From Electrons to Elephants and Elections*, pp. 597–640. Springer.

Smith, N., & Wilson, D. 1991. *Modern Linguistics: The Results of Chomsky's Revolution*. Indiana University Press.

Smolensky, P. 2001. Optimality theory: frequently asked 'questions'. In Fukazawa, H., & Kitahara, M. (eds.), *Gengo*, pp. 1–72. Taishukan.

Smolensky, P., & Dupoux, E. 2009. Universals in cognitive theories of language. *Behavioral & Brain Sciences* 32: 468–9.

Sperber, D. 2010. The Guru effect. *Review of Philosophy & Psychology* 1: 583–92.

Sperber, D., & Wilson, D. 1986. *Relevance: Communication and Cognition*. Blackwell.

1994. Outline of relevance theory. *Hermes* 1: 85–106.

1995. *Relevance: Communication and Cognition* (2nd ed.). Blackwell.

Sporns, O. 2013. Structure and function of complex brain networks. *Dialogues in Clinical Neuroscience* 15: 247–62.

2014. Contributions and challenges for network models in cognitive neuroscience. *Nature Neuroscience* 17: 652–60.

Sprouse, J. 2018. Acceptability judgments and grammaticality, prospects and challenges. In Hornstein, N., Lasnik, B., Patel-Grosz, P., & Yang, C. (eds.), *Syntactic Structures after 60 Years: The Impact of the Chomskyan Revolution in Linguistics*, pp. 195–224. De Gruyter Mouton.

Stalnaker, R. 1970. Pragmatics. Synthese 22. Reprinted in *Context and Content: Essays on Intentionality in Speech and Thought*. Oxford University Press, 1999.

1976. Possible worlds. *Nous* 10(1): 65–75.

1978. Assertion. *Syntax and Semantics* (New York Academic Press) 9: 315–32.

1984. *Inquiry*. MIT Press.

1997. Reference and necessity. In Hale, B., & Wright, C. (eds.), *A Companion To Philosophy of Language*, pp. 534–54. Blackwell.

1999. *Context and Content*. Oxford University Press.

2002. Common ground. *Linguistics & Philosophy* 25: 701–21.

2014. *Context and Content*. Oxford University Press.

Stanley, J., & Szabó, Z. 2000. On quantifier domain restriction. *Mind & Language* 15(2–3): pp. 219–61.

Stanton, K. 2020. Linguistics and philosophy: break up song. In Nefdt, R., Klippi, C., & Karstens, B. (eds.), *The Philosophy and Science of Language: Interdisciplinary Perspectives*, pp. 409–36. Palgrave Macmillan.

Starr, W. 2020. A preference semantics for imperatives. *Semantics & Pragmatics* 13(6): 1–60.

Steedman, M. 2017. The emergence of language. *Mind & Language* 32: 579–90.

Stokoe, W. 1960. Sign language structure: an outline of the visual communication system of the American deaf. *Studies in Linguistics, Occasional Papers*, 8. University of Buffalo.

1980. Sign language structure. *Annual Review of Anthropology* 9: 365–470.

1991. Semantic phonology. *Sign Language Studies* 71: 99–106.

Stojnić, U. 2017. Content in a dynamic context. *Nous* 53(2): 394–432.

Stokhof, M. 2012. The role of artificial languages. In Russell, G., & Fara, D. (eds.), *The Routledge Companion to Philosophy of Language*, pp. 553–4. Routledge.

Schwartz, J., Boë, L., & Abry, C. 2007. Linking the dispersion-focalization theory (DFT) and the maximum utilization of the available distinctive features (MUAF) principle in a Perception-for-Action-Control Theory (PACT). In Solé, M., Beddor, P., & Ohala, M. (eds.), *Experimental Approaches to Phonology*, pp. 104–24. Oxford University Press.

Strevens, M. 2020. *The Knowledge Machine*. Liveright Publishing Corporation.

Szabó, Z. 2000. *Compositionality*. Routledge.

(ed.) 2005. *Semantics versus Pragmatics*. Oxford University Press.

2009. The distinction between semantics and pragmatics. In Lepore, E., & Smith, B. (eds.), *The Oxford Handbook of Philosophy of Language*, pp. 361–90. Oxford University Press.

2011. The case for compositionality. In Hinzen, W., Machery, E., & Werning, M. (eds.), *The Oxford Handbook of Compositionality*, pp. 64–80. Oxford University Press.

2022. *Possible Human Languages*. Unpublished manuscript.

Szabó, Z., & Thomason, R. 2019. *The Philosophy of Language*. Cambridge University Press.

Tallerman, M. 1998. Understanding Syntax. Hodder Arnold.

Tarski, A. 1933. The concept of truth in the languages of the deductive sciences.

Tiede, H., & Stout, L. 2010. Recursion, infinity and modeling. In van der Hulst, H. (ed.), *Recursion and Human Language*, pp. 147–58. Mouton de Gruyter.

Thomas, J. 2012. *Meaning in Interaction: An Introduction to Pragmatics*. Routledge.

Thomason, R. 1974. *Formal Philosophy: Selected Papers by Richard Montague*. New Haven Press.

Thurner, S., Hanel, R., & Klimekl, P. 2018. Introduction to the Theory of Complex Systems. Oxford Academic.

Tomalin, M. 2006. *Linguistics and the Formal Sciences*. Cambridge University Press.
2007. Reconsidering recursion in syntactic theory. *Lingua* 117: 1784–800.

Tomasello, M. 2000. *Origins of Human Communication*. MIT Press.

Travis, C. 1994, On constraints of generality. In *Proceedings of the Aristotelian Society*, New Series 44, pp. 165–88. Aristotelian Society Publications.

Trubetzkoy, N. 1958 [1939]. *Grundzüge der Phonologie*. Vandenhoeck & Ruprecht.

van der Hulst, H. 1993. Units in the analysis of signs. *Phonology* 10: 209–41.
(ed.) 2010. *Recursion and Human Language*. De Gruyter Mouton.

van Heijenoort, J. 1967. Logic as calculus and logic as language. *Synthese* 17(3): 324–30.

van Rooij, R., & Franke, M. 2022. Optimality-theoretic and game-theoretic approaches to implicature. In Zalta, E. (ed.), *The Stanford Encyclopedia of Philosophy*. Metaphysics Research Lab, Stanford University.

Vaswani, A., Shazeer, N., Parmar, N., Uszkoreit, J., Jones, L., Gomez, A. N., Kaiser, Ł., & Polosukhin, I. 2017. Attention is all you need. *Advances in Neural Information Processing Systems* 30.

Varela, F., Thompson, E., & Rosch, E. 1991. *The Embodied Mind: Cognitive Science and Human Experience*. MIT Press.

Veltman, F. 1996. Defaults in update semantics. *Journal of Philosophical Logic* 25: 225–61.

Veres, C. 2022. Large language models are not models of natural language: they are corpus models. https://arxiv.org/abs/2112.07055

Vermeerbergen, M., van Herreweghe, M., Akach, P., & Matabane, E. 2007. Constituent order in Flemish Sign Language (VGT) and South African Sign Language (SASL): a cross-linguistic study. *Sign Language & Linguistics* 10(1): 23–54.

Watts, D., & Strogatz, S. 1998. Collective dynamics of 'small-world' networks. *Nature* 393(4): 440–2.

Weisberg, M. 2007. Three kinds of idealization. *Journal of Philosophy* 104(12): 639–59.
2013. *Simulation and Similarity: Using Models to Understand the World*. Oxford University Press.

Westera, M., & Boleda, G. 2019. Don't blame distributional semantics if it can't do entailment. In *Proceedings of the 13th International Conference on Computational Semantics*. Association for Computational Linguistics.

White, E., Hutka, S., Williams, L., & Moreno, S. 2013. Learning, neural plasticity and sensitive periods: implications for language acquisition, music training and transfer across the lifespan. *Frontiers in Systems Neuroscience*. https://doi.org/10.3389/fnsys.2013.00090

Wigner, E. 1960. The unreasonable effectiveness of mathematics in the natural sciences. *Communications on Pure and Applied Mathematics* 13(1): 1–14.

Wilcox, S., & Wilcox, P. 2015. The analysis of signed languages. In Heine, B., & Narrog, H. (eds.), *The Oxford Handbook of Linguistic Analysis*, pp. 843–64. Oxford University Press.

Wilcox, E., Levy, R., Morita, T., & Futrell, R. 2018. What do RNN language models learn about filler - gap dependencies? In *Proceedings of the 2018 EMNLP Workshop BlackboxNLP: Analyzing and Interpreting Neural Networks for NLP*, pp. 211–21. Association for Computational Linguistics.

Wilson, D., & Sperber, D. 1988. Representation and relevance. In Kempson, R. (ed.), *Mental Representations: The Interface between Language and Reality*, pp. 133–53. Cambridge University Press.

Wilson, D., & Sperber, D. 2012. *Meaning and Relevance*. Cambridge University Press.

Wittgenstein, L. 1953. *Philosophical Investigations*. Anscombe, G., & Rhees, R. (eds.), Anscombe, G. E. M. (trans.). Blackwell.

Woschitz, J. 2020. Scientific realism and linguistics: two stories of scientific progress. In Nefdt, R., Klippi, C., & Karstens, B. (eds.), *The Philosophy and Science of Language*, pp. 143–77. Palgrave Macmillan.

Wunderlich, D. 2012. Lexical decomposition in grammar. In Werning, M., Hinzen, W., & Machery, E. (eds.), *The Oxford Handbook of Compositionality*, pp. 307–28. Oxford University Press.

Yalcin, S. 2007. Epistemic modals. *Mind* 116: 983–1026.

2012. Introductory notes on dynamic semantics. In Fara, D., & Russell, G. (eds.), *The Routledge Companion to the Philosophy of Language*, pp. 253–79. Routledge.

Yalcin, S., & Knobe, J. 2014. Epistemic modals and context: experimental data. *Semantics and Pragmatics* 7: 1–21.

Yang, C. 2006. *The Infinite Gift*. Scribner.

Yang, Y., & Piantadosi, S. (2022). One model for the learning of language. *PNAS* 119(5): e2021865119.

Youguo, P., Huailin, S., & Tiancai, L. (2007). The frame of cognitive pattern recognition. *Chinese Control Conference*, pp. 694–6.

Zeevat, H. 1989. A compositional approach to discourse representation theory. *Linguistics & Philosophy* 12: 95–131.

2007. *Optimal Interpretation as an Alternative to Gricean Pragmatics*. Unpublished manuscript, Universiteit van Amsterdam.

2008. Where is pragmatics in optimality theory? In Kecskes, I., & Mey, J. (eds.), *Intention, Common Ground and the Egocentric Speaker-Hearer*, pp. 87–104. De Gruyter Mouton.

2014. *Language Production and Interpretation: Linguistics Meets Cognition*. Brill.

2015. Perspectives on Bayesian natural language semantics and pragmatics. In Zeevat, H., & Schmitz, H. (eds.), *Bayesian Natural Language Semantics and Pragmatics, Language, Cognition, and Mind 2*, pp. 1–24. Springer Verlag.

Zhou, J., & Hai, Z. 2019. Head-driven phrase structure grammar parsing on Penn Treebank. In *Proceedings of the 57th Annual Meeting of the Association for Computational Linguistics*, pp. 2396–408. Association for Computational Linguistics.

Zwarts, J., & Verkuyl, H. 1994. An algebra of conceptual structure; an investigation into Jackendoff's conceptual semantics. *Linguistics & Philosophy* 17: 1–28.

Index

abstract
  linguistic rules, 24
  objects, 30, 48, 115–121
  properties, 6
acquisition, 4, 38, 44, 57, 177, 200
action, 101, 111, 115, 143
  philosophical action theory, 150, 153, 155
African American Vernacular English, 14
algorithm, 25, 34, 47
anaphora, 68, 95
animal communication, 23, 105
aphasia, 2, 154
artificial intelligence, 171–180, *see also* deep
  learning
autosegmental phonology, 140–142

backpropagation, 173–174
bare phrase structure, 60
Bayesian, 133–135
Behaviourism, 159
biolinguistics, 15, 184
  biology, 14, 187–189
  minimalist, 15, 25, 57–61, 151, 166, 186,
    188
  systems biolinguistics, 193–203
brain, 15, 17, 35, 56, 191, 197–198

chereme, 145
Chomsky, Noam, 3, 5, 9, 18, 50, 56, 118, 139,
    159, 163, 165, 176, 183–186
  Chomsky Hierarchy, 10
cognition, 25, 73, 122, 155
  motor cognition, 152
  social, 125, 198
cognitive science, 17, 73, 85
competence, 3, 39, 55, 144, 163
  competence–performance distinction, 8,
    179, 190
complexity science, 190–203
compositionality, 57, 74, 85–92, 96, 179
  co-compositionality, 102–103
  probabilistic, 169

computational
  computation, 143, 172
  linguistics, 101, 157, 168, 171, 176
  theory of mind, 10
construction grammar, 73
context, 108–111, 114, 120–124
  change potential, 95
  dependence, 83
  radical contextualism, 118
context-free grammar, 6, 10–13, 28, 45, 169,
    196
constituency, 12, 32–33, 66, 68, 195
convention, 4, 19, 24, 39, 200
  conventional meaning, 93, 109, 130, 133
c-structure, 69

deep learning, 171–180
dependency grammar, 65–71, 202
dependency length minimisation, 54
descriptive adequacy, 57, 159
discrete infinity, 28, 30–35, 59, 183
distributional hypothesis, 97

E-language, 14, 39
empty categories, 176
evolution, 59–63, 186–189
explanation, 157–158
explanatory adequacy, 57, 159

faculty of language, 60–63, 184–186, 199
  broad faculty of language (FLB), 28
  narrow faculty of language (FLN), 59
f-structure, 69, 197
feature structure, 71–73, 78
finite-state grammar, 10–11, 28, 54, 159
formal language theory, 6, 10, 65, 192, 196
functional application, 85–89, 99

Galilean style, 164–167
game theory, 116, 130
generative grammar, 2–9, 12, 34, 54, 59, 70,
    168, 180, 184, 196–198